Have You Heard...

A Tasteful Medley of Memphis

SUBSIDIUM, INCORPORATED
benefitting
The Memphis Oral School for the Deaf

Have You Heard...*A Tasteful Medley of Memphis*

Photo Acknowledgments

Memphis Museum System
The Peabody
The Orpheum
"Gates of Graceland"
"Used by permission, Elvis Presley Enterprises, Inc."
"Hunt-Phelan image(s) used by permission, © Hunt-Phelan"
Mark Lombardo
W.C. Handy image used by permission of Estate of W.C. Handy

Thank you to Memphian Jeff Atnip for his original cover design –
your creativity inspired us all!

For additional copies write to:

SUBSIDIUM PUBLICATIONS
SUBSIDIUM, INC.
4711 Spottswood
Memphis, TN 38117

ISBN 0-9658361-0-X

First Printing   10,000   September, 1997

Proceeds from the sale of **Have You Heard...** support the volunteer efforts of
SUBSIDIUM, INC., on behalf of the Memphis Oral School for the Deaf.

Thank You for Your Support!

Printed in the USA by
WIMMER
The Wimmer Companies
Memphis

Subsidium

SUBSIDIUM stands apart from other organizations. With few requirements, the commitment of the members comes from the heart and is the most impressive component of this group of volunteers. While balancing their own family life and work, they devote extra hours in their day to seeing that the dream of every hearing-impaired student at the Memphis Oral School for the Deaf (MOSD) is realized: the opportunity to learn to speak.

During the past 30 years, **SUBSIDIUM** has given over $2,000,000 to the school through numerous fundraisers and endless hours as classroom aides to the MOSD staff. Both large and small fund-raising projects have occupied the members over the years. The two most closely identified with **SUBSIDIUM** are the Gigantic Rummage Sale, which was discontinued in 1992, and the Carrousel of Shoppes, which celebrates its 20th anniversary in October, 1997. This 3-day shopping extravaganza has expanded four times, currently using the entire Mid-South Coliseum as a venue for merchants from around the country. Specialty items for every whim and taste are available as is daily lunch in the Café Carrousel, staffed by our volunteers, and a glamorous Preview Gala,

A Memphis Oral School for the Deaf student, wearing his amplification devices, enjoys a carrousel ride with a **SUBSIDIUM** volunteer.

Have You Heard...*A Tasteful Medley of Memphis*

held the Thursday evening before the next morning's grand opening. With the publication of **Have You Heard...** *A Tasteful Medley of Memphis*, we have added another dimension to our fundraising on behalf of the Memphis Oral School.

The difference between ordinary and extraordinary is "that little extra." Working in the classrooms alongside the teachers and speech therapists allows members to become involved with the progress of every student. Whether forming letters in sand, reading a story out loud, or helping the students with their juice cartons, each classroom volunteer knows she is needed. **SUBSIDIUM** is a Latin word meaning "troops stationed in reserve in the third line of battle." Members do think of themselves as a third line of defense, after the parents and teachers, in the struggle to give a hearing-impaired child the gift of speech.

Our volunteers have heard the silence of our special children and, for as many reasons as we have members, give of their time and energy. Making a difference in a child's life and cherishing lifelong friendships sum up why **SUBSIDIUM** is so great!

Have You Heard...*A Tasteful Medley of Memphis*

Cookbook Committee

Co-Chairs   Kathy Christiansen
                Sylvia Creedon

Committee Members

Pat Casbarro
Donna Christian
Susan Edmonds
Sherry Edmundson
Suzy Erstine
Sandra Flatt
Ann Frayser
Elaine Hare
Terry Hassell
Donna Hoffman
Carmel Hopper
Cheryl Johnson
Sandy King
Angela Lindsay
Cheryl Lombardo
Nancy Magill
Maureen Myers
Barbara Olson
Margaret Pendrich
Beth Perkins
Kimberly Ring
Beth Skudder
Beth Webb
Kyle Wiltse

Have You Heard...*A Tasteful Medley of Memphis*

Cookbook Contributors

B.B. King's
Bogies
Shelley Boden
Suzanne Bowlin
Christy Britcliffe
Rita Brown
Ann Burt
Café Society
Donna Callaway
Pat Casbarro
Diane Chambliss
Shiree Charles
Donna Christian
Julie Christiansen
Kathy Christiansen
Libbee Clifford
Becky Coleman
Sylvia Creedon
Linda Dismuke
Susan Edmonds
Sherry Edmundson
Evelyn Egan
Mary Frances Erstine
Suzy Erstine
Jason Flatt
Sandra Flatt
Susan Fleetwood
Kay Forbes
Ann Frayser
Cindy Gambrell
Sue Greenly
Frank Grisanti's Restaurant
Elaine Hare

Judy Hart
Terry Hassell
Roberta Hefley
Charolette Hesse
Emarie Higgins
Shirley Hodge
Donna Hoffman
Carmel Hopper
Eileen Huffman
Sr. Jeanine Jaster, S.C.N.
Helen H. Jenkins
Jim's Place East
Cheryl Johnson
Sue Johnson
Eva Keathley
Mikyun Kim
Sandy King
Dana Kittleson
Suzanne Lax
Pam Laycook
Angela Lindsay
Tina Liollio
Hope Logan
Cheryl Lombardo
Nancy Keathley Long
Nancy Magill
Theresa Magill
Lisa Marcom
Barbara Mayo
Hynie McDowell
Pat McGhee
Tyler McFarland
Jean Miller
Donna Moffatt
Sherri Morgan

MOSD Staff
Maureen Myers
Bunnie Olivere
Barbara Olson
Robbie O'Neil
Pam Ott
Adrienne Pakis-Gillon
Toby Parker
The Peabody Hotel
Margaret Pendrich
Beth Perkins
Cindy Peterson
Tish Pierce
Elizabeth & Robert Renfro
Kristen Reynolds
Carolyn Riley
Kim Ring
Deb Scharff
Nancy Scott
Sally Seward
Fran Shannon
Jean Simpson
Beth Skudder
Lisa Stimpson
Mary Stone
H.M. Tillman
Beth Wade
Beth Washington
Beth Webb
Kim Williams
Lee Williams
John Willingham
Kyle Wiltse
Nancy Wood

Have You Heard...*A Tasteful Medley of Memphis*

Table of Contents

Appetizers & Beverages

Appetizers & Beverages

Have You Heard …

...about the Mississippi River

The lure of the Mississippi River as it flows by Memphis is an attraction to the native as well as to the visitor. "Mecha" (great) and "Ceba" (river) combine two Algonquin words, becoming Mechacebe or Mississippi. DeSoto crossed this river 66 years before the founding of Jamestown. At the foot of the Chickasaw bluffs, the river is 80 feet deep under the bridges and just under a mile wide. For over 35,000 years, the river has flowed from Lake Itasca, Minnesota, 2,340 miles to the Gulf of Mexico. In 1917, during a particularly harsh winter, the river froze from bank to bank. Jefferson Davis and Confederate Parks are located on the right and left of Riverside Drive just south of Poplar Avenue. From these vantage points, citizens watched the Battle of Memphis on June 6, 1862. The city was captured and remained under Federal control until the Civil War ended in 1865. South of Confederate Park is the Wolf River Channel with its famous cobblestones which came from Ireland. Mud Island and its amenities are easily viewed from here.

Monroe, one of Riverside Drive's cross streets, was built to allow mule-drawn wagons with bales of cotton to make the steep climb up the bluff. Just south, alongside the river, is Tom Lee Park where a 30-foot granite obelisk monument stands out against the water's swift current. In 1925, Tom Lee rescued 32 engineers and their families from the wrecked steamer M.E. Norman. He was in a small skiff, and ferried survivors to the bank with little regard for his own life. Today, it is the site of most of the outdoor celebrations of the Memphis in May festival including the annual Sunset Symphony. A lovely view of "Ole Muddy" can be seen from Ashburn Park at Riverside and Georgia Streets, where the dogwoods bloom each Spring. Bridges cross the river at Memphis: the newest is the Hernando DeSoto Bridge, built in 1972. The first railroad crossing south of St. Louis, Missouri, was built in 1892, and the Harahan Bridge for rail and automobile traffic opened in 1916. The Memphis-Arkansas Bridge opened in 1949 as the nation and the city prospered in a post-war boom. Many changes have occurred in Memphis during the last 150 years, but one thing remains constant – the mighty Mississippi River.

Fried Pickles

1 cup milk
1 egg, lightly beaten
1 cup flour
1 teaspoon pepper
1 teaspoon salt
1 (16-ounce) jar sliced kosher dill pickles, drained
Oil for frying
Horseradish sauce

Combine milk and eggs to make an egg wash. Combine flour, pepper and salt. Place pickles in egg wash, then in seasoned flour. Shake off excess flour and deep fry in oil heated to 350° until crispy. Serve with horseradish sauce.

B. B. King's Restaurant

Cheese Canapés

1 pound soft margarine
4 jars Old English cheese
1 tablespoon Beau Monde seasoning
1 teaspoon Worcestershire sauce
15 drops hot pepper sauce
3 loaves party-size extra thin white bread,
    crusts removed

Combine all ingredients except bread and mix thoroughly. Spread generously on bread. Stack bread in 3 layers and cut each stack into 4 pieces. Freeze on baking sheet and store in plastic bags. When ready to serve, place frozen quarters on lightly greased baking sheets and bake in preheated 475° oven for 5 to 6 minutes.
Yield: 100 canapés.

Green Chile Cheese Puffs

6 eggs, beaten
1 cup grated cheddar cheese
1 cup grated Monterey Jack cheese
1 (4-ounce) can diced green chiles, drained
Salt, pepper and garlic salt to taste

Combine all ingredients. Spoon by tablespoon into small muffin pans. Bake in preheated 350° oven for 20 minutes.
Yield: 4 dozen.

Sound Information

As the mother of a young, hearing impaired child, I have many worries concerning my child's ability to assimilate what he is taught with his everyday surroundings. At school one day, he saw a video and heard a discussion of safe driving and alcohol. Several weeks later, my son and I were in the car, finishing errands. I had a cola can in my hand, and Alex tapped my arm and said, "Mom, you shouldn't drink and drive!" I was delighted that he applied what he knew to my driving! –A MOSD Parent

Sound Bites

Cutting onions
without tears–
Freeze or
refrigerate before
chopping or peel
under cold water.

Stuffed Baked Brie

1 package puff pastry sheets
1 jar pesto sauce
1 (8-ounce) brie round
1 egg white, beaten with 2 tablespoons water

Thaw 1 sheet of puff pastry according to package directions. Reserve remaining sheet for other uses. Drain oil from pesto. Cut brie in half horizontally and spread pesto on cut side of bottom layer. Top with other brie half, cut side down. Roll out dough slightly. Place brie in center of pastry. Brush corners and edges with egg white wash. Fold up edges to completely enclose cheese. Brush top with egg white wash and bake in preheated 375° oven for 25 minutes. Let stand 25 minutes before serving. Serve with crackers.

Variations: *Substitute pepper jelly, chutney or dill for pesto.*

Herbed Boboli with Peppers and Goat Cheese

¼ cup olive oil
1 small red onion, chopped
6 large cloves garlic, thinly sliced
½ large red bell pepper, coarsely chopped
½ large yellow or green bell pepper, coarsely
    chopped
¼ teaspoon crushed red pepper
Salt and pepper
4 small boboli crusts
5 ounces goat cheese
Dried thyme

Heat oil in large skillet and sauté onion and garlic until soft, about 15 minutes. Add bell peppers and cook another 5 minutes. Stir in crushed red pepper and season with salt and pepper. Brush boboli with any oil left in skillet. Divide pepper mixture evenly over crusts. Cut into wedges and place on a baking sheet. Top each piece with a generous dollop of goat cheese and sprinkle with thyme. Bake at 450° for 12 to 15 minutes.

Variation: *To make this a main dish, add left over roasted lamb. Shredded Mexican cheese may also be substituted for the goat cheese.*

Cashew Chicken with Lime Marmalade Dipping Sauce

¼ cup cooking sherry
¼ cup soy sauce
1 tablespoon sesame oil
2 tablespoons fresh lime juice
Finely grated zest of 1 lime
2 cloves garlic, minced
1½ tablespoons chopped fresh ginger
2 pounds boneless, skinless chicken
1½ cups toasted cashews
½ cup sesame seeds
½ cup cornstarch

Lime Marmalade Dipping Sauce:
1 jar lime marmalade
1 (5-ounce) jar prepared white cream-style
   horseradish
3 tablespoons chopped fresh cilantro

Combine sherry, soy sauce and sesame oil in a small bowl. Stir in lime juice, lime zest, garlic and ginger. Cut chicken into 2 x 1-inch pieces and marinate in sherry mixture for at least 2 hours, or overnight.

Place cashews, sesame seeds and cornstarch in a food processor. Process until finely ground and pour into a shallow dish. Drain chicken and dredge in nut mixture. Place chicken on a lightly oiled baking sheet, leaving a little space between pieces. Bake in preheated 375° oven for 15 minutes.

For sauce, heat marmalade in a saucepan over low heat until melted. Stir in horseradish and cilantro and serve. **Serves 4 to 6.**

Sound Bites

Seeds and nuts, both shelled and unshelled, keep best and longest when stored in the freezer. Nuts in the shell crack more easily when frozen. Nuts and seeds can be used directly from the freezer.

Curried Chicken Almond Canapés

1 cup minced cooked chicken or
   2 (5-ounce) cans chunk white chicken, drained
1 cup mayonnaise
¾ cup shredded Monterey jack cheese
⅓ cup ground almonds
¼ cup chopped parsley
2 large shallots, minced
2 teaspoons fresh lemon juice
1½ teaspoons curry powder
⅛ teaspoon hot sauce
Salt and freshly ground pepper to taste
5 to 6 dozen 1½-inch diameter thinly sliced
   bread rounds
5 to 6 dozen almond slices

Combine all ingredients except bread rounds and almond slices. Refrigerate until chilled. Spread about 1½ teaspoons mixture on each bread round, mounding in center. Top with almond slice. Place on baking sheet and bake in preheated 500° oven until lightly browned and sizzling, about 5 to 8 minutes. **Yield: 5 to 6 dozen.**

Crab Nachos

1 (8-ounce) package cream cheese, softened
1 (8-ounce) package shredded Monterey
   Jack cheese
¼ teaspoon cumin powder
Garlic powder to taste
1 (13-ounce) can artichoke hearts,
   drained and sliced
1 (6-ounce) can crab meat, drained
Corn chips
Sliced jalapeño peppers (optional)

Combine cheeses, cumin powder and garlic powder and blend well. Add artichoke hearts and crab meat. Spread corn chips on a baking sheet and top with crab mixture. Sprinkle with jalapeño, if desired. Broil 5 to 7 minutes, or until cheese is melted.

Gourmet Crab Cakes with Lemon Dill Sauce

6 tablespoons butter, divided
1 scallion, finely chopped
1 clove garlic, minced
2 tablespoons finely chopped red bell pepper
Cayenne pepper to taste
3 tablespoons whipping cream
1 tablespoon Dijon mustard
1 egg, beaten
1 teaspoon minced fresh basil
1 teaspoon minced fresh parsley
1 cup fine dry bread crumbs, divided
1 pound fresh lump crab meat, picked over to
    remove shell and cartilage
¼ cup Parmesan cheese
2 tablespoons vegetable oil

Lemon Dill Sauce:
¾ cup mayonnaise
½ cup buttermilk
2 tablespoons chopped fresh dill
1 tablespoon minced fresh parsley
2 teaspoons fresh lemon juice
1 tablespoon grated lemon peel
1 clove garlic, minced

Melt 1 tablespoon butter in a large skillet and sauté scallion, garlic and bell pepper until wilted, about 2 minutes. Add cayenne, cream and mustard. Cool slightly. Add egg, basil, parsley, ½ cup bread crumbs and crab meat. Mix lightly and mold into 16 2-inch wide patties. Combine remaining bread crumbs and Parmesan cheese in a shallow dish. Roll patties in crumb mixture and chill for at least 1 hour. (The crab cakes can be made early in the day and refrigerated, covered.) Heat remaining butter in a large skillet over moderate heat. Sauté the crab cakes 3 minutes per side. Serve with sauce.

For the sauce, combine all ingredients in a medium bowl. Chill until sauce thickens. **Yield: 16 cakes.**

Sound Information

Hearing impairment is the single most prevalent chronic physical disability in the United States.

Cheese and Shrimp Appetizers

15 slices firm white bread
1 (4½-ounce) can shrimp, drained and chopped
1 cup shredded Swiss cheese
½ cup mayonnaise
1 tablespoon milk
½ teaspoon dried dill
Parsley sprigs, optional

Cut 30 circles from bread with a 2-inch fluted cookie cutter. Lightly toast. Combine shrimp, cheese, mayonnaise, milk and dill in a small bowl. Spread on toast and broil 6 inches from heat until hot and bubbly, 3 to 4 minutes. Garnish with parsley, if desired. (May be made ahead and frozen until ready to use.) **Yield: 2½ dozen.**

Prosciutto-Wrapped Shrimp with Garlic Dipping Sauce

18 thin slices prosciutto
18 fresh basil leaves
18 extra large shrimp, peeled and deveined
18 bamboo skewers, soaked in water 30 minutes

Garlic Dipping Sauce:
⅓ cup red wine vinegar
2 tablespoons Dijon mustard
1 tablespoon chopped garlic
1 cup olive oil
Salt and pepper

Place 1 prosciutto slice on work surface, short end parallel to edge. Place 1 basil leaf at short end of prosciutto and top basil with 1 shrimp. Roll up and thread onto skewer. Repeat with remaining prosciutto, basil and shrimp. (This can be done one day ahead. Wrap tightly in plastic wrap and refrigerate.)

Grill shrimp on a prepared barbecue grill or broil until shrimp is opaque in center, turning frequently, about 6 minutes. Serve hot or at room temperature with dipping sauce.

For Sauce: *Combine vinegar, mustard and garlic in a blender. Gradually add oil and blend well. Place in a small bowl and season with salt and pepper to taste.* **Yield: 1½ dozen.**

Teriyaki Shrimp with Hot Plum Sauce

24 large shrimp (about ¾ pound), peeled and
   deveined
⅓ cup **vegetable oil**
¼ cup **lemon juice**
¼ cup **soy sauce**
2 tablespoons dry sherry
2 cloves garlic, minced
½ teaspoon freshly ground pepper
12 slices bacon, cut in half crosswise

Hot Plum Sauce:
1 cup plum preserves
2 tablespoons brown sugar
2 tablespoons lemon juice
1 tablespoon ketchup
1 tablespoon Dijon mustard

Place shrimp in a large bowl. Combine oil, lemon juice, soy sauce, sherry, garlic and pepper. Pour over shrimp. Cover and refrigerate 3 hours, stirring occasionally.

Cook bacon in a large skillet until limp but not crisp. Drain. Remove shrimp from marinade and discard marinade. Wrap 1 bacon slice around each shrimp, securing with a wooden pick. Place on a rack in a roasting pan and bake in preheated 450° oven until shrimp turn pink and bacon is crisp, about 8 to 10 minutes. Serve immediately with Hot Plum Sauce.

For Sauce: *Combine all ingredients in a small saucepan. Bring to a boil. Reduce heat and simmer 10 minutes, stirring occasionally.* **Yield: 2 dozen shrimp and 1¼ cups sauce.**

Sound Bites

When serving hors d'oeuvres on a silver tray, you may wish to protect it from acids by covering it with a layer of leafy green lettuce.

Tomato Crostini

1 (1-inch thick) slice day-old Italian bread
1 tablespoon red wine vinegar
2 large cloves garlic, minced
1 tablespoon drained chopped capers
3 tablespoons extra virgin olive oil
3 tablespoons minced flat leaf parsley
1 tablespoon minced fresh basil
4 very ripe plum or Roma tomatoes, diced
Lightly toasted baguette slices

Soak bread slice in vinegar until vinegar is absorbed. Shred finely into a medium bowl. Add remaining ingredients except baguette slices. Mix well and let sit at room temperature for 1 to 2 hours or refrigerate until ready to use. Serve at room temperature with baguette slices.

Goat Cheese and Sun-Dried Tomato Strudel

1 package phyllo dough, thawed
½ cup olive oil
8 ounces goat or feta cheese
½ cup sun-dried tomatoes, cut into ½-inch dice
¼ cup pitted, diced Kalamata olives
2 tablespoons chopped fresh basil
1 teaspoon black pepper
2 tablespoons toasted pine nuts
Fresh baby salad greens, tossed with balsamic vinegar and olive oil

*Lay 1 sheet phyllo on work surface and brush with olive oil. Keep remaining phyllo covered with a damp cloth to prevent drying. Place a second sheet of phyllo on top and brush with olive oil. Repeat one more time. Cut cheese into ¾-inch dice and toss with sun-dried tomatoes, olives, basil pepper and pine nuts. Spoon mixture on bottom edge of phyllo and roll up. Cut into desired portion size. Brush with olive oil and place on a baking sheet in the center of a preheated 425° oven until golden brown, 8 to 10 minutes. Place on a salad plate and surround with baby greens. **Serves 4.***

Mushroom Stuffed Mushrooms

3 dozen mushrooms, cleaned
¼ cup butter
1 tablespoon flour
½ teaspoon salt
½ cup half and half
2 teaspoons chopped chives
1 teaspoon lemon juice

*Remove stems from mushrooms and chop. Heat butter in a small skillet and sauté chopped stems until tender. Add flour, salt, half and half, chives and lemon juice. Cook over low heat until thickened, stirring constantly. Stuff mushrooms with this mixture. Place on a baking sheet which has been lightly coated with nonstick vegetable spray and bake in preheated 400° oven for 8 minutes. **Yield: 3 dozen.***

Sound Information

28 million Americans have been identified as having some degree of hearing-impairment.

Champagne Mushrooms

6 tablespoons butter, divided
1 tablespoon minced garlic
1½ pounds mushrooms, cleaned and stems removed
1½ cups Brut champagne
Salt and pepper to taste
1 to 2 tablespoons minced fresh parsley or mixed fresh herbs

*Melt 3 tablespoons butter in a medium skillet over medium heat. Sauté garlic until lightly browned. Add mushrooms and cook, stirring occasionally, until lightly browned, about 5 minutes. Add champagne and bring to a boil. Reduce heat and simmer until liquid is reduced to ⅓ cup, about 10 minutes. Season with salt and pepper to taste. Remove from heat and whisk in remaining butter until sauce is slightly thickened. Arrange mushrooms on a serving dish with toothpicks inserted in each. Pour sauce over mushrooms and garnish with parsley or fresh herbs. **Serves 6.***

Beef Horseradish Roll-ups

1 (No. 303) can Bavarian-style sauerkraut, drained
1 (8-ounce) package cream cheese, softened
1 tablespoon prepared horseradish
½ teaspoon seasoned salt
½ teaspoon garlic salt
4 jars sliced dried beef

Combine sauerkraut, cream cheese, horseradish and salts. Separate beef slices and spread ½ to 1 teaspoon cheese mixture over each slice. Roll beef tightly and refrigerate overnight to enhance flavor.

To serve: *Arrange on a platter with mustard dip in center.* ***Yield: 5 dozen.***

Genoa Triangles

1 (8-ounce) package cream cheese, softened
4 ounces mascarpone cheese
½ teaspoon dried thyme
1 teaspoon garlic powder
1 pound Genoa salami, very thinly sliced

Blend together cheeses, thyme and garlic powder. Divide salami into groups of 8 slices. Spread 7 pieces of each group with cheese mixture. Stack the 7 slices, and top with the eighth slice (without cheese). Cut each stack into 8 wedges and serve. ***Yield: 100 triangles.***

Chicken Tortilla Pinwheels

1 (8-ounce) package cream cheese, softened
2 (4-ounce) cans chopped green chiles, drained
1 (4½-ounce) can chopped ripe olives, drained
½ teaspoon garlic powder
¼ teaspoon hot pepper sauce
6 (8-inch) flour tortillas
2 (2½-ounce) packages thinly sliced chicken

Combine cream cheese, chiles, olives, garlic powder and hot sauce in a small bowl. Stir well. Spread ¼ cup cheese mixture over each tortilla. Arrange 3 slices of chicken over cheese mixture and roll tortilla up jelly-roll fashion. Wrap tightly in plastic wrap and chill at least 2 hours. To serve, slice into 1-inch rounds. ***Yield: 3 dozen.***

Marinated Shrimp, Mushrooms and Artichokes

1 package bleu cheese salad dressing mix
1 package Italian salad dressing mix
1 package cheese garlic salad dressing mix
1 (2¼-ounce) bottle capers, drained
2 to 3 pounds shrimp, cooked and peeled
2 (4-ounce) cans whole button mushrooms, drained
2 (14-ounce) cans tiny artichoke hearts or
    quartered large artichoke hearts, drained
2 cans hearts of palm, drained
2 to 3 teaspoons salt

Prepare salad dressings according to package directions, omitting water and replacing with vinegar. Place remaining ingredients in a large bowl and top with dressings. Cover and refrigerate overnight, gently stirring occasionally. **Serves 20.**

Marinated Cheese

½ cup olive oil
½ cup white wine vinegar
1 (2-ounce) jar diced pimento, drained
3 tablespoons chopped fresh parsley
3 tablespoons minced green onions
3 cloves garlic, minced
1 teaspoon sugar
¾ teaspoon dried whole basil
½ teaspoon salt
½ teaspoon freshly ground black pepper
1 (8-ounce) 5½ x 2 x 1-inch block sharp
    Cheddar cheese, chilled
1 (8-ounce) package cream cheese, chilled
Fresh parsley sprigs, optional

Combine all ingredients except cheeses and parsley sprigs in a jar. Cover tightly and shake vigorously. Cut Cheddar cheese in half lengthwise. Cut crosswise into ¼-inch thick slices. Repeat procedure with cream cheese. Arrange cheese slices alternately in a shallow baking dish, standing slices on edge. Pour marinade over cheese, cover and refrigerate at least 8 hours. Transfer cheese slices to a serving platter in the same alternating fashion and cover with marinade. Garnish with parsley sprigs, if desired. Serve with assorted crackers. **Serves 16.**

Sound Bites

If potato chips lose their freshness, place under the broiler for a few moments. Care must be taken not to brown them.

Sesame Pork Appetizers with Ginger Sauce

2 (¾-pound) pork tenderloins
½ cup dry sherry
1 tablespoon soy sauce
½ cup honey
½ cup sesame seeds
Fresh spinach leaves

Ginger Sauce:
⅓ cup soy sauce
1 green onion, finely chopped
1 tablespoon dry sherry
1 tablespoon dark sesame oil
1 small clove garlic, crushed
½ teaspoon peeled, grated fresh ginger

Place pork in a large zip lock bag. Combine sherry and soy sauce. Pour over pork and seal bag. Refrigerate 1 to 2 hours. Remove pork from marinade and discard marinade. Brush pork with honey and roll in sesame seeds. Place on a rack in a roasting pan lined with heavy-duty foil. Bake, uncovered, in preheated 350° oven until meat thermometer inserted into thickest part of tenderloins registers 160°, about 40 to 45 minutes. Thinly slice and arrange on a spinach-lined serving platter. Serve with Ginger Sauce.

For Ginger Sauce: *Combine all ingredients in a small serving bowl. Stir well.* ***Serves 10 to 12.***

Panhandle Shrimp Dip

2 tablespoons lemon juice
2 tablespoons prepared horseradish
1 teaspoon Worcestershire sauce
1 teaspoon hot pepper sauce
½ cup ketchup
½ cup chili sauce
½ cup mayonnaise
½ cup sour cream
2 pounds cooked, peeled shrimp, chopped,
   or 3 cans shrimp, drained

Combine all ingredients except shrimp and blend well. Fold in shrimp and chill. Serve with crackers. ***Serves 12.***

Pesto Cheesecake

Crust:
¾ cup bread crumbs
⅓ cup ground pine nuts or walnuts
¼ cup Parmesan cheese
⅓ cup melted butter

Filling:
⅔ cup prepared pesto sauce
3 (8-ounce) packages cream cheese, softened
3 eggs
¼ cup milk
Sun-dried tomatoes (optional)

For crust: *Combine all ingredients and press on bottom and up sides of an 8-inch springform pan.*

For filling: *Drain oil from top of pesto sauce. Beat cream cheese on high speed of mixer until light and fluffy. Add eggs one at a time, beating well after each addition. Add milk and pesto and mix well. Pour into crust. Bake in preheated 300° oven until set, about 1 hour. Turn oven off and partially open door for 1 hour. Remove from oven and cool on wire rack. Cover and chill before serving. Serve garnished with sun-dried tomatoes, if desired.*

Party Shrimp Mousse

1½ tablespoons unflavored gelatin
¼ cup cold water
1 can tomato soup
1 (8-ounce) package cream cheese, softened
1½ cups chopped cooked shrimp
1 cup mayonnaise
¾ cup finely chopped celery
½ cup finely chopped onion

Soften gelatin in cold water. Heat soup and add gelatin and cheese. Stir until cheese is melted and mixture is smooth. Remove from heat and cool. When cooled, add remaining ingredients and pour into a greased 4-cup mold. Chill overnight. Unmold and serve with crackers.
Serves 15 to 20.

Variation: *May substitute lobster or crab for shrimp.*

Elegant Seafood Dip

3 tablespoons butter
4 tablespoons chopped celery
2 tablespoons finely chopped green onion
3 tablespoons flour
1½ cups half and half
½ teaspoon salt
Dash of Worcestershire sauce
Dash of hot pepper sauce
½ pound fresh crab meat
½ pound cooked, shelled shrimp
¼ cup dry vermouth
2 cups grated New York State Cheddar cheese

Melt butter in a large skillet over medium heat. Sauté celery and onion until tender, about 5 minutes. Add flour and cook 2 minutes more, stirring constantly. Gradually add half and half. Reduce heat to a simmer and cook, stirring frequently, until thick. Add remaining ingredients except cheese. Pour into a greased casserole. Top with cheese and bake in preheated 350° oven until cheese is melted and dip is bubbling, about 20 to 30 minutes. Transfer to a chafing dish and serve with assorted crackers.

Sun-Dried Tomato Hummus

1 (15-ounce) can chick peas, drained
4 ounces oil-packed sun-dried tomatoes, drained
¼ cup tahini
⅓ cup lemon juice
2 tablespoons chopped fresh parsley
2 tablespoons chopped onion
1 tablespoon reduced-sodium soy sauce
1 clove garlic
1½ teaspoons ground cumin
¼ teaspoon cayenne pepper

Place all ingredients in food processor. Pulse until well blended. Serve with quartered pita bread, corn chips or bagel chips.

Beer Cheese

1 (8-ounce) package cream cheese, softened
4 ounces pasteurized process cheese spread
3 ounces garlic cheese
½ cup beer
1 loaf Hawaiian bread

Place cheeses and beer in a blender and process until smooth. Hollow out bread, leaving a 1-inch shell. Cut bread which has been removed into cubes. Pour cheese mixture into hollowed out loaf and serve with bread cubes and tortilla chips.

Curry Vegetable Dip

1 cup mayonnaise
2 tablespoons Durkee's sauce
1 tablespoon prepared horseradish
1 teaspoon celery seed
1 teaspoon curry powder
1 teaspoon seasoning salt
½ teaspoon Worcestershire sauce
¼ clove garlic, crushed
Dash of hot pepper sauce

Combine all ingredients in a small bowl. Chill and serve with assorted raw vegetables. **Yield: 1 cup.**

Feta and Walnut Dip

½ pound feta cheese
2 tablespoons olive oil
8 tablespoons milk
1 cup walnuts
Cayenne pepper to taste

Combine all ingredients except cayenne in processor and pulse until blended. Add cayenne to taste. Serve with crackers or corn chips.

Sound Information

What I like best about the Memphis Oral School for the Deaf: "The optimism that is generated by the teaching staff, as well as the people involved in administration; the creativity exhibited by the teachers in implementing the learning process; the way in which the teacher knows each student without ever having to refer to a chart or a record."

–A MOSD Parent

Mango Chutney

1 (8-ounce) package cream cheese, softened
1 cup shredded sharp Cheddar cheese
1 teaspoon curry powder
1 jar mango chutney
¼ cup chopped pecans
¼ cup fresh coconut
¼ cup chopped green onions

Combine cream cheese, Cheddar cheese and curry powder. Shape into a disk and chill for 1 to 2 hours. Top with remaining ingredients and serve with butter crackers.

Fancy Chicken Log

2 (8-ounce) packages cream cheese, softened
1 tablespoon bottled steak sauce
½ teaspoon curry powder
1½ cups minced cooked chicken
⅓ cup minced celery
¼ cup chopped fresh parsley, divided
¼ cup chopped almonds

Combine cream cheese, steak sauce and curry powder. Add chicken and celery and 2 tablespoons parsley. Blend well. Refrigerate remaining parsley. Shape chicken mixture into a 9-inch log. Wrap in plastic and chill for four hours. Combine remaining parsley and almonds in a shallow dish. Roll log in mixture to coat. Serve with crackers.

Worcestershire Clam Dip

1 (8-ounce) package cream cheese, softened
1 (7½-ounce) can minced clams, drained
   and juice reserved
1 tablespoon chopped parsley
2 teaspoons onion powder
2 teaspoons Worcestershire sauce
¾ teaspoon lemon juice
⅛ teaspoon salt
Hot pepper sauce to taste

Combine all ingredients except reserved clam juice and blend well. Add enough juice to achieve desired consistency. Serve with crackers or chips.

Layered Mexican Dip

1 can refried beans
2 cups sour cream
1 package taco seasoning
2 cups shredded mozzarella cheese
2 cups shredded Cheddar cheese
2 avocados
¼ cup picante sauce
Lemon juice
4 tomatoes, chopped
4 green onions, chopped
1 small can sliced black olives, drained

Spread refried beans in bottom of a springform pan. Combine sour cream and taco seasoning. Spread over beans. Sprinkle with cheeses. Mash avocados and mix in picante sauce. Add lemon juice to taste. Spread over cheeses. Top with layers of tomatoes, green onions and black olives. Cover with plastic wrap and refrigerate overnight. Remove collar from pan and serve with corn chips.

Sound Bites

To reduce the calories in dips, substitute non-fat yogurt for sour cream and light mayonnaise for regular mayo.

Mexican Cheesecake

1 cup crushed tortilla chips
3 tablespoons butter, melted
2 (8-ounce) packages cream cheese, softened
2 eggs
2 (4-ounce) cans diced green chiles, drained
4 tablespoons chopped jalapeño peppers
4 ounces Colby cheese, shredded
4 ounces Monterey Jack cheese, shredded
¼ cup sour cream
¼ cup chopped tomatoes
¼ cup chopped green onions
¼ cup diced black olives

Combine tortilla chips and butter. Press into bottom of a 9-inch springform pan. Bake in preheated 325° oven for 15 minutes. Remove from oven, leaving oven on. Beat cream cheese until light and fluffy. Add eggs one at a time, beating well after each addition. Add chiles, jalapeño and cheeses. Pour into crust and bake 30 minutes. Remove from oven and cool in pan. Run knife around edge and remove collar from pan. Spread with sour cream and decorate with tomatoes, green onions and olives. Serve with chips.

Artichoke Crab Dip

1 cup mayonnaise
2½ cups grated Parmesan cheese
1 (7-ounce) can Alaska King crab, drained
  and flaked
1 (14-ounce) can artichoke hearts, drained
  and chopped
Dash of hot pepper sauce

Combine mayonnaise and cheese. Stir in crab and arti-chokes. Place in a glass baking dish and chill overnight. To serve hot, bake in preheated 350° oven until bubbling, about 30 minutes. Place in a chafing dish and serve with chips. This dip is also good cold, served with crackers.

Hot Bleu Cheese Dip

7 slices bacon
2 cloves garlic, minced
4 ounces bleu cheese, crumbled
1 (8-ounce) package cream cheese, softened
¼ cup half and half
2 tablespoons chopped chives
Toasted sliced almonds

Cook bacon until brown and crispy. Crumble. Combine garlic, cheeses and half and half. Fold in bacon and chives. Place in a baking dish which has been coated with nonstick vegetable spray. Bake in preheated 350° oven for 30 minutes. Top with almonds and serve with crackers.

Chocolate Pecan Ball

1½ cups chocolate chips, melted
½ cup crème de menthe liqueur
3 (8-ounce) packages cream cheese, softened
1 teaspoon cinnamon
2 cups chopped pecans

Combine all ingredients except pecans and mix until smooth. Cover and refrigerate until firm enough to handle. Divide into 3 balls and roll in pecans. Refrigerate until chilled. Serve with chocolate or vanilla wafers, animal crackers or sugar cookies.

Pepperoni Pizza Dip

1 (8-ounce) package cream cheese, softened
½ cup sour cream
⅛ teaspoon dried oregano
⅛ teaspoon garlic powder
⅛ teaspoon crushed red pepper
½ cup prepared pizza sauce
½ cup quartered pepperoni slices
¼ cup chopped green bell pepper
½ cup shredded mozzarella cheese

Combine cream cheese, sour cream and spices. Spread over bottom of a 9-inch quiche dish. Top with pizza sauce. Sprinkle with pepperonis and bell pepper. Bake in preheated 350° oven for 10 minutes. Top with cheese and bake an additional 10 minutes. Serve with bite-size tortilla chips.

Sound Bites

Soften 1 (8-ounce) package of cream cheese by microwaving at 30% power for 2 minutes.

Baked Crab Meat with Melba Toast

1 (16-ounce) can white crab meat
1 tablespoon milk
2 (8-ounce) packages cream cheese, softened
¼ cup finely chopped onion
½ teaspoon salt
1 teaspoon Worcestershire sauce
1 teaspoon prepared horseradish
3 to 4 drops hot pepper sauce
1 cup toasted sliced almonds
Melba toast

Place crab meat and milk in top of a double boiler. Heat over hot water. Add cream cheese and stir gently until cheese melts. Add remaining ingredients except almonds and melba toast. Pour into a casserole which has been coated with nonstick vegetable spray. Sprinkle with almonds. Bake in preheated 375° oven for 15 minutes. Serve with melba toast.

Orange Cheese Ball

2 (8-ounce) packages cream cheese, softened
4 tablespoons powdered sugar
1 tablespoon grated lemon rind
1 tablespoon grated orange rind
2 tablespoons orange liqueur
1 cup sliced almonds, toasted
1 tablespoon orange juice

Combine all ingredients except almonds. Mix well and shape into a ball. Roll ball in almonds and chill. Serve with sweet wafers.

Butterscotch Apple Dip

1 can sweetened condensed milk
1 cup butterscotch morsels
1 tablespoon vinegar
¼ teaspoon salt
¼ teaspoon cinnamon
Apples
Lemon juice

Combine milk, morsels, vinegar, salt and cinnamon in a medium saucepan. Cook over medium heat until melted, stirring frequently. Slice apples and sprinkle with lemon juice to prevent discoloration. Drain on paper towels. Serve with warm dip.

Coconut Fruit Dip

1 (8-ounce) package light cream cheese, softened
1 can cream of coconut
1 (8-ounce) container frozen whipped topping, thawed

Combine cream cheese and cream of coconut. Blend until smooth. Fold in whipped topping. Serve with strawberries, grapes, kiwi and melons.

Fresh Strawberries with Cream Dip

1 (8-ounce) package cream cheese, softened
1 cup sour cream
⅓ cup powdered sugar
2 teaspoons orange liqueur
1 quart strawberries, rinsed and hulled

Combine cream cheese and sour cream in a small bowl. Beat at medium speed until smooth. Add powdered sugar and liqueur, mixing well. Chill 1 hour. Serve with strawberries. **Yield: 2 cups dip.**

Coffee Liqueur-Cinnamon Fruit Dip

2 (3-ounce) packages cream cheese, softened
6 tablespoons powdered sugar
6 tablespoons sour cream
8 teaspoons coffee liqueur
½ teaspoon cinnamon

Beat cream cheese in a small bowl until fluffy. Add remaining ingredients and mix well. Serve with fresh fruit.

Strawberries Extraordinaire

20 large strawberries, rinsed and patted dry
6 ounces chocolate chips
1 tablespoon vegetable oil

Melt chocolate chips in top of double boiler. Stir in oil and reduce heat to low. Dip strawberries in melted chocolate and allow to harden on waxed paper. Do Not Refrigerate. Eat the same day.

Variation: *Pretzels or bananas may be substituted for strawberries.*

Sound Information

Three out of every 100 school children are affected by hearing loss.

Sound Bites

A different flavoring for tea: Instead of sugar, dissolve old-fashioned lemon drops or hard mint candy in your tea. They melt quickly and keep the tea clean and brisk!

Friendship Tea

18 ounces instant orange-flavored drink
1 cup sugar
½ cup presweetened lemonade mix
½ cup instant tea mix
1 package apricot gelatin
2½ teaspoons cinnamon
1 teaspoon ground cloves or nutmeg

Mix all ingredients and store in airtight jars. To prepare tea, mix one slightly rounded teaspoon or more to taste with hot water.

Plantation Tea

2 tea bags
⅔ to ¾ cup sugar
¼ cup lemon juice
2 cups boiling water plus 2 cups water
½ teaspoon almond extract
½ teaspoon vanilla

Place tea, sugar and juice in a 1-quart container. Add boiling water and steep for 10 minutes. Remove tea bag or leaves. Add remaining ingredients and stir. Chill overnight. Serve over ice. **Yield: 1 quart.**

Almond Punch

Great for tea or bridal reception.

1 small package lemon gelatin
2 cups boiling water
2½ cups sugar
5 cups cold water
1 large can unsweetened pineapple juice
1 cup lemon juice
1 (1-ounce) bottle almond extract
2 liters ginger ale

Dissolve gelatin in 2 cups boiling water in a large container. Add remaining ingredients except ginger ale. Pour into 2 1-gallon plastic bags and freeze. Defrost 2 to 3 hours before serving. It should still be slushy. Just before serving, add ginger ale. **Yield: 25 5-ounce cups.**

Tangy Tea

2 family size tea bags
3 cups boiling water
1½ cups sugar
1 (6-ounce) can frozen limeade
1 (6-ounce) can frozen lemonade
Enough water to make 1 gallon

Place tea bags in a 1-gallon container. Pour boiling water over tea and steep for 10 minutes. Remove tea bags and add remaining ingredients. Serve over ice. **Yield: 1 gallon.**

Banana Punch

6 cups water
4 cups sugar
1 (3-ounce) can frozen lemonade concentrate
5 ripe bananas
1 large can pineapple juice
2 cups orange juice
3 (2 liter) bottles ginger ale

Combine water and sugar in a saucepan. Bring to a boil, then cool. Place lemonade concentrate and bananas in a blender. Purée. Add to sugar water. Stir in pineapple juice and orange juice. Mix well and freeze. Zip lock bags work well. **When ready to serve, add ginger ale.**

Hot Cranberry Punch

2 quarts cranberry juice
3 quarts apple juice
½ cup firmly packed brown sugar
4 cinnamon sticks
⅛ teaspoon salt
1 tablespoon whole cloves

Combine all ingredients and heat. To make in a coffee pot, place brown sugar, cinnamon sticks, salt and cloves in coffee filter. Let coffee pot perk. **Yield: 30 cups.**

Hot Sherry Punch

1 orange
Whole cloves
1 (48-ounce) bottle apple juice
1 (750 ml) bottle sherry

Stud orange with cloves. Mix apple juice and sherry in a saucepan (for stove top), a Dutch oven (for oven) or a crock pot (for table top). Add orange. Heat and keep hot over low heat. Serve hot in mugs or cups.

Cranberry Spritzer

2 cups cranberry juice cocktail, chilled
1½ cups Sauterne, chilled
½ cup triple sec or other orange-flavored liqueur
2 cups club soda, chilled

*Combine all ingredients except club soda in a pitcher. Just before serving, add club soda. Serve over crushed ice. **Yield: 1½ quarts.***

Torrejon O Club Sangria

This recipe was given by the bartender at Torrejon A. F. Base in Spain, who said the cheapest red wine makes the best sangria.

1½ liters burgundy
1 liter club soda
3 jiggers brandy
Sugar
1 orange, sliced
1 lemon, sliced

Mix burgundy and club soda in a large pitcher or punch bowl. Add brandy. Sweeten to taste with sugar and garnish with fruit slices.

Champagne Punch

3 cups sugar
2 cups lemon juice
1 fresh pineapple, cut in bite size pieces, or
   2 large cans pineapple chunks, drained
1 quart fresh hulled strawberries or
   1 package whole frozen strawberries
1½ quarts club soda, chilled
1 quart Sauterne, chilled
2 to 3 bottles champagne, chilled
1 block of ice or an ice ring

Dissolve sugar and lemon juice in sauce pan over low heat. Cool. Place pineapple on cookie sheets and freeze. When ready to serve, combine all ingredients in a punch bowl. **Yield: 2 gallons.**

Sound / Bites

To make an ice ring– Pour club soda and water in a mold or ring. When partially frozen add pineapple chunks and strawberries to decorate. Return to freezer until frozen solid.

Apricot Brandy Slush

Make 4 days in advance.

9 cups water, divided
2 cups sugar
4 regular-size tea bags
1 (12-ounce) can frozen orange juice concentrate
1 (12-ounce) can frozen limeade concentrate
2 cups apricot brandy

Combine 7 cups water and sugar. Bring to a boil and let cool. Bring remaining 2 cups water to a boil. Add tea bags and let steep until water cools. Combine sugar water, tea and remaining ingredients in a nonmetallic container. Cover and freeze. Stir daily for 2 to 3 days.

When ready to serve, place 3 scoops in a glass. Drink as is, or pour a little lemon-lime soft drink over it.

Breakfast, Brunch & Breads

Breakfast, Brunch & Breads

Have You Heard ...

... about The Peabody Hotel

If you are in Memphis for any length of time, you will at some point be directed to The Peabody. It is referred to as the "South's Grand Hotel" and the home of the world-famous marching ducks. Many special memories are made in the ballrooms of this grand hotel. It is where many of us went to our first prom, our first wedding reception, our first ladies' luncheon, our first college dance, our first gala. Sitting in the lobby, having an iced tea or a julep is a must in order to absorb the elegance of The Peabody.

The original hotel was located at Main and Monroe. It was built in 1869 by Robert C. Brinkley and was named for financier George Peabody. The present building, considered a gracious example of Italian Renaissance Revival architecture, was opened in 1925. A complete renovation in the mid '90s added to the reputation that "the Delta begins in the lobby of The Peabody Hotel." It is listed on the National Register of Historic Places and is a recipient of Mobil's Four Star rating. Delightful dining, tempting gift shops, the daily morning presentation of the ducks, and its location in downtown Memphis would persuade anyone who visits "The Peabody" that something grand is about to occur.

Peabody's Molasses Bread

6 cups bread flour
1 cup whole wheat flour
3 tablespoons active dry yeast
2 teaspoons salt
6 tablespoons unsalted butter, softened
1½ cups light unsulphured molasses
2 cups warm water

Place bread flour, wheat flour and yeast in bowl of an electric mixer fitted with a dough hook. (If one is not available, the dough can also be mixed and kneaded by hand.) Blend flour mixture. Fit mixer with dough hook, add butter, molasses, salt and water. Knead for 10 minutes. Turn dough onto a floured work surface and form it into a ball. Place dough in a lightly greased large bowl, cover, and let rise in a warm place for 1½ to 2 hours, until doubled in volume. Punch down and form into 2 loaves. Place in 2 greased 9 x 5-inch loaf pans, cover and let rise again until doubled in volume. Preheat oven to 350°. Bake loaves 35 minutes. Remove from pans and cool on wire racks. The loaves should sound hollow when tapped. **Yield: 2 loaves.**

Eggs Amandine

10 slices bread, crusts removed
½ cup grated Cheddar cheese
6 large eggs
1⅔ cups milk
1 cup whipping cream
¼ cup sherry
1¼ teaspoons cornstarch
¼ teaspoon almond extract
4 tablespoons butter
½ cup sliced almonds

Cube bread and layer alternately with cheese in a 2-quart casserole which has been coated with nonstick vegetable spray. Combine eggs, milk, cream, sherry, cornstarch and almond extract in a large bowl. Beat until well blended. Pour over bread and cheese. Melt butter and pour over egg mixture. Cover and refrigerate at least 8 hours.

Sprinkle with almonds and bake in preheated 325° oven for 1 hour. **Serves 12.**

Baked Eggs Benedict

Sauce:
¼ cup butter
¼ cup flour
1 teaspoon salt
1 teaspoon paprika
⅛ teaspoon nutmeg
⅛ teaspoon fresh ground black pepper
2 cups milk, heated
½ cup white wine
2 cups grated Swiss cheese (about 8 ounces)

Eggs:
4 English muffins, split
Butter
2 tablespoons unsalted butter
1 (6-ounce) package sliced Canadian bacon
8 eggs

Crumb Topping:
1 cup crushed corn flakes
¼ cup unsalted butter, melted

For Sauce: *Melt butter in heavy saucepan over low heat. Add flour and cook and stir one minute. Stir in salt, paprika, nutmeg and pepper until well blended. Stir in milk. Heat to a boil, and cook, stirring constantly, until smooth and thickened, about 2 minutes. Reduce heat to low. Add wine and cheese. Cook, stirring, just until cheese is melted. Cover and remove from heat.*

For Eggs: *Toast and butter muffin halves. Butter a 9 x 13-inch baking dish. Place muffins in dish. Melt 2 table-spoons butter in skillet and brown bacon on each side. Place 2 slices bacon on each muffin. Heat 3 inches of water in Dutch oven to simmer. Break 1 egg at a time into small cup. Holding cup close to water's surface and at edge of Dutch oven, slip egg into simmering water. Cook until egg is set, about 2 to 3 minutes. Remove with slotted spoon and let water drip off. Gently place egg on top of muffin. Continue with remaining eggs. Spoon prepared sauce over each egg, dividing evenly. Sprinkle with crumb mixture. Cover with plastic wrap and refrigerate overnight.*

To finish dish, remove from refrigerator and let stand 45 minutes to 1 hour. Heat oven to 375°. Uncover dish and bake 15 minutes or until heated through. **Serves 8.**

Egg and Artichoke Casserole

2 (6½-ounce) jars marinated artichoke hearts
1 bunch green onions
1 clove garlic, minced
4 eggs, beaten
8 ounces Cheddar cheese, shredded
10 round buttery crackers, rolled into crumbs

Drain artichokes and reserve marinade. Cut artichokes into thirds. Mince green onions, using half of tops. Heat reserved marinade in a small skillet over medium heat. Sauté green onions and garlic until tender. Combine all ingredients and pour into a greased 9-inch square glass baking dish. Bake in preheated 350° oven for 40 minutes. **Serves 4.**

Sausage Breakfast Pizza

1 (8-ounce) package crescent rolls or packaged pizza dough
1 pound mild or hot sausage
½ cup sliced scallions
¼ cup chopped green bell pepper
1 cup shredded Monterey Jack or mozzarella cheese
1 cup frozen hash brown potatoes, thawed
4 large eggs
¼ cup milk
¼ cup minced fresh parsley
⅛ teaspoon nutmeg
Salt and freshly ground black pepper
⅓ cup grated Parmesan cheese

Roll out dough on a lightly floured surface into a circle to fit a medium pizza pan or 11-inch quiche pan. Press dough into bottom and up sides of pan. If using pizza pan, make a rim with dough. Cook sausage in a medium skillet until lightly browned, about 10 minutes, breaking up sausage while cooking. Pour off excess fat. Add scallions and green pepper. Cook until vegetables are soft, stirring frequently, about 5 minutes. Spoon mixture into bottom of prepared shell. Sprinkle Monterey Jack cheese over top. Distribute potatoes evenly over cheese. Beat eggs, milk, parsley, nutmeg and salt and pepper to taste in a small bowl. Pour over mixture in shell and sprinkle evenly with Parmesan cheese. Bake in preheated 350° oven until set and lightly browned on top, about 45 minutes. Cut into wedges to serve. **Makes 8.**

Sound Bites

When a recipe calls for adding raw eggs to hot mixture always begin by adding a small amount of hot mixture to the beaten eggs slowly to avoid curdling.

Egg, Sausage and Potato Casserole

2 pounds mild or hot sausage
1 (15-ounce) package frozen hash brown
    potatoes, thawed
12 eggs
1¼ cups half and half
½ teaspoon salt
¼ teaspoon pepper
4 to 5 drops hot pepper sauce

Brown sausage in a skillet, breaking it up while stirring. Drain well on paper towel. Drain skillet, leaving a small amount of sausage drippings. Add potatoes and cook until soft. Mix sausage with potatoes. Combine eggs and half and half in a large bowl. Beat until well blended. Add seasonings. Add sausage mixture and stir to mix. Pour into a 9 x 13-inch casserole dish which has been coated with nonstick vegetable spray. Bake, uncovered, in preheated 350° oven for 25 to 30 minutes. **Serves 10 to 12.**

Easy Eggs Florentine

1 (10-ounce) package frozen chopped spinach,
    thawed and well drained
¼ cup minced onions
8 hard-cooked eggs, sliced ⅛-inch thick
1 cup shredded Swiss or Jarlesberg cheese
    (about 4 ounces)
⅔ cup condensed cream of mushroom soup
⅔ cup sour cream
2 tablespoons butter
½ cup crushed herb-seasoned stuffing mix
¼ cup grated Parmesan cheese
Paprika

Spread spinach evenly in bottom of a lightly buttered 1½-quart casserole. Sprinkle with onions and layer egg slices on top. Combine cheese, soup and sour cream in a small bowl. Stir until well mixed and spread on top of eggs. Melt butter in a small saucepan. Add stuffing mix and stir until well combined. Sprinkle evenly over cheese sauce. Sprinkle with Parmesan cheese and paprika. Bake, uncovered, in preheated 350° oven until lightly browned on top and bubbly, about 35 to 45 minutes. **Serves 4 to 6.**

Scrambled Eggs for a Brunch

½ pound butter, divided
2 cups minced green onions
½ cup flour
2½ cups evaporated milk
2½ cups milk
2 cups grated sharp cheese
1 cup sherry
1 teaspoon seasoned salt
½ teaspoon curry powder
½ teaspoon white pepper
½ teaspoon cayenne
½ teaspoon dry mustard
3 dozen eggs
2 cups water
Salt and pepper to taste

Melt ¼ pound butter in a large saucepan. Sauté onions lightly and stir in flour. Gradually add milk and cook, stirring constantly, until thickened. Blend in cheese and remove from heat. Stir in sherry and seasonings. Beat 1½ dozen eggs with 1 cup water and season lightly with salt and pepper. Melt 4 tablespoons butter in skillet. Scramble eggs until they barely hold together. Do not overcook eggs or casserole will be too firm when baked. Set aside to cool. Repeat with remaining eggs. Grease 2 3-quart casseroles lightly and pour one-fourth of the white sauce in bottom of each casserole dish. Place scrambled eggs evenly on top of sauce and cover with remaining sauce, being careful to entirely cover bottom and top of eggs with sauce. Cover tightly and refrigerate up to 2 days.

When ready to finish, bring casseroles to room temperature. Bake, covered, in preheated 275° oven for 1 hour. Keep warm over hot water until ready to serve.

Sound Bites

To keep scrambled eggs moist, take them up moments before they reach to degree of doneness that you desire

Sound Bites

If crust browns before inside cooks fully, cover edges of crust lightly with strips of foil.

Breakfast Quiche

2 (9-inch) pie shells, unbaked
1 pound sausage, browned
8 ounces mozzarella cheese, shredded
8 eggs, beaten
1½ cups milk
1 teaspoon salt
½ teaspoon pepper

Divide sausage between pie shells and spread evenly over bottom. Top with cheese. Combine remaining ingredients in a medium bowl and mix thoroughly. Pour half into each shell. Bake in preheated 375° oven until set, 25 to 35 minutes. **Serves 8 to 10.**

Ham Quiche

3 eggs
1 cup half and half
4 slices ham, torn into pieces
½ pound Swiss cheese, grated
1 tablespoon flour
¼ cup chopped onion
¼ cup chopped green bell pepper
Salt and pepper to taste
1 (9-inch) pie shell, unbaked

Beat eggs in a medium bowl. Stir in half and half. Add remaining ingredients except pie crust and blend well. Pour into pie crust and bake in preheated 325° oven until a knife inserted in center comes out clean, about 30 minutes.

Sausage and Apple Ring

2 pounds pork sausage
1½ cups cracker crumbs
2 eggs, beaten
½ cup minced onion
1 cup grated peeled apple

Combine all ingredients in a medium bowl. Mix well, using hands. Press lightly into a greased Bundt pan and bake in preheated 350° oven for 30 minutes. Drain and invert onto serving dish. Garnish with parsley sprigs or fill middle of ring with scrambled eggs. **Serves 8 to 10.**

Sausage and Spinach Casserole

Good for brunch or as an appetizer.

1½ cups grated sharp Cheddar cheese
3 tablespoons flour
⅔ cup mayonnaise
3 eggs, lightly beaten
1 (10-ounce) package frozen chopped spinach, cooked and drained
1 (4-ounce) can sliced mushrooms, drained
½ pound mild sausage, cooked and drained
½ teaspoon salt

Toss cheese with flour in a large bowl. Add remaining ingredients and mix well. Pour into a greased 9-inch square baking dish and bake in preheated 350° oven until set, about 30 minutes. Cut into squares to serve.

Recipe can be doubled and baked in a 9 x 13-inch baking dish.

Texas Eggs

10 eggs
3 tablespoons sour cream
Salt and pepper to taste
½ pound hot sausage
½ pound mild sausage
Sliced mushrooms
1 green bell pepper, chopped
1 medium onion, chopped
1 can diced tomatoes and green chiles
8 ounces pasteurized process cheese spread
8 ounces Cheddar cheese
8 ounces mozzarella cheese

Place eggs, sour cream, salt and pepper in a blender and blend until smooth. Pour into a greased 9 x 13-inch baking dish. Bake in preheated 400° oven for 7 minutes.

Sauté sausage, mushrooms, bell pepper and onions in a large skillet until sausage is cooked through, breaking up sausage while cooking. Drain well. Stir in diced tomatoes and green chiles. Pour over egg mixture. Melt cheeses together and spread over sausage mixture. Cover and refrigerate overnight.

When ready to finish, bake, uncovered, in preheated 350° oven until hot and bubbly.

Sound Bites

Separating an egg–
Eggs separate more easily when cold, but must be allowed to attain room temperature after separating, before they are used in a recipe.

Sour Cream Coffee Cake

1 cup margarine, softened
2 cups sugar
2 eggs
1 cup sour cream
2 tablespoons milk
½ teaspoon vanilla
2 cups flour, sifted
1 teaspoon baking powder
¼ teaspoon salt

Topping:
1 cup finely chopped pecans
2 teaspoons sugar
1 teaspoon cinnamon

*Cream margarine, sugar, eggs, sour cream, vanilla and milk until light and fluffy. Sift together flour, baking powder and salt. Add to creamed mixture. Pour one-third of batter into a greased and floured Bundt pan. Combine topping ingredients and sprinkle half over batter. Top with second third of batter. Sprinkle with remaining topping. Pour remaining batter over topping and bake in preheated 350° oven until a toothpick inserted in center comes out clean, about 50 to 60 minutes. Remove from pan immediately and cool on wire rack. **Serves 8 to 12.***

Bundt Cinnamon Rolls

1 package frozen roll dough
¼ cup firmly packed brown sugar
2 teaspoons cinnamon
1 (3-ounce) package butterscotch pudding
   (not instant)
½ cup chopped pecans
½ cup margarine, melted

Roll slightly thawed rolls in a mixture of cinnamon and sugar. Place rolls in a greased Bundt pan. Sprinkle dry pudding mix and pecans over rolls and drizzle with margarine. Cover pan with a light cloth and let stand overnight or all day. Do not refrigerate.

*When ready to finish, bake in preheated 325° oven for 35 minutes. Invert onto serving dish and serve immediately. **Serves 8 to 10.***

***Variation:** Vanilla pudding may be substituted for butterscotch.*

Pecan Apple Danish Coffee Cake

2 (8-ounce) packages crescent rolls
2 (8-ounce) packages cream cheese, softened
1½ cups sugar, divided
2 teaspoons vanilla
1 egg
½ cup butter or margarine, melted
1 Granny Smith apple, peeled and chopped
1 cup chopped pecans
1½ teaspoons cinnamon

Preheat oven to 350°. Unroll one package crescent rolls in bottom of a 9 x 13-inch baking pan which has been coated with nonstick vegetable spray. Press out to cover bottom. Pinch seams and roll 1 inch up sides. Combine cream cheese, 1 cup sugar, vanilla and egg in a bowl. Mix well to blend. Pour over crust. Unroll second package of rolls on a cutting board. Roll out and pinch seams together. Place over cream cheese mixture and pinch top and bottom crusts together. Combine butter, apple, pecans, remaining ½ cup sugar and cinnamon in a bowl. Spread evenly over top crust. Bake until crust is brown, about 30 minutes. Let rest at least 1 hour before serving.
Serves 12.

Sound Bites

To reduce fat, applesauce can be substituted for up to half the oil, margarine or butter required in many recipes for muffins, quick breads, cake mixes and cakes made from scratch. Eliminating all the fat, however, can result in an overly dry baked product.

Cherry Kringle

2 cups flour
1 cup butter
1 cup sour cream
Dash of salt
1 can cherry pie filling
Powdered sugar
Water

Cut flour and butter together with a pastry fork until mixture resembles coarse meal. Add sour cream and a dash of salt. Mix well, cover and refrigerate overnight.

The following day, divide dough into 2 balls. Roll each ball into a rectangle the size of a baking sheet. Spread pie filling over center of dough and fold each side to center. Place on ungreased baking sheet. Bake in preheated 375° oven for 35 minutes. Add water to powdered sugar until of a glaze consistency. Pour over kringle.

Lemon Blueberry Muffins

1 large egg
2 cups biscuit baking mix
¼ cup sugar
2 tablespoons vegetable oil
6 ounces lemon yogurt
¾ cup fresh or frozen blueberries

Preheat oven to 400°. Break egg into a medium bowl and beat lightly with a fork. Stir in remaining ingredients except blueberries just until baking mix is moistened. Don't stir too much; the batter will be thick. Gently fold in blueberries. Line a muffin pan with paper liners or coat bottoms with nonstick vegetable spray. Fill cups two-thirds full with batter. Bake until golden brown, 15 to 18 minutes. Remove immediately from pan. Serve warm or cool. **Yield: 1 dozen.**

Morning Glory Muffins

2 cups flour
1 cup sugar
2 teaspoons baking soda
2 teaspoons cinnamon
¼ teaspoon salt
½ cup raisins, soaked in hot water for 30 minutes
    and drained thoroughly
2 cups shredded carrots
1 large apple, grated
½ cup chopped nuts
½ cup shredded coconut
3 eggs
⅔ cup vegetable oil
2 teaspoons vanilla

Combine flour, sugar, baking soda, cinnamon and salt in a large bowl. Stir in raisins, carrots, apples, nuts and coconut. In a separate bowl, beat eggs, oil and vanilla until well blended. Add to flour mixture and blend just enough to moisten dry ingredients. Pour into 12 large muffin cups and bake in preheated 350° oven for 20 to 22 minutes. **Yield: 1 dozen.**

Raspberry Bran Muffins

2½ cups flour
1¾ cups sugar
2 teaspoons baking powder
½ teaspoon baking soda
½ teaspoon salt
2 cups buttermilk
½ cup vegetable oil
2 large eggs
8 cups bran flakes cereal
½ cup raspberry jam

*Preheat oven to 350°. Combine flour, sugar, baking powder, baking soda and salt in a medium bowl. Whisk buttermilk, oil and eggs in a large bowl to blend. Add flour mixture and cereal and stir just until blended. Line muffin tins with paper muffin cups. Spoon ¼ cup batter into each muffin cup. Make a well in center of each with a small spoon and fill well with 1 teaspoon jam. Spoon remaining batter over. Bake until tester inserted into centers comes out clean, about 25 minutes. Turn out onto racks and cool slightly. Serve warm or at room temperature. **Yield: 2 dozen.***

Sound Bites

Substituting two egg whites for one whole egg lightens a recipe by 5 grams of fat and 213 milligrams of cholesterol.

Sweet Potato Muffins

2 cups sifted flour
2 teaspoons baking powder
½ teaspoon baking soda
1 teaspoon salt
1¼ teaspoons cinnamon
½ teaspoon nutmeg
1 cup cooked, mashed sweet potatoes
1 cup sugar
½ cup milk
2 eggs
¼ cup butter, melted
¾ cup chopped pecans

*Sift together flour, baking powder, baking soda, salt, cinnamon and nutmeg. Combine sweet potatoes, sugar, milk and eggs in a medium bowl. Add flour mixture and butter. Mix until well blended. Stir in nuts. Fill greased muffin cups one-half full. Bake in preheated 350° oven until a toothpick inserted in center comes out clean, about 20 minutes. **Yield: 2 dozen.***

Company French Toast with Strawberry Topping

12 (1½-inch thick) slices French bread
1 (8-ounce) package cream cheese, softened
2 tablespoons sugar
½ teaspoon nutmeg
½ teaspoon cinnamon
6 eggs, beaten
1 cup half and half
½ cup milk

Strawberry Topping:
1 cup powdered sugar
2 tablespoons cornstarch
½ cup butter, melted
⅓ cup Grand Marnier
3 cups sliced strawberries

Preheat oven to 350°. Slice each piece of bread horizontally to form a pocket. Combine cream cheese, sugar, nutmeg and cinnamon. Spread 1½ tablespoons of cream cheese mixture inside pocket. Place bread in a greased casserole dish. Combine eggs, half and half and milk. Pour over bread and turn slices to coat. Bake 35 minutes.

For Topping: *Combine all ingredients except strawberries in a medium saucepan. Cook over medium heat, stirring constantly, until sugar and cornstarch are dissolved. Add strawberries and heat through. Serve over French toast. **Serves 12.***

French Toast Italian Style

1 (12-ounce) can evaporated milk
1 cup sugar
4 eggs
1 teaspoon almond extract
2 tablespoons hazelnut liqueur
1 loaf Italian or French bread, sliced ¾-inch thick
¼ cup powdered sugar

*Combine milk, sugar, eggs, almond extract and liqueur. Beat with a wire whisk until well blended. Dip both sides of bread in milk mixture, draining excess. Cook on a griddle which has been coated with nonstick spray. Cook until golden brown on both sides. Serve sprinkled with powdered sugar. **Serves 12.***

Blueberry Pancakes

1 cup flour
1½ teaspoons baking powder
½ teaspoon salt
1 tablespoon sugar
¼ teaspoon cinnamon
1 egg, separated
2 tablespoons margarine, melted
¾ cup milk
¾ cup fresh blueberries

Combine flour, baking powder, salt, sugar and cinnamon in a medium bowl. In a separate bowl, beat egg yolk until thick and lemon colored. Add margarine and milk and stir until blended. Add dry ingredients, stirring just until moistened. Beat room temperature egg white in a clean bowl until stiff peaks form. Fold into batter. Gently fold in blueberries. For each pancake, pour ¼ cup batter onto hot, lightly greased griddle. Turn when edges appear cooked.
Yield: 8 4-inch pancakes.

Cranberry Orange Bread

2 cups sifted flour
1 cup sugar
1½ teaspoons baking powder
1 teaspoon salt
½ teaspoon baking soda
¼ cup butter or margarine
1 egg, beaten
1 teaspoon grated orange peel
¾ cup orange juice
1½ cups light raisins
1½ cups fresh or frozen cranberries, chopped

Sift flour, sugar, baking powder, salt and baking soda into a large bowl. Cut in butter until mixture is crumbly. Add egg, orange peel and orange juice all at once. Stir just until mixture is evenly moist. Fold in raisins and cranberries. Spoon into greased 9 x 5 x 3-inch loaf pan. Bake in preheated 350° oven until a toothpick inserted in center comes out clean, about 1 hour and 10 minutes. Remove from pan and cool on a wire rack.

Variation: *Substitute cranberries for raisins for an all-cranberry bread.*

Sound Bites

Peel over-ripened bananas, leave whole and place in a freezer bag. Freeze for later use.

Sour Cream Banana Bread

¼ cup butter, softened
1¼ cups sugar
2 eggs, beaten
4 tablespoons sour cream
1½ cups flour
1 teaspoon baking soda
1 teaspoon vanilla
1 cup mashed banana

Cream butter and sugar in a large bowl until light and fluffy. Add eggs one at a time, beating well after each addition. Add remaining ingredients and blend. Pour into a greased loaf pan and bake in preheated 350° oven until a tester inserted in center comes out clean, about 45 minutes.

Orange Poppy Bread

3 cups flour
1½ teaspoons baking powder
1½ cups milk
2¼ cups sugar
1½ teaspoons vanilla
1½ teaspoons butter flavoring
1½ teaspoons salt
3 eggs, beaten
1⅛ cups vegetable oil
1½ teaspoons poppy seeds
1½ teaspoons almond extract

Glaze:
½ teaspoon butter flavoring
½ teaspoon vanilla
¾ cup sugar
½ teaspoon almond extract
¼ cup orange juice

Preheat oven to 350°. Combine all bread ingredients in a large mixing bowl. Beat on medium speed for 2 minutes. Pour into 2 greased loaf pans and bake 1 hour. Combine glaze ingredients and pour over hot bread. **Yield: 2 loaves**.

Lemon Bread

1 cup sugar
⅓ cup butter, melted
1 teaspoon lemon extract
¼ cup fresh lemon juice
2 eggs
1½ cups flour
1 teaspoon baking powder
1 teaspoon salt
½ cup milk
Grated rind of 1 large lemon
½ cup chopped pecans

Glaze:
½ cup powdered sugar
¼ cup fresh lemon juice

Preheat oven to 350°. Cream sugar, butter, lemon extract and juice in a medium bowl. Add eggs, one at a time, beating well after each addition. Sift together flour, baking powder and salt. Stir into creamed mixture alternately with milk. Add lemon rind and pecans. Pour into a buttered 8-inch loaf pan and bake until a toothpick inserted in center comes out clean, about 1 hour.

For Glaze: *Place sugar and lemon juice in a small saucepan. Heat over low, stirring constantly, until sugar is dissolved.*

Remove bread from oven and pierce top in several places with a sharp knife blade or a thin fork. Pour glaze over top and cool in pan for 1 hour. Remove from pan, wrap in foil and let stand 24 hours before cutting. This bread keeps 2 to 3 months in the refrigerator.

Strawberry Bread

Great with cream cheese.

2 cups flour
2 cups sugar
1 teaspoon baking soda
1 teaspoon salt
1 tablespoon cinnamon
4 eggs, beaten
1¼ cups vegetable oil
1¼ cups chopped pecans
2 cups sliced strawberries

Sift together flour, sugar, baking soda, salt and cinnamon in a large bowl. Add eggs, oil, berries and pecans. Stir just enough to moisten. Spoon into 2 well-greased 9 x 5 x 3-inch loaf pans. Bake in preheated 350° oven until a toothpick inserted in center comes out clean, about 1 hour to 1 hour and 10 minutes. Cool on wire racks. **Yield: 2 loaves.**

Hot Cheese Toast

8 slices bacon
⅓ cup mayonnaise
1 cup shredded sharp Cheddar cheese
1 small onion, grated
1 egg, lightly beaten
½ teaspoon Worcestershire sauce
Several dashes hot pepper sauce
⅛ teaspoon dry mustard
Dash of black pepper
8 slices firm white bread, toasted and crusts
    removed
Paprika
10 cherry tomatoes, sliced

Bake bacon in preheated 350° oven until crispy, about 20 minutes. Drain and crumble. Combine mayonnaise, cheese, onion, egg, Worcestershire sauce, hot pepper sauce, dry mustard and pepper. Add bacon. Spread on toast and cut into 3 strips or 4 squares. Sprinkle with paprika. Bake until cheese melts. Top with tomatoes. **Serves 8.**

Pumpkin Roll

3 eggs
1 cup sugar
⅔ cup canned pumpkin
1 tablespoon lemon juice
¾ cup flour
1 teaspoon baking powder
2 tablespoons cinnamon
1 teaspoon ginger
½ teaspoon nutmeg
½ teaspoon salt
1 cup chopped pecans
Powdered sugar

Filling:
2 (3-ounce) packages cream cheese, softened
4 tablespoons butter, softened
½ teaspoon vanilla
1 cup powdered sugar

Place eggs in a medium bowl and beat for 5 minutes. Add sugar, lemon juice and pumpkin and stir to blend. Add flour, baking powder, cinnamon, ginger, nutmeg and salt. Stir until dry ingredients are moistened. Spread batter on a greased and floured jelly roll pan. Sprinkle with nuts. Bake in preheated 375° oven for 15 minutes. Invert onto a clean dish towel which has been heavily sprinkled with powdered sugar. Roll towel and cake up together, jelly-roll style. Allow bread to cool. Unroll and remove towel. Combine all filling ingredients and spread over bread. Reroll, wrap in foil and chill.

Parmesan Biscuits

½ cup margarine, melted
2 tablespoons grated Parmesan cheese
½ teaspoon garlic powder
1 tablespoon dill
2 cans large refrigerator biscuits

*Combine all ingredients except biscuits. Cut biscuits in half and dip in margarine mixture. Bake according to package directions. **Yield: 40 biscuits.***

Savory Cheese Bread

2 cups flour
2 teaspoons baking powder
1 tablespoon sugar
½ teaspoon salt
¼ cup butter or margarine, cut into 4 parts
1 cup grated Cheddar cheese
1 tablespoon grated onion
1 teaspoon dill
¾ cup milk
1 egg, lightly beaten

Preheat oven to 350°. Combine flour, baking powder, sugar and salt in a large bowl. Cut in butter with a pastry blender or 2 knives until mixture resembles coarse meal. Stir in cheese, onion and dill. Mix well. Combine milk and egg in a small bowl. Pour into flour mixture all at once. Stir quickly with a fork just to moisten dry ingredients. Turn into a lightly greased 9 x 5 x 3-inch loaf pan. Bake until tooth-pick inserted in center comes out clean, 40 to 45 minutes. Cool in pan 10 minutes, then invert onto a wire rack to finish cooling.

Southern Oyster Dressing

1½ pints oysters
1 cup butter
¾ cup diced onion
12 cups fresh white bread crumbs (about 17 slices)
1½ cups chopped celery with leaves
1 teaspoon salt
1 teaspoon pepper
½ teaspoon thyme
½ teaspoon poultry seasoning

Drain oysters, reserving ½ cup liquid. Melt butter in Dutch oven over medium heat. Sauté onion for 5 minutes. Add oysters and reserved liquid and remove from heat. Add bread crumbs and remaining ingredients to Dutch oven. Stir. Place in greased 9 x 13-inch glass baking dish and cover with foil. Bake in preheated 350° oven for 40 minutes. Remove foil and bake an additional 20 minutes.

Broccoli Cornbread

1 (9-ounce) package frozen chopped broccoli,
   thawed and drained
1 large onion, chopped
1 (12-ounce) carton cottage cheese
½ cup margarine, melted
4 eggs
1 teaspoon salt
2 small boxes corn muffin mix

Combine all ingredients and pour into a 9 x 13-inch baking pan which has been coated with nonstick vegetable spray. Bake in preheated 400° oven for 10 minutes. Reduce oven temperature to 350° and bake an additional 35 to 40 minutes.

Oven Buttered Corn Sticks

4 tablespoons butter
2 cups biscuit baking mix
1 (8¾-ounce) can cream-style corn

Melt butter in 9 x 13-inch baking pan. Combine biscuit mix and corn. Stir until soft dough is formed. Knead for 15 strokes and roll on floured surface to ½-inch thickness. Cut into 1 x 3-inch strips and place in prepared pan. Roll in melted butter to coat well. Bake in preheated 450° oven 10 to 15 minutes.

Southwestern Spoon Bread

1 (16½-ounce) can yellow cream-style corn
1 cup yellow cornmeal
¾ cup milk
⅓ cup corn oil
2 eggs, lightly beaten
1 teaspoon baking powder
½ teaspoon salt
1 cup shredded sharp Cheddar cheese
1 (4-ounce) can chopped green chiles

Combine all ingredients except cheese and chiles in a mixing bowl. Blend well. Pour half of batter into a greased 2-quart baking dish. Sprinkle with cheese and chiles. Pour remaining batter over all. Bake in preheated 375° oven until just set, about 45 minutes. Serve warm. **Serves 6 to 8.**

Sound Bites

*To thaw frozen bread loaves and rolls–
Place in brown paper bag and put in 325° oven for 5 minutes.*

Salads, Soups & Sandwiches

Salads, Soups & Sandwiches

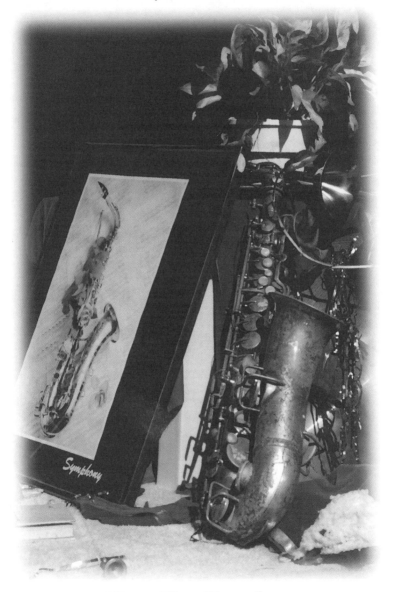

Have You Heard ...

. . . about Beale Street

*W*hat made Beale Street famous? In his "Beale Street Blues" W.C. Handy immortalized this historic area of downtown Memphis and he queried, "If Beale Street could talk...". Responses to this are as varied as the people who developed the area, and are as many as those who work and party there today! In the 1800's, on the docks where Beale met the Mississippi, riverboats and barges filled with cotton and agricultural offerings were unloaded; the river men then celebrated by enjoying their evenings on Beale. Music, bootlegging and games of chance added to the legends which gave the street its shocking reputation.

After the area was raided in the 1930's, dry-good stores, pawn shops and restaurants attempted to lure the more proper to the area. Nearby cross streets still had unsavory businesses but parts of Beale, particularly the eastern end, became the setting for Victorian mansions and antebellum homes of great grandeur. Today, Beale Street pulses with retail shops, museums, restaurants and, of course, musical establishments. W.C. Handy Park is a national historic landmark. Listen carefully – the Blues, jazz, zydeco, rock 'n roll, and even Gershwin echo the infamous past of this Memphis tourist attraction from early morning to...early morning of the next day as modern Beale Street adds to its legend.

Bogie's Gourmet Chicken Salad with Grapes and Almonds

2½ cups cubed cooked chicken breast
1 cup diced celery
1 cup green grapes, halved
½ cup slivered almonds, toasted
1 teaspoon salt
½ cup whipping cream, whipped
½ to ¾ cup mayonnaise

Combine chicken, celery, grapes, almonds and salt. Gently fold in whipped cream. Add enough mayonnaise to achieve desired consistency.

Tarragon Chicken Salad

8 large chicken breasts, boiled and shredded
3 green onions, chopped
1 to 2 cups mayonnaise
½ cup Dijon mustard
1 to 2 tablespoons dried tarragon, or to taste
Salt and pepper to taste

Combine all ingredients, adding enough mayonnaise to reach desired consistency. Great served on croissants or French baguettes.

Party Chicken Pasta

8 ounces rotini, cooked according to package
   directions
2 cups cooked, cubed chicken
1½ cups seedless grapes
½ large cucumber, chopped
¾ cup chopped celery (optional)
1 cup mayonnaise
½ cup sour cream
1½ teaspoons onion salt

Place rotini, chicken, grapes, cucumber and celery, if desired, in a salad bowl. Combine mayonnaise, sour cream and onion salt. Mix thoroughly and pour over salad. Toss well, cover and refrigerate overnight.

Sound Information

"We wanted to pick the kind of program that best suited our son. We preferred an auditory-oral program because we felt that he would be able to function better with skills that he learned there (at MOSD). If we could use the limited hearing that our son had, and teach him to speak, then he would be able to communicate better with others."

Overnight Layered Chicken Salad

6 cups shredded iceberg lettuce
¼ pound fresh bean sprouts
1 (8-ounce) can water chestnuts, drained
    and sliced
½ cup thinly sliced green onions, including
    some tops
1 medium cucumber, thinly sliced
4 cups cooked (may be grilled) chicken cut in
    2 to 3-inch strips
2 (6-ounce) packages frozen pea pods, thawed

Dressing:
2 cups mayonnaise
2 teaspoons curry powder
1 tablespoon sugar
½ teaspoon ground ginger

Garnish:
½ cup Spanish peanuts
12 to 18 cherry tomatoes

Distribute lettuce in an even layer in bottom of large salad bowl. Layer in order: bean sprouts, chestnuts, onion, cucumber and chicken. Pat pea pods dry and arrange on top. Combine all dressing ingredients. Mix until smooth. Spread evenly over top of salad. Cover and refrigerate at least overnight, and up to 24 hours. Toss before serving and garnish with peanuts and cherry tomatoes. **Serves 10 to 12.**

Crab Pasta Salad

6 ounces vermicelli, cooked according to
    package directions
3 green onions, chopped
¼ cup chopped green bell pepper
¼ cup chopped red bell pepper
½ cup mayonnaise
1 package crab meat, cut into bite-size pieces
Seasoned salt, to taste

Combine all ingredients in a large salad bowl and toss to mix well. If dry, add water, 1 tablespoon at a time, until desired moistness is reached. Cover and chill.

Lima Bean Salad

1 (10-ounce) package frozen small lima beans
1 small onion, chopped
1½ teaspoons salt, divided
2 teaspoons lemon juice
2 tablespoons extra virgin olive oil
1½ tablespoons minced fresh parsley
1 clove garlic, minced
½ teaspoon freshly ground black pepper

*Place lima beans, onion and 1 teaspoon salt in a sauce-pan. Add water just to cover and bring to a boil over high heat. Cover, reduce heat and cook until barely tender. Drain well and place in salad bowl. Whisk together lemon juice, remaining salt, olive oil, parsley, garlic and pepper. Pour over warm beans and let marinate until room temperature, tossing occasionally. **Serves 4.***

Green Salad with Grilled Szechuan Chicken

1 pound boneless, skinless chicken breast
Seasoned pepper
1 (8-ounce) can pineapple slices
3 tablespoons vegetable oil
2 tablespoons hot soy sauce
1 tablespoon white vinegar
1 tablespoon honey
¼ teaspoon ground ginger
1 head lettuce, torn in bite-size pieces
2 cups broccoli florets
1 bunch green onions, chopped
1 medium bell pepper, chopped

Lightly sprinkle chicken with seasoned pepper and grill until done. Slice into strips. Drain pineapple, reserving 2 tablespoons juice. To make dressing, combine reserved juice, vegetable oil, soy sauce, vinegar, honey and ginger in a covered jar. Shake well. Brush pineapple slices with a small amount of dressing and grill 2 to 3 minutes. Place lettuce, broccoli, green onions and bell pepper in a large salad bowl. Arrange chicken and pineapple over top. Pour dressing over and toss to coat.

Sound Information

*"Thank you,
Subsidium, and
the excellent staff
at the Memphis
Oral School for
the Deaf for your
outstanding
efforts to help
hearing-impaired
children. The
Memphis Oral
School has not
only given our son
the gift to verbally
communicate,
but also has
provided a
challenging
learning
environment. The
very existence of
the Memphis Oral
School would not
be possible
without the
tremendous
support and
dedication of
Subsidium."*

Potato and Chicken Salad

1 pound small new potatoes
Salt
¼ pound bacon, diced (optional)
1 head roasted garlic
¾ cup mayonnaise
1 teaspoon red wine vinegar
Pinch of crushed red pepper flakes
3 cups cubed cooked chicken
¼ packed cup large basil leaves, chopped

Scrub potatoes, but do not peel. Bring a large pot of water to boil. Add a pinch of salt and potatoes. Cook until potatoes are just tender when pierced with a sharp knife. Drain and rinse under cold water. Set aside. Cook bacon until crisp and drain well. Remove roasted garlic cloves from skin and place in food processor. Add mayonnaise, vinegar and crushed pepper and process until creamy. Halve or quarter potatoes. Place in salad bowl with bacon and chicken. Toss gently to combine. Pour dressing over and toss again. Sprinkle with chopped basil. **Serves 4 to 6.**

To Roast Garlic: *Cut top off head to expose flesh at top of each clove. Remove papery outer leaves, but keep head intact. Drizzle with ½ teaspoon olive oil, cover with foil, and bake in preheated 325° oven for 30 minutes. Remove foil and bake an additional 15 minutes. When cool enough to handle, pinch each clove to release the roasted garlic.*

Marinated Bleu Cheese Cabbage Salad

1 medium cabbage, shredded
4 green onions, chopped
1 cup mayonnaise
1 tablespoon prepared horseradish
4 ounces Bleu cheese, crumbled
½ cup sour cream
2 to 3 tablespoons fresh lemon juice
Salt and pepper to taste
½ green bell pepper, julienned
½ red bell pepper, julienned

Combine all ingredients except bell pepper in a large bowl. Toss well, cover and chill at least one hour. Garnish with bell pepper strips. **Serves 6 to 8.**

Chinese Pasta Salad

3 chicken breasts, cooked and cubed
½ pound ham slice, cubed
1 bunch scallions, chopped
1 red bell pepper, julienned
Snowpeas, parboiled
1 pound spaghetti, cooked according to package
  directions

Dressing:
¾ cup safflower oil
2½ tablespoons sesame oil
1 teaspoon hot chili oil
2 tablespoons sesame seeds
3 tablespoons ground coriander
¾ cup soy sauce

Place all salad ingredients in serving bowl.

For Dressing: *Place the 3 oils in a small saucepan and heat. Add sesame seeds and brown, stirring constantly. Remove from heat and add coriander and soy sauce. Pour over salad and toss. Serve hot or cold.* **Serves 8 to 10.**

Broccoli Salad

1½ pounds seedless red grapes, halved
1 bunch fresh broccoli, chopped
1 pound bacon, cooked crisp and crumbled
1 cup almond pieces
1 cup walnut pieces

Dressing:
2 cups mayonnaise
4 tablespoons white vinegar
⅔ cup sugar

Place salad ingredients in a salad bowl. Combine dressing ingredients in another bowl and blend well. Pour over salad and toss to coat. Cover and chill several hours or overnight.

Variation: *Cauliflower may be added for more color. Red onion may be used instead of grapes.*

BLT Chicken Pasta Salad

1 pound boneless, skinless chicken breasts
1 pound bacon, cooked crisp and crumbled
3 cups torn, bite-size lettuce (Boston, Romaine or iceberg)
1 large tomato, coarsely chopped
8 ounces pasta twists, cooked according to package directions

Dressing:
1 cup mayonnaise
⅓ cup water
2 tablespoons barbecue sauce
1 tablespoon white vinegar
1 tablespoon freeze-dried chives
½ teaspoon garlic powder
½ teaspoon pepper

Place chicken in a 6-quart pot and add just enough water to cover. Bring to a boil, reduce heat to low and simmer until chicken is no longer pink in center, 8 to 10 minutes. Remove to cutting board to cool. When cool enough to handle, cut into bite-size pieces. Place in salad bowl and add remaining salad ingredients. Add dressing and toss thoroughly.

For Dressing: *Combine all ingredients and mix until well blended.*

Spicy Black Bean Salad

3 (15-ounce) cans black beans, rinsed and drained
1 red onion, minced
2 large tomatoes, seeded and chopped
½ cup chopped fresh cilantro
3 jalapeño peppers, seeded and minced
3 cloves garlic, minced
2 tablespoons lime or lemon juice
1½ teaspoons ground cumin
1 tablespoon red wine vinegar
½ cup olive oil
1 teaspoon salt
¼ teaspoon freshly ground black pepper

Combine all ingredients in a large salad bowl. Toss gently until mixed. Cover and refrigerate for up to 2 days. Adjust seasonings before serving. **Serves 8.**

Variation: *Add 1 small can yellow corn, drained, for color.*

Penne with Grilled Tomato Vinaigrette

Grilled Tomato Vinaigrette:
2 medium tomatoes, peeled, halved and seeded
2 teaspoons minced garlic
⅓ cup red wine vinegar
2 tablespoons lemon juice
1 teaspoon salt
1 teaspoon freshly ground black pepper
½ cup vegetable oil

Salad:
8 ounces penne pasta, cooked according to
  package directions
5 tablespoons finely chopped green onions
1 medium red bell pepper, cored, seeded and
  chopped
18 fresh snow peas, trimmed and halved
½ cup halved black olives or oil-cured olives
1 (14-ounce) can water-packed artichoke hearts,
  drained and chopped
¼ cup chopped red onion
1 boneless, skinless chicken breast half (4 ounces),
  grilled and sliced (optional)

For Vinaigrette: *Preheat grill to medium-high. Grill tomato halves until soft and slightly charred. Remove from grill and chill. Place chilled tomatoes, garlic, vinegar, lemon juice, salt and pepper in a food processor. Process until smooth. With processor running, slowly add oil and continue processing until well blended.*

For Salad: *Combine all ingredients in a large bowl. Pour in half of vinaigrette and toss to coat. Add additional dressing if needed.* **Serves 4 to 6 as a main dish, 8 as side dish.**

Fettuccine Salad

½ **pound spinach fettuccine, cooked according to package directions**
½ **pound egg fettuccine, cooked according to package directions**
⅓ **cup olive oil**
½ **cup chopped red onion**
¾ **pound snow peas**
20 **cherry tomatoes**
2 **red bell peppers, seeded and chopped**
8 **scallions, chopped**
½ **cup chopped fresh chives**
½ **cup chopped fresh basil**
¾ **cup vinegar**
¼ **cup Parmesan cheese**
Grated zest of 1 orange, lemon or lime
Salt and pepper to taste

Make dressing by combining oil, vinegar, salt and pepper. Combine remaining ingredients in a large salad bowl. Top with dressing and toss well. Cover and refrigerate for one hour before serving. **Serves 8.**

Variation: *Add cooked shrimp or chicken.*

Tomato Mozzarella Salad

1 **medium red onion, very thinly sliced**
2 **tablespoons white wine vinegar**
3 **very ripe tomatoes, thinly sliced**
8 **ounces fresh mozzarella, sliced**
⅓ **cup extra virgin olive oil**
2 **tablespoons red wine vinegar**
½ **teaspoon salt**
½ **teaspoon pepper**
1 **tablespoon drained tiny capers**
3 **to 4 large basil leaves, torn**
Sliced black olives

Place onion slices in a small bowl and sprinkle with white wine vinegar. Add enough cold water to barely cover. Add 2 ice cubes. Let sit at room temperature for one hour. Drain well and pat dry. Arrange tomatoes and mozzarella in alternating slices on a serving platter. Top with onion slices. Whisk together oil, red wine vinegar, salt and pepper in a small bowl. Pour over salad. Garnish with capers, basil and olives. This can be done up to an hour before serving. Serve at room temperature. **Serves 6.**

Tortellini Salad

If making more than 3 hours ahead, reserve half of dressing and toss with salad just before serving.

10 ounces fresh cheese tortellini, cooked according
   to package directions
¼ cup minced fresh parsley
¼ pound salami, cubed
¼ pound Havarti cheese, cubed
1 red or green bell pepper, seeded and chopped
½ cup sliced black olives
2 green onions including tops, sliced

Dressing:
3 tablespoons red wine vinegar
1 teaspoon dried basil
1 teaspoon Dijon mustard
¼ teaspoon salt
¼ teaspoon coarsely ground black pepper
1 clove garlic, minced
½ cup virgin olive oil

Combine all salad ingredients in a large bowl. Place all dressing ingredients in a food processor and blend well. Pour over salad and toss thoroughly. Cover and refrigerate at least 1 hour. **Serves 4 to 6.**

Sound Bites

Shallots, like onions, are members of the lily family. They have a mild onion flavor with just a hint of garlic. Use in place of onions when a milder flavor is desired.

Gazpacho Salad

1 large cucumber, thinly sliced
2 medium tomatoes, chopped
1 large carrot, thinly sliced
1 large celery stalk, thinly sliced
1 small red onion, thinly sliced

Dressing:
⅓ cup vegetable oil
2 tablespoons red wine vinegar
2 tablespoons vegetable juice
1 teaspoon sugar
Salt and pepper

Place salad ingredients in a large bowl. Combine oil, vinegar, juice and sugar in a jar with a tight-fitting lid. Season with salt and pepper to taste. Seal lid and shake well. Pour over salad and toss to combine. Cover and refrigerate overnight, stirring occasionally. Serve cold. **Serves 4 to 6.**

Almond Brittle Salad

Almond Brittle:
⅔ cup sugar
½ cup slivered almonds

Salad:
1 head Romaine lettuce, torn into bite-size pieces
½ cup chopped celery
1 tablespoon minced parsley
1 bunch green onions, chopped
1 to 2 cans mandarin orange slices, drained

Dressing:
½ teaspoon salt
2 tablespoons sugar
2 tablespoons vinegar
¼ cup olive oil
¼ teaspoon hot pepper sauce
Dash of pepper

For Almond Brittle: *Heat sugar in a heavy skillet over low heat until melted and slightly brown. Add almonds and stir to coat. Cool on foil. Break into pieces when cool enough to handle.*

Place salad ingredients in a large bowl. Top with almond brittle. Combine dressing ingredients and blend well. Pour over salad and toss to coat.

Tropical Fruit Salad

4 cantaloupes, cut in cubes or balls
4 honeydew melons, cut in cubes or balls
8 to 10 bananas, peeled and sliced
3 pounds seedless green grapes
3 pounds seedless red grapes
1 watermelon, cut in cubes or balls
Dressing:
1 cup sour cream
¼ cup grated coconut
¼ cup apricot preserves
2 tablespoons dry white wine
½ cup chopped macadamia nuts

Combine all fruit in a large salad bowl. Combine dressing ingredients in another bowl. Mix well. Serve sauce separately. A hollowed-out coconut shell makes a fun presentation. **Serves 20.**

Romaine Salad with Feta Cheese Toast

Also called Christmas Salad for obvious reasons, but wonderful all year round.

4 ½-inch thick slices French bread
6 tablespoons olive oil, divided
¼ pound feta cheese
2 tablespoons red wine vinegar
¼ teaspoon salt
⅛ teaspoon pepper
1 head Romaine lettuce, torn into bite-size pieces
2 tablespoons minced bottled roasted red peppers

For Toast: *Preheat oven to 350°. Brush both sides of bread with 1 tablespoon olive oil. Toast in oven, turning once. Crumble cheese over toast and broil until cheese begins to melt.*

For Dressing: *Place vinegar, salt and pepper in a jar with a lid. Close and shake until salt is dissolved. Add 5 tablespoons oil and shake again to combine. Place Romaine in a bowl and top with dressing. Toss to coat. Divide among 4 serving plates. Top each plate of salad with a piece of toast and garnish with red peppers.* **Serves 4.**

Kiwi, Orange and Romaine Salad

1 head Romaine lettuce, torn in bite-size pieces
3 kiwis, peeled and sliced
1 (11-ounce) can mandarin orange sections, drained
1 large red onion, sliced
½ cup olive oil
¼ cup lime juice
3 tablespoons red wine vinegar
3 tablespoons orange marmalade
Salt and freshly ground black pepper to taste
Croutons
⅓ cup halved pecans
3 ounces bleu cheese, crumbled

Place lettuce, kiwi, orange sections and onion in a salad bowl. Combine olive oil, lime juice, vinegar, marmalade, and salt and pepper. Blend well and pour over salad just before serving. Toss well and top with croutons, nuts and cheese. **Serves 6 to 8.**

Sound Bites

Keep fresh sliced apples from turning brown— soak in a 7up/Sprite type drink before serving.

Fruity Tossed Green Salad

1 head Bibb lettuce, torn in bite-size pieces
1 head Romaine lettuce, torn in bite-size pieces
2 (11-ounce) cans mandarin orange sections, drained
¼ cup slivered almonds, toasted
½ cup chopped red onion

Strawberry Dressing:
1 (16-ounce) package frozen strawberries, thawed
1½ teaspoons honey
¼ teaspoon dried thyme
¼ teaspoon pepper
3 tablespoons raspberry vinegar
½ cup water
2 teaspoons canola oil
1 teaspoon soy sauce

Place salad ingredients in a large bowl. Place all dressing ingredients in a blender and purée until thoroughly blended. Pour into a covered container and refrigerate. When ready to serve, pour dressing over salad and toss to coat. **Serves 10 to 12.**

Chinese Cabbage Salad

3 tablespoons red wine vinegar
2 tablespoons sugar
½ teaspoon salt
¼ teaspoon pepper
½ cup vegetable oil
1 small head Napa or Chinese cabbage, cut in bite-size pieces
3 ounces chicken-flavor Ramen noodles, crushed
½ cup chopped green onion
4 ounces almonds, toasted

Place vinegar and sugar in a small saucepan. Cook over medium heat, stirring, until sugar is dissolved. Remove from heat and stir in salt, pepper and flavor packet from noodle mix. Cool. Whisk in oil. Place cabbage in a large bowl. Top with noodles, green onions and almonds. Stir dressing mixture to combine and pour over salad. Toss to coat and serve immediately. **Serves 8.**

Variation: *Top with thinly sliced grilled chicken breast.*

Spinach Salad with Strawberries

Dressing:
½ cup sugar
¾ teaspoon paprika
¼ teaspoon dry mustard
1 teaspoon Worcestershire sauce
¾ cup canola or light vegetable oil
1 teaspoon vinegar
2 tablespoons poppy seeds
2 tablespoons sesame seeds, toasted
1 teaspoon minced onion

Salad:
1 pound fresh spinach, torn into bite-size pieces
1 pint fresh strawberries, sliced
4 bananas, sliced
1 cup chopped walnuts or almonds

*Combine all dressing ingredients in a blender. Process until well mixed. Layer spinach, fruit and nuts on a plate. Top with dressing just before serving. **Serves 10**..*

Sound Bites

Soak banana slices in citrus or pineapple juice to prevent discoloration.

Springtime Fruit Salad

1 fresh pineapple, chopped
1 quart strawberries, quartered
½ cup blueberries
½ cup raspberries
1 (11-ounce) can mandarin oranges, drained
2 cups orange juice
1 cup sugar
¼ cup cream sherry
¼ teaspoon almond extract
½ teaspoon vanilla

Place fruit in a salad bowl and toss gently. Combine remaining ingredients in a small bowl and stir until sugar dissolves. Pour over fruit and toss lightly. Cover and refrigerate for 2 to 3 hours before serving.

Sound Bites

When trying to
select a ripe
pineapple, pull
out a leaf from
the pineapple
crown. If the leaf
comes out easily,
the pineapple is
ripe.

Marinated Artichoke Salad

Dressing:
¾ cup vegetable oil
1 tablespoon cider vinegar
¼ teaspoon garlic salt
1 tablespoon Dijon mustard
1 tablespoon grated Parmesan cheese, or more to
   taste
1 teaspoon salt
¼ teaspoon pepper
¼ teaspoon dill

Salad:
1 green bell pepper, thinly sliced
1 small onion, thinly sliced
1 (8½-ounce) can artichoke hearts, drained
½ cup chopped celery
1 cucumber, unpeeled and thinly sliced
1 cup cubed mozzarella cheese
½ pound fresh mushrooms, sliced
1 (15-ounce) can hearts of palm, drained
Lettuce leaves
2 slices bacon, cooked crisp and crumbled

*Place dressing ingredients in a food processor and pro-
cess until well blended. Layer all salad ingredients except
lettuce and bacon in a bowl. Top with dressing and toss to
blend. Cover and refrigerate for several hours. When
ready to serve, arrange on lettuce leaves and garnish
with bacon. **Serves 8.***

Holiday Cranberry Salad

1 package cranberries, finely chopped
1 cup sugar
1 large can crushed pineapple, drained
1 cup chopped pecans
1 cup miniature marshmallows
½ large container frozen whipped topping, thawed

*Sprinkle cranberries with sugar, cover, and refrigerate
overnight.*

*The following day, combine cranberry-sugar mixture,
pineapple, pecans and marshmallows. Gently fold in
whipped topping. Cover and refrigerate until chilled.*

Vegetable Salad

Dressing:
¾ cup vinegar
½ cup vegetable oil
¾ cup sugar
1 teaspoon salt
1 teaspoon pepper

Salad:
1 can tiny peas, drained
1 can French-cut green beans, drained
1 can white corn kernels, drained
1 can Chinese vegetables, drained
1 small jar pimentos, drained
1 green bell pepper, seeded and diced
1 cup diced celery
1 small bunch green onions, chopped

Combine all dressing ingredients in a saucepan. Bring to a boil. Remove from heat and cool. Place salad ingredients in a large bowl. Top with dressing and toss. Cover and refrigerate overnight. Drain before serving. **Serves 16.**

Sound Bites

Peeling
thin-skinned fruit–
Place fruit in a
bowl, cover with
boiling water
and let set for
1 minute. Peel
with a paring
knife.

Blueberry Salad

1 large package grape gelatin
1 large can crushed pineapple, drained
1 can or jar blueberry pie filling

Topping:
1 (8-ounce) package cream cheese, softened
1 cup sour cream
½ cup sugar
1 tablespoon vanilla
½ cup chopped pecans
Lettuce leaves

Dissolve gelatin in boiling water according to package directions. Do not add cold water. Add pineapple and pie filling and pour into a 9 x 13-inch glass dish. Refrigerate until set. Beat cream cheese by hand until smooth. Add sour cream, sugar and vanilla and stir until smooth. Pour over congealed fruit and sprinkle with pecans. Cover and chill overnight. To serve, cut in squares and place on lettuce-lined salad plates.

Summer Fruit Salad with Creamy Lemon Dressing

Creamy Lemon Dressing:
1 cup half and half
1 tablespoon vinegar or lemon juice
3 tablespoons frozen lemonade concentrate, undiluted
½ teaspoon vanilla

Salad:
2 fresh plums, sliced
1 fresh peach, sliced
1 fresh nectarine, sliced
1 fresh Bartlett pear, sliced
Lettuce leaves
Toasted coconut

Combine half and half and vinegar or lemon juice and let sit ½ hour to sour. Add lemon concentrate and vanilla and mix well. Arrange fruit on a lettuce-lined platter. Serve with dressing and garnish with coconut.

To Toast Coconut: *Spread coconut on a baking sheet and place under broiler until coocnut is lightly browned, about 1 to 2 minutes. Watch carefully, as it will burn easily.*

Frozen Fruit Salad

16 ounces sour cream
¾ cup sugar
2 tablespoons lemon juice
⅛ teaspoon salt
1 cup chopped pecans
¼ cup halved maraschino cherries
2 cups crushed pineapple
2 large bananas, sliced

Combine sour cream, sugar, lemon juice and salt in a large bowl. Blend until sugar is dissolved. Add remaining ingredients. Spoon into muffin tins or a salad mold and freeze overnight.

Apricot Salad

2 (3-ounce) packages apricot gelatin
2 cups boiling water
2 cups cold water
1 medium can crushed pineapple, drained
    and juice reserved
2 bananas, sliced
½ cup chopped nuts

Topping:
2 tablespoons margarine
2 tablespoons flour
½ cup sugar
½ cup reserved pineapple juice
1 egg, beaten
1 (3-ounce) package cream cheese, softened
1 package whipped topping mix, prepared

Dissolve gelatin in boiling water. Add cold water and cool. Add pineapple, bananas, and nuts. Pour into salad mold and refrigerate until congealed.

For Topping: *Place margarine, flour, sugar, pineapple juice and egg in a saucepan. Cook over medium heat, stirring constantly, until thick. Remove from heat and cool. Add cream cheese and blend thoroughly. Fold in whipped topping. Spread over salad. Chill before serving.*

Spiced Orange Salad

1 (11-ounce) can mandarin oranges, drained and
    juice reserved
½ cup water
¼ cup sugar
1 cinnamon stick
8 whole cloves
1 (3-ounce) package lemon gelatin
¾ cup orange juice
3 tablespoons lemon juice

Combine reserved juice, water, sugar, cinnamon and cloves in a saucepan. Heat to boiling. Reduce heat and simmer 5 minutes. Remove from heat and discard cinnamon stick and cloves. Pour hot liquid over gelatin and stir until dissolved. Add oranges, lemon juice and orange juice. Pour into mold and refrigerate overnight.

Sound Bites

Exposure to direct sunlight softens tomatoes instead of ripening them. Leave the tomatoes, stem-up, in any spot where they will be out of direct sunlight.

Sound Bites

Ripen green bananas or green tomatoes by wrapping in a wet dish towel and placing in a paper sack.

Honey-Celery Seed Dressing

⅔ cup sugar
⅓ cup cider vinegar
⅓ cup honey
¼ cup cold water
1 teaspoon dry mustard
1 teaspoon celery seed
1 teaspoon paprika (optional)
¼ teaspoon salt
½ cup vegetable oil

Place all ingredients except oil in blender. Process on low speed until smooth. Gradually add oil while still running. Increase speed to medium and process until thickened and thoroughly combined. Cover and chill. Serve on fruit salad, or a combination of Bibb lettuce, red onion and grapefruit slices. Keeps well in refrigerator. **Serves 2 cups.**

Easy Thousand Island Dressing

¾ cup mayonnaise
¼ cup ketchup
2 tablespoons sweet pickle relish or more to taste
¼ teaspoon onion juice
Salt and pepper to taste

Combine all ingredients and chill.

Roquefort Salad Dressing

1 cup mayonnaise
½ cup buttermilk
¼ cup sour cream
¼ cup cottage cheese
2 cloves garlic, minced
3 ounces Roquefort cheese, crumbled
Juice of ½ lemon
Salt and cracked pepper to taste

Combine all ingredients in a blender and process until smooth. **Yield: 2 cups.**

Caesar Salad Dressing

2 egg yolks
1 tablespoon Dijon mustard
1 teaspoon ground anchovies
1 tablespoon chopped garlic
1 tablespoon Worcestershire sauce
1 teaspoon lemon juice
¼ cup red wine vinegar
¾ cup olive oil
Black pepper to taste
1 cup grated Romano cheese

Blend egg yolks, mustard, anchovies, garlic, Worcestershire sauce, lemon juice and vinegar in a mixing bowl with a whisk. Mixing continuously, slowly add olive oil and whisk until thoroughly combined. Season with pepper to taste and add cheese.

Sound Bites

Bury avocados in a bowl of flour to ripen.

Sweet and Sour Dressing

1 cup sugar
½ cup white vinegar
1 cup vegetable oil
1 teaspoon celery seed
¼ teaspoon dill seed
¼ teaspoon mustard seed
¼ teaspoon paprika
¾ teaspoon salt

*Combine sugar and vinegar in a small saucepan. Bring to a boil over high heat. Remove from heat and add remaining ingredients, blending thoroughly. Cool and pour into a lidded jar. Cover and chill overnight. Great on spinach salad. **Yield: 1½ cups.***

Honey–Mustard Dressing

½ cup mayonnaise
4 teaspoons spicy brown mustard
1 tablespoon white vinegar
1 tablespoon honey
1 tablespoon prepared horseradish
Dash of paprika
Dash of hot pepper sauce

*Combine all ingredients in a small bowl. Whisk until blended. Serve over salad greens. **Yield: ¾ cup.***

German-Style Dressing

1 tablespoon flour
¾ cup sugar
½ teaspoon salt
¼ teaspoon pepper
1 egg
1 cup cider vinegar
1 tablespoon bacon drippings*
2 tablespoons mayonnaise
*1 tablespoon salad oil and 1 teaspoon real bacon bits may be substituted for drippings

Place flour, sugar, salt and pepper in a small saucepan. Stir in egg and gradually add vinegar until well combined. Cook over medium-low heat until mixture thickens, about 3 minutes, stirring often. Remove from heat and stir in bacon drippings and mayonnaise. Good on potato salad, three bean salad or cabbage slaw. Mix well.

Honey-Lime Dressing

1 cup sugar
2 tablespoons dry mustard
1 tablespoon ground ginger
½ cup honey
⅓ cup lime juice
⅓ cup water
2 cups vegetable oil

Place all ingredients except oil in blender. Process on high speed 30 seconds. Scrape down sides and process on high 30 more seconds. With blender on high speed, gradually add oil in a slow, steady stream, processing until thickened. Cover and chill. Serve over fresh fruit. **Yield: 3⅔ cups.**

Black Bean Soup

1 pound dried black beans
9 cups chicken broth
1 pound smoked turkey sausage, sliced
1½ teaspoons butter, margarine or oil
½ cup chopped carrot
½ cup chopped celery
1 large onion, chopped
3 to 4 cloves garlic, minced
1 tablespoon cumin
1 tablespoon oregano
½ to ¾ cup dry sherry
Salt and pepper

Rinse and pick over beans. Soak in cold water to cover for 14 hours. Place chicken broth in a saucepan and add sausage. Heat until boiling, then reduce to low and simmer for 2 hours. Degrease the broth.

Melt butter in a large saucepan and sauté carrots, celery and onion for 5 minutes. Add garlic and sauté 1 more minute. Add drained beans and 6 cups of the broth. Add at least half of the sausage. The more you add, the more intense the flavor. Stir in cumin and oregano. Bring to a boil, stirring occasionally. Reduce heat and simmer, partially covered, until beans are tender, about 1½ hours. Add sherry and simmer 5 more minutes. Puree soup in blender or processor. Return to saucepan and reheat over very low heat, stirring frequently. Thin with reserved stock if necessary. Season with salt and pepper, if desired. Garnish as desired with chopped hard-cooked egg, rice, grated cheese, sliced lemon, chopped red onion, and sour cream.

Sound Information

The cochlear implant miracle is not just the result of surgery. Specialized training is needed to enable these children to recognize and understand the new sounds which they now hear for the first time. The MOSD can provide educational back-up and outreach services to any child with an implant in the Mid-South area.

Sound Bites

Soup can be topped with a variety of garnishes such as crisp bacon bits, grated cheese, sliced stuffed olives, thin lemon slices, chopped parsley or green onions, or fresh chopped tomatoes.

Baked Potato Soup

4 large baking potatoes, baked and cubed
⅔ cup butter or margarine
⅔ cup flour
6 cups milk or half and half
Salt and pepper
2 tablespoons chopped green onions
½ cup crisp-cooked crumbled bacon
1 cup shredded Cheddar cheese
1 (8-ounce) carton sour cream

Melt butter in a large saucepan over low heat. Add flour and stir until smooth. Gradually add milk and continue cooking over low heat until bubbly, stirring frequently. Salt and pepper to taste. Stir in green onions, bacon, cheese and potatoes. Slowly fold in sour cream and continue cooking until heated through. **Serves 4 to 6.**

Sweet Corn Chowder

5 ears fresh sweet white corn
3 bacon slices, chopped
½ onion, diced
4 cups chicken stock
1½ teaspoons minced fresh thyme or
  ½ teaspoon dried, crumbled
1 bay leaf
2 tablespoons cornstarch
2 tablespoons water
2 cups whipping cream
¾ cup cooked wild rice
Salt and pepper

Cut kernels from corn and reserve cobs. Cook bacon in heavy large saucepan over medium-high heat until fat is rendered. Add onion and sauté until onion is tender, about 3 minutes. Add corn cobs, chicken stock, thyme and bay leaf. Cover and simmer 20 minutes. Remove cobs. Dissolve cornstarch in 2 tablespoons water. Stir into soup. Add corn kernels, cream and rice. Bring to a boil, stirring constantly. Reduce heat and simmer until corn is tender, about 5 minutes. Season with salt and pepper to taste. Can be made 1 day ahead and refrigerated, covered. Bring to a simmer before serving. **Serves 6.**

Butternut Squash Soup with Ginger and Lime

1¼ cups finely chopped onion
3½ tablespoons minced fresh ginger root
7 tablespoons unsalted butter
10 cups peeled, seeded and thinly sliced
  butternut squash (about 3¾ pounds)
5 cups chicken broth
5 cups water
7 garlic cloves
5 tablespoons fresh lime juice, or to taste
Salt and pepper

Garnish:
¾ cup vegetable oil
7 tablespoons 1½-inch-long julienne strips
  peeled ginger root
10 thin slices lime

Sauté onion and ginger in butter in a large saucepan over moderately low heat, stirring occasionally, until onion is softened. Add squash, broth, water and garlic. Bring to a boil, cover and reduce heat. Simmer until squash is tender, about 15 to 20 minutes. Remove from heat and puree in batches in a blender or food processor. Return puree to saucepan and add lime juice and salt and pepper to taste. Reheat over moderately low heat until hot. Soup may be made 2 days in advance and refrigerated, covered.

For Garnish: *Heat oil in a skillet over moderately high heat until it is hot but not smoking. Fry the ginger, stirring, until it is pale golden, about 1 minute. Transfer with a slotted spoon to paper towels to drain. Divide the soup among 10 bowls, float a lime slice on each and top with fried ginger. Serve soup hot or at room temperature.* **Serves 10.**

Sound Bites

*Too salty—
For soups and
stews, add
a teaspoon
each of cider
vinegar and
sugar.*

Sound Bites

Soup stock
should not be
salted until the
end, since it might
become too salty
as the stock is
reduced.

La Montaña Tortilla Soup

1 tablespoon olive oil
⅓ cup sliced onion
1 teaspoon minced garlic
1 jalapeño pepper, seeds removed and minced
8 cups chicken stock
1 cup fresh diced tomatoes
2 tablespoons chili powder
1 tablespoon cumin
2 teaspoons oregano
2 tablespoons chopped cilantro
Tortilla chips, broken
Grated Monterey Jack cheese or sour cream

Heat olive oil in a large saucepan over moderately high heat. Sauté onion, garlic and jalapeño until onion is transparent. Add chicken stock, tomatoes, chili powder, cumin and oregano. Bring to a boil, reduce heat and simmer for 30 minutes. Add cilantro and simmer 5 minutes more. Place tortilla chips in serving bowls. Ladle soup over chips and top with grated cheese or sour cream. **Serves 6.**

Old-Fashioned Split Pea Soup

1½ cups quick-cooking split green peas
1 quart water
1 (2½-pound) fully cooked ham shank
⅔ cup coarsely chopped onion
¼ cup diced carrot
½ cup coarsely chopped celery
2 sprigs parsley
1 clove garlic
1 bay leaf, crumbled
½ teaspoon sugar
⅛ teaspoon dried thyme
⅛ teaspoon pepper
1 (13¾-ounce) can chicken broth

Place peas and 1 quart water in a large stock pot. Bring to a boil, reduce heat and simmer covered for 45 minutes. Add more water if necessary. Add remaining ingredients and simmer, covered, for 1½ hours. Remove ham shank from soup and cool. Cut ham from bone and dice. If a smooth soup is desired, press vegetables and liquid through a coarse sieve. Return to stock pot, add ham and reheat slowly, uncovered, until hot, about 15 minutes. **Serves 8.**

Minestrone

1 (1 pound, 11-ounce) can red
   kidney beans, undrained
1 teaspoon salt
½ teaspoon garlic salt
1 clove garlic
¼ teaspoon pepper
1 tablespoon vegetable oil
¼ cup chopped fresh parsley
1 small zucchini, unpeeled, cubed
2 stalks celery, chopped
1 small carrot, sliced
2 green onions, chopped
4 to 5 leaves Swiss chard
3 tablespoons butter
1 (8-ounce) can tomato sauce or
   1 can tomatoes, mashed
2½ cups water
½ cup dry sherry
¼ cup elbow macaroni
Parmesan cheese, optional

Place undrained beans in a large stock pot. Mash about two-thirds, leaving one-third whole. Add salt, garlic salt, pepper, oil and parsley. Heat. Add vegetables, butter, tomato sauce and water. Bring to a boil, reduce heat and simmer 1 hour. Add sherry and macaroni and simmer until macaroni is cooked, 10 to 15 minutes. Serve garnished with Parmesan if desired. **Serves 6 to 8.**

Variation: *Substitute pinto or great northern beans for kidney beans.*

Asparagus Soup

1 (10¾-ounce) can chicken broth
1 (10-ounce) package frozen cut asparagus
¼ cup sliced green onions
⅛ teaspoon ground mace
Pepper to taste
1 cup water

Combine all ingredients except water in a saucepan. Bring to a boil, then cover and cook over low heat until asparagus is tender, about 5 minutes. Pour mixture into a blender and process until smooth. Return to saucepan and add water. Heat, stirring occasionally. **Yield: 3 cups.**

Sound Bites

Adding water to the soup stock must be left to the wisdom of the cook. If the stock boils too rapidly, the water evaporates before it is seasoned. If cooked insufficiently, the stock will not derive enough flavor from the meat and herbs.

Beef Broth Soup

1 large soup bone with some meat on bone, or
   3 to 4 pieces short ribs
1 (28-ounce) can whole peeled tomatoes, mashed
1 large onion, quartered
2 ribs celery, quartered
2 chicken bouillon cubes
1 teaspoon salt or to taste
⅛ teaspoon pepper
1 (16-ounce) package extra wide noodles,
   cooked according to package directions

Combine all ingredients except noodles in a large stock pot. Add 5 quarts water and bring to a boil. Reduce heat and simmer until soup cooks down about 2 inches in pot, about 2 hours. Strain broth, discarding vegetables and bones. Reheat broth and serve over noodles.

Don't add noodles to the broth because they will absorb all the liquid. Store leftover noodles and broth separately.

Taco Soup

1 pound lean ground beef
1 large onion, chopped
1 can kidney beans, undrained
1 can black beans, undrained
1 can chili beans, undrained
1 can shoe peg corn, undrained
1 (16-ounce) can chopped tomatoes, undrained
1 (15-ounce) can tomato sauce
1½ cups water
1 (4½-ounce) can chopped green chiles
1 (1½-ounce) package taco seasoning mix
1 (1-ounce) envelope ranch-style dressing mix
Garnish: tortilla chips, shredded cheese, shredded
   lettuce, chopped tomatoes, sour cream,
   chopped avocado

Cook ground beef and onion in a large Dutch oven over medium high heat until meat is browned. Drain. Stir in remaining ingredients. Bring to a boil, reduce heat and simmer 30 minutes. Garnish as desired.

Mushroom Bisque

1 pound fresh mushrooms
1½ cups whipping cream
1 (6-ounce) bottle clam juice
2 tablespoons minced shallot
6 fennel seeds
3 cups chicken stock
¼ teaspoon salt
A few grates of nutmeg
4 tablespoons butter
4 tablespoons flour
2 tablespoons dry sherry
Sprigs of fennel or chopped hazelnuts

Grind mushrooms in a meat grinder if possible, to achieve the best texture. If a meat grinder is not available, chop very finely with a knife or use a food processor, being careful not to overprocess. Bring mushrooms, cream, clam juice, shallots and fennel to a boil in a large saucepan. Reduce heat and simmer 10 minutes. Make a roux by melting butter in a small skillet. Allow foam to subside and stir in flour. Cook over low heat for 5 minutes, stirring frequently. Set aside to cool. Add chicken stock, salt and nutmeg to mushrooms. Stir one cup of mushroom mixture into the cooled roux until smooth. Whisk back into the soup, bring to a simmer and cook 15 minutes. Serve garnished with sprigs of fennel or chopped hazelnuts. **Serves 6.**

Sound Bites

Stock and broth are used interchangeably. The word **broth** is usually used when a plain soup is made from chicken or beef and served as is. **Stock** is the basic liquid obtained by long cooking of meat, poultry, or fish with vegetables.

Clam Chowder

6 large quahogs plus 10 small cherrystone clams
  or 3 cans chopped clams, if fresh clams are
  not available
½ cup water
½ cup clarified butter
1 clove garlic, minced
1 medium onion, chopped
1 stalk celery, chopped
½ teaspoon white pepper
1 small bay leaf
¼ teaspoon dried thyme
½ cup flour
40 ounces clam juice
1 large potato, cubed
1 pint whipping cream
Salt and pepper

Wash clams thoroughly. Place quahogs in a pot with ½ cup water. Cover tightly and steam until clams open. Repeat process with cherrystones. Remove clams from shell, chop coarsely and reserve broth in a separate container. Add butter and garlic to pot. Sauté 2 to 3 minutes. Add onion, celery and spices. Sauté until onions are translucent. Add flour to make roux, stirring constantly. Cover over low heat for 5 minutes. Do not brown. Slowly add clam juice, stirring constantly to avoid lumps. Simmer for 10 minutes, stirring frequently to avoid burning. Add potatoes and cook until tender. Add cream and clams and bring back to a boil. Season to taste. **Serves 10.**

Note: Quahog is the American Indian name for the largest of the hard-shell clam.

Chicken Gumbo

2 tablespoons flour
½ cup vegetable oil
3 slices bacon, diced
1 chopped onion
½ green bell pepper, chopped
1 clove garlic, minced
1 teaspoon soy sauce
1 tablespoon Worcestershire sauce
1 teaspoon salt
Dash of pepper
Dash of hot pepper sauce
1 (28-ounce) can tomatoes
4 chicken breasts with skin and bone
2 to 3 cups water
1 to 2 cups frozen okra
1½ teaspoons filé powder
Cooked rice

Combine flour and oil in a large stock pot. Cook over medium heat until lightly browned. Add bacon and cook 1 minute. Add onion, garlic, and green pepper. Sauté until onion is translucent. Add soy sauce, Worcestershire sauce, salt, pepper, hot pepper sauce, tomatoes, chicken and water. Bring to a boil, reduce heat and simmer until chicken is cooked through and tender, about 45 minutes. Remove chicken to a cutting board. Debone, skin and chop chicken. Return to soup and add okra and filé powder. Simmer 20 to 30 minutes. Serve over rice.

Note: Boneless, skinless chicken may be used.

Sound Bites

Bouillon is a cooking term derived from the French that is used to describe the strained and clear liquid from the stockpot.

Seafood Gumbo

¾ cup bacon drippings or vegetable oil
¾ cup flour
1 large onion, finely chopped
2 pounds okra, thinly sliced
1 medium green bell pepper, finely chopped
1 clove garlic, minced
3 quarts beef or chicken stock
1 (28-ounce) can tomatoes, finely chopped
3 pounds shrimp
2 cans crab meat
1 tablespoon Worcestershire sauce
Hot pepper sauce, to taste
Salt and pepper
Cooked rice

Make a roux by combining bacon drippings and flour in a heavy skillet. Cook, stirring constantly, over medium heat until flour is browned. Add onions, okra, bell pepper and garlic. Sauté until vegetables are limp and beginning to brown. Combine stock and tomatoes in a large stock pot. Bring to a boil, reduce heat and simmer. Add vegetable mixture and cook 2 hours, stirring frequently. Add seafood and remaining ingredients except rice. Cook an additional 15 minutes. Serve over rice. **Yield: 1 gallon.**

This gumbo freezes well.

Grilled Eggplant Sandwich

1 large eggplant, sliced lengthwise into
    ¼-inch thick slices
¼ cup olive oil
Salt and freshly ground black pepper
4 baguette rolls, sliced lengthwise
¼ cup basil pesto
1 ripe tomato, sliced
8 ounces fresh mozzarella cheese, sliced

Preheat grill to high. Brush both sides of eggplant slices with olive oil and season with salt and pepper to taste. Grill until tender but not mushy, about 5 minutes. Spread rolls lightly with pesto and top with eggplant, tomato slices and cheese. **Serves 4.**

Chicken Hero

¾ cup mayonnaise
5 green onions, including tops, thinly sliced
1 (8-ounce) can water chestnuts, drained and
   coarsely chopped
4 teaspoons Dijon mustard
1 teaspoon Worcestershire sauce
1 teaspoon salt
5 to 6 drops hot pepper sauce
4 cups diced, cooked chicken
2 cups shredded Monterey Jack cheese, divided
1 baguette loaf French bread
1 cup chopped tomato

Garnish:
Minced fresh parsley
Sliced green onions
Sliced black olives

*Combine mayonnaise, green onions, water chestnuts, mustard, Worcestershire, salt and hot pepper sauce in a large bowl. Stir in chicken and 1 cup Monterey Jack cheese. This can be done ahead, covered and refrigerated for up to 24 hours. Split French loaf in half lengthwise. Trim any uneven crust from bottom so loaf rests evenly. Place bread, cut side up, on baking sheet. Add tomato to chicken mixture. Spread evenly over each bread half and sprinkle with remaining cheese. Bake in a preheated 375° oven until cheese is bubbly and lightly browned, about 10 minutes. Transfer to a long cutting board and divide into serving portions. Garnish with parsley, green onions and olives. **Serves 6 to 8.***

Sound Bites

How to roast and peel bell peppers–

1. Preheat the broiler.

2. Choose perfect peppers that have no dark or soft spots. Wash thoroughly and dry with paper towels.

3. Place the whole peppers in a baking or broiler pan about 4 inches from the heat. Turn the peppers often until they have charred black all over, about 5 minutes.

4. Wrap the peppers in dampened paper towels to steam or place them in a closed paper bag to cool for about 10 minutes. This helps to loosen the skin.

5. When the peppers have cooled, cut them in half. Discard seeds, membranes, and stem. Peel off the loosened skin with a sharp paring knife.

Crab Croissants

½ cup mayonnaise
¼ teaspoon dried dill
2 cloves garlic, minced
¼ cup minced fresh parsley
⅛ teaspoon cayenne pepper
⅔ pound crab meat
1 cup shredded Cheddar cheese
1 cup shredded Monterey Jack cheese
1 (2¼-ounce) can sliced black olives, drained
1 (10-ounce) package frozen artichoke hearts, cooked and quartered
4 large croissants

Combine all ingredients except croissants in a medium bowl. Cover and refrigerate until ready to use. Split croissants horizontally. Spread each half with crab mixture. Place on baking sheet and broil 5 inches from heat until heated through, 3 to 4 minutes. **Serves 8.**

Broiled Sicilian Sandwich

½ teaspoon olive oil
¼ cup thinly sliced onion
½ small zucchini, halved lengthwise and thinly sliced (about ½ cup)
½ teaspoon minced garlic
½ cup seeded, coarsely chopped tomato
¼ cup roasted red bell peppers, peeled and coarsely chopped
¼ teaspoon dried thyme
⅛ teaspoon freshly ground black pepper
¾ cup shredded provolone cheese, divided
4 (1-inch thick) slices Italian bread
2 tablespoons freshly grated Parmesan cheese

Heat olive oil over medium-low heat in a medium skillet. Add onion, zucchini and garlic and sauté until vegetables are tender, about 5 minutes. Add tomato, roasted bell pepper, thyme and pepper. Cook 1 to 2 minutes. Sprinkle 2 tablespoons provolone on each bread slice. Top with ¼ cup onion mixture. Combine remaining provolone and Parmesan and sprinkle evenly over top. Preheat broiler and broil sandwiches, 3 inches from heat, until cheese melts. Serve immediately. **Serves 4.**

Chicken Breast Sandwich with Melted Jarlsberg

½ cup mayonnaise
1 cup salsa fresca, divided (recipe below)
8 (8-ounce) skinless, boneless chicken breasts
8 (½-inch-thick) slices Texas toast or hard French
  rolls, lightly toasted
16 thin slices Jarlsberg cheese

Combine mayonnaise and ½ cup salsa fresca. Cover and refrigerate 1 hour. Grill, broil or sauté chicken breasts. Spread bread with salsa mayonnaise. Place chicken on bread, top with cheese and melt under broiler. Serve open-face with a dollop of salsa fresca. **Serves 8.**

Salsa Fresca

1 ½ pounds tomatoes, seeded and cut into
  ½-inch dice
¼ cup finely chopped onion
¼ cup chopped fresh cilantro
1 jalapeño, seeded and finely chopped
3 tablespoons fresh lime juice
Salt and pepper

Combine all ingredients in a small bowl. Let stand at least 30 minutes before serving. Use within 24 hours.

Ham and Cheese Sandwich

1 cup butter, melted
¼ cup poppy seeds
2 tablespoons prepared mustard
¼ cup instant minced onions
1 loaf French bread, halved horizontally
1 pound Virginia baked ham, sliced
1 pound baby Swiss cheese, sliced

Combine butter, poppy seeds, mustard and onion in a small bowl. Cover and refrigerate overnight. Spread cut sides of bread with butter mixture. Layer ham and cheese on bottom half of bread. Place top half over cheese, wrap in foil and bake in preheated 350° oven for 1 hour. **Serves 6 to 8.**

We've had this at many Subsidium meetings and everyone loves this sandwich.

Sound Bites

To keep party sandwiches or other food hot for a picnic, wrap in foil then in several sheets of newspaper. Store in insulated ice chest.

Muffuletta

¼ pound thinly sliced ham
¼ pound sliced Genoa salami
4 slices Swiss cheese
6 ounces sliced provolone cheese
1 (10 inch) round loaf Italian bread, halved horizontally
1½ cups olive salad (recipe below)

Layer ham, salami, Swiss and provolone cheese on bottom half of bread. Place bread halves on a baking sheet and bake in preheated 350° oven until thoroughly heated, 5 to 10 minutes. Spread cheese with chilled olive salad. Place remaining bread half on top and cut into quarters to serve. **Serves 4.**

Olive Salad

3 (10-ounce) jars pimento-stuffed olives, drained and coarsely chopped
3 stalks celery, chopped
2 carrots, grated
2 cloves garlic, minced
1 (4-ounce) jar diced pimento, drained
3 tablespoons drained capers
½ cup olive oil
¼ cup red wine vinegar

Combine all ingredients in a medium bowl. Cover and chill. May be kept in refrigerator up to 1 week. **Yield: 7 cups.**

Pineapple Pimento Spread

1 pound grated medium Cheddar cheese
2 (4-ounce) jars chopped pimentos, drained
1½ cups mayonnaise (do not use light)
2 tablespoons black pepper
1 cup drained, crushed pineapple

Combine all ingredients. **Serves 16.**

Great for feeding crowds at tailgate parties or family reunions.

Sauced Stack-Ups

3 English muffins, split and toasted
6 slices Canadian bacon, ham or turkey
1 cup shredded Swiss cheese
1 (10-ounce) package frozen asparagus
    spears, cooked
1 (1-ounce) package white sauce mix
1 tablespoon Durkee's sauce
½ teaspoon Worcestershire sauce

Place muffins on a baking sheet and top each half with a slice of Canadian bacon, ham or turkey. Sprinkle with half of the cheese. Divide asparagus among muffins and sprinkle with remaining cheese. Bake in preheated 425° oven for 15 minutes. Meanwhile, prepare white sauce according to package directions. Stir in remaining ingredients. Spoon warm sauce over sandwiches. **Serves 6.**

Tailgate Picnic Sandwich

½ cup olive oil
¼ cup balsamic vinegar
1 teaspoon minced garlic
6 large red bell peppers, roasted, peeled
    and cut into ¾-inch strips
2 (1½-pound) sourdough bread rounds
Coarse grain Dijon mustard
4 ounces thinly sliced hard salami, divided
¼ pound fresh spinach, washed and
    stemmed, divided
6 ounces sliced provolone cheese, divided
12 thin slices red onion, separated into
    rings, divided
4 ounces thinly sliced cooked turkey breast, divided
4 ounces thinly sliced ham, divided

Combine oil, vinegar and garlic in a medium bowl. Add roasted pepper strips and turn to coat evenly. Let stand at room temperature 3 hours. (This may be done up to 2 days in advance.) Cover and refrigerate. Cut tops off bread rounds and reserve. Hollow loaves, leaving ½-inch thick shells and discarding insides. Spread inside and top of each loaf with mustard. Layer half of each of the following ingredients: salami, spinach, marinated peppers, cheese, onion rings, turkey and ham in each loaf. Replace bread tops. Wrap in plastic wrap and then in foil. Chill overnight. Cut each loaf into 6 wedges to serve. **Serves 12.**

Entrées

Entrées

Have You Heard …

... about the Hunt-Phelan Home

*O*pening the door to the Hunt-Phelan Home in the 500 block of Beale Street affords a visitor glimpses of antebellum decor and Civil War history. Started in 1828, it took four years to complete the home which was part of a large estate and the site of many social events in Memphis prior to the Civil War. Lavish appointments and furniture from the period are lovingly displayed along with precious family photos, books and heirlooms which carefully chronicle this fascinating era of the Old South. The Battle of Vicksburg was planned in the home's library by General Ulysses S. Grant who used the estate as his headquarters after the Battle of Memphis. Hunt-Phelan may be the only home to boast having Grant and Confederate President Jefferson Davis both sleep there – of course at different times. A camp for yellow fever victims is also part of the storied history of this picturesque mansion which had running water and one of the first swimming pools in the city. Spend a few hours strolling through the gardens and the home to relive a bygone era.

John Willingham's World-Champion Ribs

2 slabs spareribs (6 to 7 pounds)
½ cup apple cider vinegar
½ cup water
6 to 7 tablespoons mild seasoning mix

Lay ribs in a non-reactive pan. Combine vinegar and water and brush on both sides of ribs. Sprinkle with seasoning mix and rub it in with fingertips. Cover and refrigerate at least 12 hours.

Start the cooker and allow it to reach 250°. Place slabs in cooker and cook for 4½ to 5½ hours, turning every 15 minutes. The ribs are done when the internal temperature of the meat reaches 180°, the ribs are flexible, the meat is fork tender and the ends of the bone extend about ⅜ inch below meat. Cut slabs into individual bones or 3-rib racks. Serve immediately with or without your favorite sauce. **Serves 4.**

Dry Memphis Ribs

1 cup plus 2 tablespoons salt
1 cup plus 2 tablespoons sugar
¼ cup plus 3½ tablespoons black pepper
¼ cup plus 2 tablespoons garlic powder
¼ cup plus 2 tablespoons monosodium glutamate
3 tablespoons paprika
1 teaspoon cayenne pepper
10 pounds lean pork ribs
Vinegar

Combine all ingredients except pork in a 1-quart lidded jar. Seal and punch holes in lid. Sprinkle generously over ribs. Cook ribs on a grill with the cover down. Do not let the fire get too hot. Turn ribs every hour. Sprinkle more seasoning on ribs after second hour. Add more charcoal to grill after third hour. After cooking for 3 hours, baste ribs with vinegar and continue cooking 1 more hour, basting frequently. **Serves 8.**

Sound Bites

Vegetables that
are good with
Pork–
Broccoli
Brussels sprouts
Braised red and
white cabbage
Celery (au gratin
or almondine)
Green beans
Leeks
Lima Beans
Mushrooms
Glazed onions
Mashed potatoes
Roast potatoes
Tomatoes
Turnips

Roasted Pork Tenderloin Stuffed with Spinach, Sun-Dried Tomatoes and Goat Cheese

1½ pound whole pork tenderloin
1 bunch spinach, washed and stems removed
3 tablespoons butter
4 cloves garlic, crushed
½ cup champagne
¼ cup sun-dried tomatoes
¼ cup goat cheese, crumbled
1 tablespoon olive oil
Salt and freshly ground black pepper

Cut a pocket lengthwise in pork. Melt butter over medium heat in a medium sauté pan. Sauté garlic and spinach. Remove with a slotted spoon and cool. Squeeze out any excess liquid and blot dry. Chop roughly. Preheat oven to 375°. Warm champagne in a small saucepan over medium heat. Remove from heat and add tomatoes. Soak until softened, about 15 minutes. Drain tomatoes and chop roughly. Combine spinach, tomatoes and goat cheese and stuff into pocket in pork. Securely tie tenderloin with kitchen string. Heat olive oil in a large sauté pan. Sear meat on all sides, then place in a shallow roasting pan and roast in oven until a meat thermometer inserted in center of pork registers 140° to 150°, about 25 to 30 minutes. The pork will be slightly pink in the center. Slice pork into ½ inch medallions and fan on serving plates. **Serves 4.**

Peppered Pork

2 (1-pound) pork tenderloins
1 tablespoon coarsely ground pepper
½ cup white wine
½ cup chicken broth
½ cup low fat sour cream
2 teaspoons country-style Dijon mustard

Roll tenderloins in pepper to coat. Place in roasting pan and bake in preheated 350° oven for 30 to 40 minutes. Remove from oven, place pork on a cutting board and drain fat from pan. Pour wine into pan and place over high heat, scraping up any browned bits with a wooden spoon. Add broth and cook until reduced by half. Remove from heat and stir in sour cream and mustard. Slice pork and top with sauce.

Roast Pork with Fruit Sauce

1 (3 to 4) pound pork loin roast
1 cup apple juice
½ cup apple jelly
1 teaspoon ground cardamom
¾ cup dried fruit (cranberries, peaches or
   apricots), chopped

Place pork in shallow roasting pan. Combine juice, jelly and cardamom in a small saucepan. Heat, stirring, until jelly is melted. Pour over roast. Cook until a meat thermometer inserted in center of pork registers 160°, basting frequently. Remove from pan and slice. Add fruit to pan drippings and simmer over low heat until fruit is softened, about 5 minutes. Pour over pork.

Crown Roast of Pork with Creole Mustard Sauce

2 teaspoons dried thyme, crumbled
2 teaspoons salt
Pepper
1 tablespoon vegetable oil
1 (12-rib) crown roast of fresh pork
   (about 6¾ pounds), patted dry
¼ cup dry white wine
¼ cup whipping cream
⅓ cup Creole mustard
Flat-leafed parsley sprigs
Cherry tomatoes

*Combine thyme, salt, pepper to taste and oil in a small bowl. Mix well. Rub on all sides of pork. Place pork in a lightly oiled shallow roasting pan and roast in a preheated 450° oven for 20 minutes. Reduce heat to 325° and continue baking until a meat thermometer inserted in center registers 160°, about 2¼ hours more. Transfer to a platter and let stand for 15 minutes. Add wine to the roasting pan and deglaze over moderately high heat, scraping up the brown bits. Strain mixture through a fine sieve into a small saucepan. Add ½ cup water and boil mixture until it is reduced to about ⅔ cup. Add cream and boil, stirring, until it is reduced to about ¾ cup. Whisk in mustard and salt and pepper to taste. Arrange parsley sprigs and tomatoes around pork and serve with mustard sauce. **Serves 6.***

Pork with Grapes and Wine Sauce

1 (3-pound) pork butt roast, boned and tied
1 onion, sliced
2 cloves garlic, minced
1 teaspoon dried thyme
¼ teaspoon dried rosemary
1 bay leaf
2¼ teaspoons pepper
2 tablespoons olive oil
¼ cup brandy
2 tablespoons butter or margarine
2 tablespoons vegetable oil
1 cup dry white wine
2 pounds white seedless grapes, divided
½ cup whipping cream or half and half

Place roast in a large bowl and top with onion slices, garlic, thyme, rosemary, bay leaf, pepper, olive oil and brandy. Cover and marinate 3 hours. Remove pork from marinade, reserving marinade. Melt butter with oil in a Dutch oven. Brown meat on all sides. Strain marinade into pot and add wine. Cover and bring to a boil. Reduce heat and simmer 2 hours. Add 1¾ pounds grapes. Cover and cook 5 minutes. Remove meat to a cutting board. Stir cream into Dutch oven and cook for 2 minutes, stirring constantly. Slice meat and arrange on a serving platter. Pour sauce with grapes over meat. Garnish with remaining grapes. **Serves 6.**

Stuffed Pork Chops

3 tablespoons butter
1 tablespoon minced onion
¼ cup thinly sliced mushrooms
½ cup crumbled bleu cheese
¾ cup fine dry bread crumbs
Salt
6 (2-rib thick) pork chops, with pockets

Melt butter in a saucepan over medium-high heat. Sauté onions and mushrooms for 5 minutes. Remove from heat and stir in cheese, bread crumbs and salt to taste. Stuff into pork chops and secure with toothpicks. Bake in preheated 350° oven for 1 hour. **Serves 6.**

Apple Brandy Pork Chops

6 (½ to 1-inch-thick) pork chops
¾ teaspoon salt
1 tablespoon vegetable oil
⅓ cup apple brandy
½ cup whipping cream
2 tablespoons chopped fresh parsley or
1 tablespoon dried
¼ teaspoon pepper

Sprinkle chops with salt. Coat an ovenproof skillet with nonstick vegetable spray. Preheat skillet, add oil and brown chops over medium heat for 4 to 5 minutes per side. Remove chops and pour brandy into skillet. Deglaze pan, scraping up any browned bits. Add cream and bring to a boil. Cook until reduced, about 3 minutes. Stir in parsley and pepper and return chops to sauce. Place in 350° oven for about 45 minutes. Good over egg noodles. **Serves 6.**

Sound Bites

The full flavor of fresh herbs or spices is best released if you add it to the dish just before serving.

Parmesan Pork Chops with Potatoes

6 (½ to 1-inch-thick) boneless pork chops
Salt and pepper
Flour
Vegetable oil
1 cup grated Parmesan cheese, divided
4 to 5 medium potatoes, thinly sliced
½ onion, sliced and separated into rings
2 beef bouillon cubes
½ cup hot water
2 tablespoons lemon juice

Season chops with salt and pepper and dust with flour. Film a large skillet with oil and heat over medium-high heat. Brown chops on all sides and transfer to a 9 x 13-inch baking dish. Sprinkle with ⅓ cup Parmesan. Arrange potatoes around chops and sprinkle with salt and ⅓ cup cheese. Arrange onion rings over potatoes. Dissolve bouillon cube in hot water and add lemon juice. Pour over all. Sprinkle with remaining Parmesan. Cover with foil and bake in preheated 350° oven for 45 minutes. **Serves 6.**

Sound Bites

Rinse fresh herbs thoroughly, wrap them in damp paper towels, and store for up to a week in the refrigerator.

Bavarian Pork Chops

4 to 6 (1-inch-thick) pork chops
Salt and pepper
Flour
1 cup dry white wine
2 cups whole mushrooms
½ cup sour cream

Trim fat from chops, reserving fat. Season chops with salt and pepper and dust with flour. Place reserved fat in a large skillet and heat over medium-high heat until melted. Sear chops on both sides and drain any excess fat. Add wine, bring to a boil, and reduce heat. Simmer, covered, for 1 hour. Add mushrooms and cook, covered, until tender. Remove meat and mushrooms from pan. Heat wine mixture to a boil, scraping browned bits from bottom of pan and reducing liquid by half. Reduce heat to low and stir in sour cream. Heat through and serve over chops and mushrooms. **Serves 4 to 6.**

Pepper Pork en Brochette

2 large cloves garlic, crushed
3 tablespoons soy sauce
2 tablespoons sherry
1 tablespoon cracked black pepper
1 tablespoon ground coriander
1 teaspoon brown sugar
½ teaspoon ground cumin
1½ pounds lean boneless pork,
    cut into 1½-inch cubes
2 small green bell peppers, seeded and
    cut into 1½-inch pieces
2 medium onions, cut into 12 wedges
⅓ cup vegetable oil

Combine garlic, soy sauce, sherry, pepper, coriander, brown sugar and cumin in a large shallow dish. Mix well. Add pork, bell pepper and onion wedges and toss to coat. Marinate at room temperature 1 to 2 hours. Thread pork, bell pepper and onion alternately onto 4 skewers. Add oil to marinade remaining in dish and mix well. Broil pork 4 inches above coals, turning frequently and brushing with marinade until brown but not dry, about 10 to 12 minutes. **Serves 4.**

Pork Tenderloin with Mustard Sauce

½ cup soy sauce
½ cup bourbon or brandy
4 tablespoons brown sugar
3 pounds pork tenderloin or loin roast

Mustard Sauce:
⅓ cup sour cream
1 cup mayonnaise
1 tablespoon dry mustard
1 tablespoon finely chopped scallions
1½ teaspoons vinegar
Salt

Combine soy sauce, bourbon and brown sugar in a container large enough to hold pork. Add pork, turn to coat, cover and marinate at least 3 hours or overnight, refrigerated.

When ready to cook, remove pork from marinade and place in a roasting pan, reserving marinade. Bake in preheated 325° oven for 1½ hours, basting frequently with marinade. Combine all sauce ingredients in a small bowl and chill. Slice pork diagonally and serve with sauce.

Pork Roast Rosemary

2 tablespoons vegetable oil
1 (5 to 6-pound) boneless pork loin roast
2 cups sherry
2 cups water
1½ tablespoons rosemary, or to taste
1 teaspoon salt
¼ teaspoon freshly ground pepper
¼ cup butter
½ cup flour

Heat oil in roasting pan over medium-high heat. Brown meat on all sides. Add sherry, water and seasonings. Cover and bake in preheated 300° oven until tender, about 4 to 5 hours. Transfer meat to a serving platter. Strain juices and skim off fat. Melt butter in a medium saucepan and blend in flour. Cook, stirring constantly, for 3 minutes. Add pan juices slowly, stirring until blended. Add additional sherry or hot water to achieve desired consistency. Serve with roast.

Ham with Cloves and Beer

1 (3 to 4-pound) boneless smoked ham half or
 1 (7 to 10-pound) ham
1 (20-ounce) can pineapple slices, undrained
1 cup firmly packed brown sugar
½ bottle beer
½ cup pancake syrup
3 to 4 tablespoons flour
40 to 50 whole cloves

Place ham in a pot large enough to hold it and cover with water. Bring to a boil, reduce heat and simmer for 1½ hours. Remove to a baking pan. Pour juice from pineapple into a large saucepan. Add brown sugar, beer, and syrup. Bring to a boil, stirring constantly. Add flour slowly. Cook, stirring, until sauce reaches consistency of a glaze. Remove from heat. Insert cloves in ham approximately ½-inch apart. Pour glaze over ham. Bake in preheated 350° oven for 1 hour, spooning glaze over ham occasionally. Serve garnished with pineapple slices.

Sausage and Rice Casserole

3 pounds pork sausage
1 onion, chopped
⅓ cup slivered almonds, salted and toasted
1 small green bell pepper, chopped
2 cups diced celery
2 cups uncooked rice
3 packages dry chicken noodle soup mix
9 cups boiling water

Brown sausage in a Dutch oven and drain excess fat. Add onion, bell pepper and celery and sauté over medium-high heat until onion is translucent. Add rice, soup mix and boiling water. Mix well and add almonds. Cover and bake in preheated 350° oven until liquid is absorbed, about 45 minutes, stirring occasionally. **Yields 10 to 12.**

Savory Roast

1 (4-pound) rump roast
6 slices bacon, diced
1 clove garlic, minced
1 tablespoon salt
1 teaspoon dried thyme leaves
¼ teaspoon nutmeg
¼ teaspoon ground cloves
1 cup brandy
1 cup dry red wine
4 leeks, cut in 1-inch pieces
8 carrots, cut in 2-inch pieces
New potatoes, optional

Preheat oven to 350°. Place roast, bacon, garlic, salt, thyme, nutmeg, cloves, brandy and wine in a Dutch oven. Cover and bake 2½ to 3 hours, basting occasionally. Add leeks, carrots and potatoes, if desired, and continue cooking until meat is tender and vegetables are done, about 1 more hour. Remove meat to a plate and vegetables to a serving bowl. Skim fat from pan and pour remaining liquid into gravy boat.

Rolled Stuffed Tenderloin

1 (3-pound) beef tenderloin or eye of round
¼ cup butter
½ small onion, chopped
1 (4-ounce) can mushrooms, drained
½ cup diced celery
1 beef bouillon cube
1 cup hot water
1½ cups soft bread crumbs
Salt and pepper
4 slices bacon

Have butcher split and flatten meat. Melt butter in a medium skillet over medium-high heat. Sauté onion, mushrooms and celery until onions are translucent. Dissolve bouillon in hot water and add to skillet. Add bread crumbs and stir to moisten. Season with salt and pepper to taste. Stuff into prepared meat and fasten edges. Place in a roasting pan and top with bacon slices. Roast, uncovered, in preheated 350° oven for 1½ hours.

Sound Bites

Vegetables that
are good with
Ham—
Artichokes
Asparagus
Dried beans
(all types)
Cabbage
(au gratin)
Celeriac
Celery
Corn
Green Beans
Kale
Lima Beans
Mushrooms
Onions or leeks
in cream
Parsnips
Peas
Sweet Potatoes
Mashed white
potatoes
Spinach
Tomatoes
Turnips
Turnip Greens
Zucchini

Sound Bites

A good and easy marinade for steaks: dry bouillon mix and soy sauce, both rubbed into meat.

Beef Tenderloin Marinated in Molasses and Black Pepper

1 cup molasses
2 tablespoons balsamic vinegar
2 tablespoons ground black pepper
2 cloves garlic, finely chopped
1 large shallot, finely chopped
2 teaspoons finely grated fresh ginger
1 teaspoon finely chopped fresh thyme
Crushed red pepper flakes to taste
2 pounds center-cut beef tenderloin, trimmed of
    all fat and silver skin
Salt
2 tablespoons vegetable oil or
    2 tablespoons unsalted butter

Combine molasses, vinegar, pepper, garlic, shallot, ginger, thyme and pepper flakes in a small bowl. Place beef in a glass dish and cover with molasses mixture. Cover and marinate in refrigerator for 24 hours, turning meat occasionally.

When ready to cook, remove meat and reserve marinade. Cut meat into 8 medallions and season lightly with salt. Heat oil in a large cast iron skillet over medium heat. Brown medallions 3 minutes on 1 side and 2 minutes on the other, or until desired doneness. Just before removing from skillet, add 4 to 6 tablespoons marinade and quickly glaze both sides of meat.

An Alternate Method: Grill entire tenderloin to desired doneness. Boil marinade in a saucepan until reduced by half. Just before serving, whisk 2 tablespoons cold, unsalted butter into sauce. Carve tenderloin and serve with sauce. **Serves 8.**

Filet Mignon with Red Wine Sauce

3 cups dry red wine
3 tablespoons cognac
3 shallots, chopped
1 tablespoon chopped fresh thyme or
   1 teaspoon dried, crumbled
6 (6-ounce) filet mignon steaks
4 cups beef stock or canned unsalted broth
4 tablespoons olive oil
5 tablespoons chilled unsalted butter,
   cut into pieces

Whisk wine, cognac, shallots and thyme in a large bowl. Place steaks in glass baking dish. Pour marinade over steaks, cover and refrigerate overnight.

The following day, remove steaks from marinade and pat dry. Transfer marinade to heavy large saucepan. Boil until reduced to 1 cup, about 20 minutes. Add stock and boil until reduced to 1¼ cups, about 20 minutes. Divide oil between 2 heavy large skillets and place over high heat. Season steaks with salt and pepper. Add 3 steaks to each skillet and brown on both sides. Reduce heat to medium-high and cook to desired doneness, about 4 minutes per side for medium-rare. Transfer to plates and tent with foil to keep warm. Add half of sauce to each skillet and bring to a boil, scraping up any browned bits. Transfer contents of both skillets to 1 skillet and bring to a simmer. Add butter and whisk until melted. Spoon over steaks and serve.
Serves 6.

Sound Bites

Vegetables that
are good with

Beef–

Artichokes

Broccoli

Brussels sprouts

Carrots

Cauliflower

Celeriac

Celery

Eggplant

Green Beans

Kale

Leeks

Lima Beans

Mushrooms

Onions

Peas

Tomatoes

Turnip Greens

White Potatoes

Yellow Squash

Zucchini

Roast Prime Rib of Beef with Herbed Crust and Madeira Sauce

1 (5 rib) standing rib roast, trimmed weight
about 12 pounds

1½ tablespoons black peppercorns

2 small bay leaves, crumbled

6 tablespoons unsalted butter, cut in pieces
and softened

⅓ cup plus 1 tablespoon flour

2½ teaspoons coarsely ground white pepper

1¼ teaspoons salt

1¼ pounds large shallots (about 1½ inches long),
peeled, leaving ends intact

2½ heads garlic, separated into cloves, unpeeled

Madeira Sauce:

¾ cup dry red wine

2½ cups canned beef broth

½ cup Madeira

1¼ tablespoons cornstarch

Let roast stand at room temperature for 1 hour. Finely grind peppercorns and bay leaves in an electric spice or coffee grinder. Place in a small bowl and add butter, flour, white pepper and salt. Mix well to form a paste. Rub over roast. Place meat rib side down in a roasting pan. Roast in preheated 500° oven for 30 minutes, then reduce heat to 350° and continue roasting for 1 hour. Add shallots and roast 10 more minutes. Add garlic cloves and roast until a meat thermometer inserted in center of meat registers 130° for medium rare, about 30 more minutes. Transfer roast to a heated platter. Transfer shallots and garlic to paper towels to drain. Keep them warm, loosely covered. Let roast rest 20 to 30 minutes before carving.

For Sauce: *Skim fat from pan drippings. Add wine and deglaze pan over moderately high heat, scraping up browned bits. Boil until liquid is reduced by half and transfer it to a saucepan. Add broth and ⅓ cup of Madeira. Boil 5 minutes. Dissolve cornstarch into remaining Madeira in a small bowl. Add to saucepan in a stream, whisking constantly. Bring to a boil, whisking, and boil for 1 minute. Season with salt and pepper and transfer to a heated sauce boat. Arrange shallots and garlic around roast and serve with sauce.*

Royal Roll-Ups with Rice

1 pound round steak
1 (2-ounce) can mushrooms, drained and
  chopped
1 medium tomato, peeled and chopped
¼ cup bread crumbs
1 teaspoon grated orange rind
1¼ teaspoons salt, divided
½ teaspoon pepper, divided
¼ cup flour
¼ cup vegetable oil
2 cups whole baby carrots
3 stalks celery, cut into 1½-inch pieces
1 cup English peas
2 cups beef broth
2 tablespoons water
Cooked rice

*Trim fat from meat and pound thin. Cut into 3¼ x 4½-inch pieces. Combine mushrooms, tomato, crumbs, orange rind, 1 teaspoon salt and ¼ teaspoon pepper in a small bowl. Place 2 tablespoons of this mixture on each piece of steak, spreading to within ½ inch of edge. Roll meat around stuffing and secure with toothpick or string. Combine flour with remaining salt and pepper. Dredge meat in flour mixture, reserving leftover flour. Heat oil in a large skillet and brown meat on all sides. Place in a shallow 2-quart casserole and add carrots, celery and broth. Cover and bake in preheated 375° oven until tender, about 1 hour. Remove toothpicks or string from meat. Place meat and vegetables over rice on a warmed serving platter. Combine reserved flour mixture and 2 tablespoons water in a small saucepan, blending until smooth. Gradually stir in pan drippings and cook over medium heat, stirring constantly, until thickened and bubbly. Serve with steak rolls. **Serves 6.***

Stir-Fry Beef with Portobello Mushrooms

1 pound beef flank steak, partially frozen
2 tablespoons soy sauce
2 tablespoons dry sherry
Dash of garlic powder
Dash of ginger
2 tablespoons cornstarch
½ cup beef broth
4 tablespoons vegetable oil, divided
1 onion, thinly sliced
1 pound portobello mushrooms, sliced
Hot cooked white rice
2 green onions, sliced diagonally

*Slice beef diagonally across the grain into thin strips. Combine soy sauce, sherry, garlic powder and ginger in a small bowl. Place beef strips in a glass dish. Pour soy sauce mixture over beef, cover and marinate at room temperature for 1 hour. Whisk together cornstarch and broth in a small bowl. Heat 2 tablespoons oil in a large skillet or wok. Drain beef and add to skillet. Cook, stirring constantly, until beef is cooked through, about 3 minutes. Remove beef and keep warm. Add remaining oil to skillet. Add onion slices and cook, stirring, until onion begins to soften. Stir in mushrooms and continue cooking, stirring constantly, for 2 more minutes. Whisk cornstarch mixture and add to skillet along with beef. Bring to a boil. Serve with rice and garnish with green onions. **Serves 4 to 6.***

London Broil with Mushroom Sauce

1 clove garlic, crushed
1 tablespoon vegetable oil
2 teaspoons chopped fresh parsley
1 teaspoon salt
1 teaspoon lemon juice
⅛ teaspoon pepper
1 (2-pound) flank steak

Mushroom Sauce:
1 cup sliced fresh mushrooms
¼ cup butter or margarine, melted and divided
1 shallot, chopped
1 clove garlic, minced
1 onion slice
2 carrot slices
1 sprig fresh parsley
6 black peppercorns
1 whole clove
1 bay leaf
2 tablespoons flour
1 (10½-ounce) can beef broth, undiluted
⅓ cup dry red wine
2 tablespoons chopped fresh parsley
¼ teaspoon salt
⅛ teaspoon pepper

Combine garlic, oil, parsley, salt, lemon juice and pepper in a small bowl. Place steak on rack in a broiler pan. Brush with half of oil mixture. Broil 6 inches from heat for 5 minutes. Turn and brush with remaining oil mixture. Broil to desired degree of doneness, 4 to 6 minutes more. Slice diagonally across grain to serve.

For Sauce: *Sauté mushrooms in 1 tablespoon butter in a skillet over medium heat until tender. Remove mushrooms to a bowl. Melt remaining butter in a saucepan and sauté shallot, garlic, onion, carrot, parsley sprig, peppercorns, clove and bay leaf over medium heat for 3 minutes. Add flour and stir until blended. Gradually add broth. Cook, stirring constantly, until mixture is thickened and bubbly. Strain through a wire-mesh sieve into a bowl, discard solids. Return to saucepan and stir in mushrooms, wine, parsley, salt and pepper. Cook over medium heat until thoroughly heated. Serve with steak.* **Yield: 6 servings steak, 1½ cups sauce.**

Beef Bourguignonne

½ pound bacon, coarsely chopped
3 pounds well-trimmed boneless beef chuck,
   cut into 1½-inch cubes
Salt and pepper
⅓ cup flour
1¼ pounds boiling onions, peeled
¾ pound large carrots, cut into 1-inch pieces
12 large cloves garlic, peeled
3 cups canned beef broth, divided
½ cup cognac or brandy
2 (750-ml) bottles red Burgundy wine
1¼ pounds mushrooms
⅓ cup chopped fresh thyme or
   2 tablespoons dried, crumbled
1 tablespoon dark brown sugar
1 tablespoon tomato paste

Preheat oven to 325°. Sauté bacon in heavy large Dutch oven over high heat until brown and crisp, about 8 minutes. Transfer to paper towels using a slotted spoon. Season beef generously with salt and pepper. Coat with flour, using all of flour. Working in 3 batches, brown beef in bacon drippings over high heat, about 5 minutes per batch. Transfer to a large bowl. Add onions and carrots to pot and sauté until light brown, about 6 minutes. Add garlic and sauté 1 minute more. Transfer to bowl with beef. Add 1 cup broth and cognac to pot. Bring to a boil and boil until reduced to a glaze, scraping up browned bits, about 8 minutes. Return meat and vegetables and their juices to pot. Add wine, mushrooms, thyme, sugar, tomato paste and remaining broth. Bring to a boil, stirring occasionally. Cover pot and place in oven. Cook until beef is tender, about 1 hour 20 minutes. Ladle liquid from stew into a large saucepan. Spoon off fat. Boil liquid until reduce to 2¾ cups, about 40 minutes. Season with salt and pepper. Pour back over beef and vegetables and rewarm over low heat before serving. Can be prepared 1 day ahead. Cover and chill. Rewarm before serving.
Serves 8.

Easy Beef Bourguignonne

3 to 5 onions, sliced
½ pound fresh mushrooms, sliced
2 tablespoons vegetable oil
2 pounds lean beef, cubed
¼ teaspoon thyme
¼ teaspoon marjoram
⅛ teaspoon pepper
1½ tablespoons flour
¾ cup beef bouillon
1½ cups Burgundy red wine

Sauté onions and mushrooms in oil in a large Dutch oven over medium-high heat. Remove to a dish. Add meat and brown on all sides. Add seasonings. Whisk flour into bouillon until blended. Add to meat and heat to boiling. Boil 1 minute. Add wine, cover, reduce heat and simmer until tender, 1½ to 2 hours. Add onions and mushrooms and cook, uncovered, 15 minutes more. Serve in soup bowls with French bread to dip in sauce.

Beef-Stuffed Potato on the Half Shell

4 large baking potatoes
½ pound ground beef, cooked and drained
¼ cup butter, softened
½ cup cooked mushrooms
4 to 5 tablespoons sour cream
2 to 3 tablespoons chopped onion
1 teaspoon seasoned salt
½ teaspoon pepper
½ cup grated Cheddar cheese
5 slices bacon, cooked, drained and crumbled

*Wash potatoes, wrap in foil and bake in preheated 350° oven until tender, 1 to 1½ hours. Remove from foil and carefully split in half lengthwise. Scoop pulp into a large mixing bowl, leaving skins intact. Add beef, butter, mushrooms, sour cream, onion, salt and pepper to bowl. Mix well. Stuff into shells and top with cheese and bacon. Return to oven and heat until cheese melts. **Serves 8.***

Sound Bites

Half portions of butter and roquefort cheese, melted together makes a tasty sauce for steak, fish, etc.

Stuffed Zucchini

4 small zucchini
6 tablespoons butter, divided
1 onion, chopped
2 cloves garlic, minced
1 pound ground beef
¾ sleeve saltine crackers, crumbled
¾ cup grated Parmesan cheese

*Halve zucchini lengthwise. Scoop out centers, reserving shells, and place in a saucepan with 3 tablespoons butter. Cook over medium heat until soft. Parboil reserved shells, drain and pat dry. Sauté onion and garlic in remaining butter until soft. Brown ground beef and drain. Place crumbled crackers in a large bowl and moisten with water. Squeeze out any excess water. Add onion, garlic, beef, zucchini pulp and Parmesan to bowl. Mix to blend thoroughly. Stuff into zucchini shells and place in a baking dish. Bake in preheated 350° oven until tops are browned, about 30 minutes. **Serves 8.***

Marinated Beef Ribs with Honey Glaze

3 cups stout beer
½ cup soy sauce
½ cup firmly packed brown sugar
¼ cup sesame oil
3 tablespoons minced garlic
1 large onion, sliced
4 pounds beef short ribs, cut crosswise
    flanken style (about ½-inch thick)

Honey Glaze:
1 cup honey
¼ cup soy sauce
2 tablespoons chopped fresh parsley
1 tablespoon minced garlic
1½ teaspoons pepper

Whisk stout, soy sauce, sesame oil and garlic together in a large bowl to blend. Add onion slices. Place ribs in a glass baking dish. Pour marinade over ribs, cover and refrigerate overnight.

For Glaze:** Whisk all ingredients in medium bowl to blend. When ready to cook, heat grill to medium. Remove ribs from marinade and place on grill. Grill until cooked through, turning occasionally, about 10 minutes. Brush with glaze and cook 1 more minute per side. Serve with remaining glaze. **Serves 6.

Veal Loin Chops with Rosemary Sauce

Rosemary Sauce:
2 tablespoons unsalted butter
1 tablespoon finely chopped shallot
1½ teaspoons minced fresh rosemary
2 tablespoons dry vermouth
½ cup veal or beef stock or canned unsalted beef
    broth
½ cup whipping cream
Salt and pepper

Veal:
3 medium zucchini
4 (8-ounce) veal loin chops (about 1 inch thick)
Salt and pepper
6 tablespoons unsalted butter, divided
1 medium tomato, peeled, seeded and diced
4 fresh rosemary sprigs

For Sauce: *Melt butter in a heavy medium skillet over medium heat. Add shallots and rosemary and cook 3 minutes, stirring occasionally. Add vermouth and boil until almost no liquid remains in pan, about 2 minutes. Add stock and boil until liquid is reduced by half, about 4 minutes. Add cream and boil until sauce thickens slightly. Season with salt and pepper. Strain into heavy small saucepan. (Can be prepared 1 day ahead. Cool, cover and chill.)*

For Veal: *Cut skin from zucchini into ¼-inch-thick pieces. Cut skin into matchstick-size strips. Reserve centers for another use. Season veal with salt and pepper. Melt 4 tablespoons butter in a heavy large skillet over medium-high heat. Add veal and cook about 3 minutes per side for medium-rare. Transfer to platter and tent with foil to keep warm. Melt remaining butter in heavy medium skillet over high heat. Add zucchini skin and sauté until crisp-tender, about 1 minute. Divide zucchini among 4 plates. Top with veal chops. Rewarm sauce over medium-low heat, stirring constantly. Spoon over veal. Sprinkle with tomatoes and garnish with rosemary sprigs.* **Serves 4.**

Sound Bites

*Vegetables that
are good with
Veal–*
Artichokes
Asparagus
Broccoli
Carrots
Cauliflower
Celeriac
Celery
Eggplant
Green Beans
Green bell
peppers
Lima Beans
Mushrooms
Onions
Peas
Tomatoes
White Potatoes
Zucchini

Veal with Sun-Dried Tomatoes, Capers and Herbs

8 (⅜-inch-thick) veal loin medallions
Salt
White pepper
¼ cup unsalted butter
¼ cup vegetable oil
2 large shallots, finely chopped
½ cup dry white wine
¾ cup drained oil-packed sun-dried tomatoes,
  sliced
3 tablespoons drained capers
1 cup canned unsalted beef broth
¼ cup chilled unsalted butter, cut into pieces
1 tablespoon minced fresh thyme or ½ teaspoon
  dried, crumbled
1 tablespoon minced fresh tarragon or ½ teaspoon
  dried, crumbled
1 tablespoon snipped fresh chives

Preheat oven to 300°. Season veal with salt and white pepper. Melt ¼ cup butter with oil in heavy large skillet over high heat. Add veal in batches and brown on all sides. Place in baking pan. Add shallots to butter and oil mixture in same skillet and sauté 2 minutes. Add wine and bring to a boil, scraping up any browned bits. Add sun-dried tomatoes and capers and boil until liquid is reduced to 2 tablespoons. Add broth and boil until liquid is reduced by one-third. Remove from heat. Bake veal about 2 minutes for medium. Gradually whisk chilled butter into warm sauce. Mix in herbs. Divide veal among plates. Spoon sauce over and serve immediately. **Serves 4.**

Veal with Prosciutto

1 pound sliced veal, pounded ¼-inch thick
   and cut into 5-inch squares
2 to 3 tablespoons minced fresh sage or
   2½ teaspoons dried, crumbled
Salt and pepper
¼ pound thinly sliced prosciutto
2 tablespoons butter
2 tablespoons olive oil
⅔ cup dry white wine

Season veal with sage, salt and pepper. Top each piece of veal with a slice of prosciutto. Roll and secure veal and prosciutto together with toothpicks. Melt butter with oil in a skillet over medium-high heat. Add veal bundles in batches and cook until golden brown, about 1 minute. Reduce heat to medium, turn veal and cook 2 minutes more. Arrange veal on a serving platter and remove toothpicks. Pour off fat from skillet. Add wine and reduce by half over medium-high heat, scraping up the browned bits. Pour sauce over veal. **Serves 4.**

Honeyed Rack of Lamb with Ginger and Rosemary

1 (2½-pound) rack of lamb
1½ teaspoons minced peeled fresh ginger
1½ teaspoons minced fresh rosemary or
   ½ teaspoon dried, crumbled
1 cup unsweetened apple cider
½ cup rich beef stock
1½ tablespoons honey, preferably clover
½ teaspoon pepper
Salt
Fresh rosemary sprigs

Preheat oven to 450°. Pat lamb dry and rub surface with ginger and minced rosemary. Arrange in shallow roasting pan. Add cider and stock to pan. Roast 10 minutes. Drizzle honey over lamb. Roast 10 minutes longer for rare, 12 minutes for medium-rare. Transfer lamb to a heated platter, sprinkle with pepper and tent with foil. Strain pan juices into a heavy small saucepan. Boil until reduced to ¾ cup, about 10 minutes. Adjust seasoning with salt. Divide sauce among plates. Carve rack into chops and arrange on sauce. Garnish with rosemary sprigs. **Serves 4.**

Sound Bites

Purchase dried herbs and spices in small quantities, keep them in tightly sealed containers away from heat and light, and try to use them within 10 to 12 months. The flavor of dried herbs fades quickly.

Grilled Veal Chops with Walnut Stuffing

1 cup walnuts, lightly toasted
1 cup packed fresh spinach leaves
1 cup packed fresh basil leaves
⅓ cup packed fresh parsley
4 tablespoons olive oil, divided
1 tablespoon white wine vinegar
1 teaspoon minced garlic
¾ teaspoon salt, divided
¾ teaspoon freshly ground pepper, divided
6 (1½-inch-thick) veal loin chops cut with pockets (about 4½ pounds)

*Place walnuts, spinach, basil and parsley in food processor. Process until finely chopped, about 30 seconds. Gradually add 3 tablespoons oil and vinegar in a steady stream, with processor running, processing just until mixture is blended. Turn mixture into a medium bowl and stir in garlic, ½ teaspoon salt and ½ teaspoon pepper. Stuff mixture evenly into pockets of chops. Secure openings with wooden picks. Brush chops with remaining oil and sprinkle evenly with remaining salt and pepper. Grill, covered, over medium-hot coals (350° to 400°) to desired degree of doneness, 8 to 10 minutes per side. Remove wooden picks before serving. **Serves 6.***

Roasted Rack of Lamb with Garlic and Herbs

2 tablespoons dried oregano
2 tablespoons dried thyme
1 tablespoon fennel seeds
1 tablespoon dried rosemary
1½ teaspoons dried rubbed sage
¼ cup olive oil
2 tablespoons chopped garlic
2 (1½-pound) racks of lamb
Salt and pepper

*Preheat oven to 400°. Combine oregano, thyme, fennel, rosemary and sage in a small bowl. Combine oil and garlic in another small bowl. Rub oil mixture over each lamb rack. Season generously with salt and pepper, then press herb mixture all over each rack. Place lamb in baking pan and roast until thermometer inserted in center registers 135° for medium-rare, about 20 minutes. Transfer lamb to platter and let stand 5 minutes. Carve into individual chops, arrange on platter and serve. **Serves 4.***

Grilled Lamb Chops with Mint Pesto

Mint Pesto:
1 cup lightly packed fresh basil leaves
1 cup lightly packed fresh mint leaves
1 shallot, chopped
1 tablespoon pine nuts
1 tablespoon honey
¼ cup plus 3 tablespoons olive oil, divided

Lamb Chops:
6 (½-inch-thick) eggplant slices
Salt and pepper
1 tablespoon fresh lemon juice
6 (3-ounce) lamb chops, about 1-inch thick

For Pesto: *Place basil, mint, shallot, pine nuts and honey in a blender and process until finely chopped. Add ¼ cup oil and blend well.*

For Lamb: *Prepare barbecue grill on medium-high heat. Sprinkle both sides of eggplant with lemon juice. Season with salt and let stand 10 minutes. Pat dry with paper towel. Brush both sides of eggplant with remaining oil. Season lamb with salt and pepper. Place eggplant and lamb on grill and cook until eggplant is tender and lamb is medium-rare, turning occasionally, about 10 minutes. Arrange eggplant slices on plates and top with lamb chops and pesto.* **Serves 2.**

Sound Bites

Pesto may be made up to 1 week ahead of time. Pour a ¼-inch-thick layer of olive oil over top, cover and refrigerate. Bring to room temperature and stir well before using.

Grilled Sesame Chicken

½ cup olive oil
½ cup white wine
½ cup soy sauce
1 to 2 tablespoons freshly grated ginger or
    2 tablespoons ground
1 tablespoon dry mustard
1 teaspoon freshly ground black pepper
4 cloves garlic, crushed, or
    2 tablespoons garlic powder
½ cup chopped green onions
3 tablespoons sesame seeds
2 whole chickens, quartered

Combine all ingredients except chicken in a bowl. Mix well to blend. Place chicken in a large zip lock bag and top with marinade. Seal and refrigerate 4 to 8 hours. Remove chicken and reserve marinade. Grill over medium-hot coals, basting frequently with marinade.

Peppercorn-Crusted Roast Lamb

1 (6-pound) leg of lamb, boned and butterflied
1 tablespoon white peppercorns, crushed
1 tablespoon green peppercorns, crushed
1 tablespoon black peppercorns, crushed
½ cup fresh mint leaves
½ cup burgundy or dry red wine
½ cup raspberry vinegar
¼ cup soy sauce
8 cloves garlic, crushed
1 tablespoon chopped fresh rosemary
2 tablespoons Dijon mustard

*Place lamb in a large shallow dish. Combine peppercorns in a small bowl and stir well. Reserve 2 tablespoons peppercorn mixture. Combine remaining peppercorn mixture with mint leaves, wine, vinegar, soy sauce and garlic. Stir well and pour over lamb. Cover and marinate in refrigerator 8 hours, turning occasionally. Remove lamb from marinade, reserving marinade. Roll lamb, tying securely with heavy string at 2-inch intervals. Coat lamb with mustard. Lightly pat reserved peppercorn mixture into mustard. Place in a shallow roasting pan and top with reserved marinade. Bake in preheated 350° oven until a meat thermometer registers 160° for medium about 2 hours and 15 minutes. Baste occasionally with pan juices. Let stand 20 minutes before slicing and serve with pan juices. **Serves 6 to 8.***

Herb Chicken and Rice

6 skinless, boneless chicken breasts
4 thin slices Swiss cheese
½ pound fresh mushrooms, sliced
1 (10¾-ounce) can cream of chicken or mushroom
   soup
1 cup sour cream
½ cup white wine or cooking sherry
2 cups herb-seasoned stuffing mix
⅓ cup margarine, melted
Hot cooked rice

*Preheat oven to 350°. Place chicken in a 9 x 13-inch baking dish which has been coated with nonstick vegetable spray. Top with cheese. Arrange mushroom slices over cheese. Combine soup, sour cream and wine in a medium bowl, blending well. Pour over mushrooms. Sprinkle with stuffing mix. Drizzle margarine over stuffing and bake for 1 hour. Serve over rice. **Serves 6.***

Chicken à la Crescents

¼ cup crushed herb stuffing mix
¼ cup chopped pecans
1 (3-ounce) package cream cheese, softened
1½ teaspoons chives
1 tablespoon butter, softened
1 teaspoon lemon pepper
1 cup chopped cooked chicken
1 (2-ounce) can mushrooms, drained
1 (8-ounce) package refrigerated crescent rolls
¼ cup butter, melted
1 can prepared chicken gravy

*Combine stuffing mix and pecans in a small bowl; set aside. Combine cream cheese, 1 tablespoon butter, chives and lemon pepper in a medium bowl. Mix well. Add chicken and mushrooms and stir to combine; set aside. Separate rolls into 8 triangles. Spread each with ¼ cup chicken mixture. Roll up starting at short side of the triangle. Roll to opposite point, tuck sides in and point under. Pinch to seal completely. Dip in melted butter, then in crumb mixture. Place on ungreased cookie sheet and bake in preheated 325° oven until golden brown, about 30 minutes. Heat gravy and serve over crescents. **Serves 8.***

Sound Bites

*Too sweet –
add salt.
If it's a main dish
or vegetable, add
a teaspoon of
cider vinegar.*

Grecian Oven-Fried Chicken

A perfect way to eat low fat without giving up the pleasure of fried food.

3 cups cornflakes
1½ teaspoons dried oregano
1 teaspoon grated lemon rind
½ teaspoon ground coriander
½ teaspoon salt
¼ teaspoon pepper
4 boneless, skinless chicken breast halves
½ cup plain fat free yogurt

*Preheat oven to 350°. Combine cornflakes, oregano, lemon rind, coriander, salt and pepper in a zip lock bag. Lightly crush mixture. Dip chicken in yogurt. Add to bag and shake to coat. Place chicken in a baking dish which has been coated with nonstick vegetable spray. Bake until juices run clear when meat is pierced with a fork, 40 to 45 minutes. **Serves 4.***

Sound Bites

3 pounds of dressed poultry yields approximately 1 pound of cooked meat. A 4½- to 5-pound hen yields 1¼ pounds meat. 1 pound of cooked poultry meat yields 3 cups cubed.

Chicken Marsala with Sun-Dried Tomatoes

1½ cups flour
1 teaspoon dried parsley flakes
¼ teaspoon salt
2 eggs, lightly beaten
½ cup half and half
6 to 8 boneless, skinless chicken breasts, pounded thin
¼ cup olive oil
¼ cup butter
1 pound fresh mushrooms, sliced
3 shallots, finely chopped
6 oil-packed sun-dried tomatoes, drained
Juice of 1 lemon
½ cup Marsala wine
Salt and freshly ground pepper to taste

Combine flour, parsley and salt on a plate. Combine eggs and half and half in a small shallow bowl. Dip chicken in egg mixture, then dredge in flour mixture. Heat olive oil in a large skillet over medium heat. Lightly sauté chicken on both sides until golden brown. Remove to a shallow baking dish and cover. Melt butter in a medium skillet over medium-high heat. Sauté mushrooms, shallots and sun-dried tomatoes for 5 minutes. Stir in lemon juice and wine and simmer gently for 5 minutes. Pour over chicken and salt and pepper to taste. Bake, covered, in a preheated 350° oven for 30 minutes. **Serves 6 to 8.**

Chicken Cashew Casserole

1 (10¾-ounce) can cream of mushroom soup
¼ cup water
1 cup diced cooked chicken
¼ pound cashews
1 cup chopped celery
¼ cup chopped onion
1 (3-ounce) can chow mein noodles, divided

Combine all ingredients reserving half of chow mein noodles. Mix well and pour into a 1½-quart casserole dish which has been coated with nonstick vegetable spray. Top with reserved noodles and bake in preheated 350° oven for 30 minutes. May be served over rice.

Chicken and Shrimp Supreme

6 to 8 skinless, boneless chicken breasts
2 tablespoons margarine
1 cup finely chopped onion
1 cup finely chopped celery
¼ cup chopped parsley
1½ cups ½-inch cubes white bread
1½ cups ½-inch cubes pumpernickel bread
2 cups mayonnaise
2 teaspoons Worcestershire sauce
2 tablespoons prepared mustard
6 teaspoons drained capers
½ cup sherry
½ teaspoon curry powder
1 cup water
2 pounds peeled, cooked shrimp

Boil chicken in seasoned water until done. Drain and cut into medium-size pieces. Melt margarine in a large skillet over medium-high heat. Sauté onion, celery and parsley until onion is translucent. Combine mayonnaise, Worcestershire sauce, mustard, capers, sherry, curry powder and water in a large bowl. Mix well to blend. Stir in chicken, sautéed vegetables, bread cubes and shrimp. Pour into a 3-quart casserole which has been coated with nonstick vegetable spray. Bake, uncovered, in a preheated 350° oven until hot and bubbling, 30 to 45 minutes. Can be prepared 1 to 2 days ahead. **Serves 8 to 10.**

Cranberry Chicken

4 to 6 large boneless, skinless chicken breast halves
1 can whole berry cranberry sauce
1 (8-ounce) bottle Catalina salad dressing
1 envelope dry onion soup mix
Hot cooked white rice

Place chicken in a baking dish. Combine cranberry sauce, salad dressing and soup mix. Pour over chicken and bake in preheated 350° oven for one hour. Serve over rice. **Serves 4 to 6.**

Variation: *French or Russian dressing also work well. May use fat free.*

To serve as an appetizer, cut chicken into bite-size pieces before baking and omit rice. Serve in chafing dish with toothpicks.

Sound Bites

Vegetables that
are good with
Poultry –
Artichokes
Asparagus
Broccoli
Carrots
Cauliflower
Celeriac
Celery
Eggplant
Green Beans
Lima Beans
Mushrooms
Onions
Peas
Potatoes, white
and sweet
Tomatoes
Yellow Squash
Zucchini

Chicken Spaghetti

5 to 6 chicken breasts
1 medium onion, chopped
1 cup chopped green bell pepper
1 (8-ounce) can sliced mushrooms, drained
1 tablespoon butter or margarine
1 (10¾-ounce) can cream of celery soup
1 (10¾-ounce) can cream of mushroom soup
¼ pound pasteurized processed cheese
1 (16-ounce) package vermicelli
2 cups grated Cheddar cheese

Boil chicken until tender. Remove from pot with a slotted spoon, reserving stock. Drain chicken, remove meat from bones and dice. Melt butter in a large skillet over medium high heat. Sauté onion, bell pepper and mushrooms until onion is translucent. Add chicken, soups and processed cheese, blending thoroughly. Cook over low heat until cheese is melted. Reheat chicken stock to a boil and cook pasta according to package directions. Drain and combine pasta with chicken mixture. Place in a greased 9 x 13-inch baking dish and top with Cheddar cheese. Bake, uncovered, in preheated 375° oven for 30 minutes.

Curried Chicken Broccoli Casserole

6 chicken breast halves
2 packages frozen broccoli florets
2 (10¾-ounce) cans cream of chicken soup
1 cup mayonnaise
1 teaspoon lemon juice
½ teaspoon curry powder
Grated Cheddar cheese
Bread crumbs
Butter

Cook chicken, debone and cut into large pieces. Cook broccoli according to package directions and drain. Place in bottom of a 3-quart casserole which has been coated with nonstick vegetable spray. Top with chicken. Combine soups, mayonnaise, lemon juice and curry powder in a medium bowl. Blend well and pour over chicken. Sprinkle with grated cheese and bread crumbs. Dot with butter and bake in preheated 350° oven for 30 minutes.
Serves 6.

Chicken with Roasted Garlic, Mushrooms and Spinach

Sound Bites

Poultry for salad or hash should be poached, not baked.

1 large head garlic, cloves separated but unpeeled
3 tablespoons olive oil, divided
4 boneless, skinless chicken breast halves
Flour
½ pound button or stemmed shiitake mushrooms, sliced
1 cup dry white wine
1 pound tomatoes, peeled, seeded and diced
2 cups packed fresh spinach leaves
2 teaspoons chopped fresh rosemary or
   1 teaspoon dried
3 tablespoons unsalted butter

*Preheat oven to 350°. Place unpeeled garlic on a small baking pan and drizzle with 1 tablespoon olive oil. Toss to coat. Bake until soft, about 20 minutes. Cool and press between fingertips to release garlic cloves from peel. Transfer to a small bowl. Pound chicken between sheets of plastic wrap using a meat mallet or rolling pin to a thickness of ½ inch. Coat with flour, shaking off excess. Heat remaining oil in a heavy large skillet over medium-high heat. Add chicken and sauté until cooked through, about 3 minutes per side. Transfer to plates and tent with foil to keep warm. Add mushrooms to skillet and sauté 4 minutes. Add wine and boil until liquid is reduced by half, about 4 minutes. Add tomatoes, spinach, rosemary and roasted garlic. Sauté until spinach wilts, about 3 minutes. Add butter and mix just until melted. Spoon over chicken and serve. **Serves 4.***

Chicken Tetrazzini

2 cups chicken broth
2 cups water
8 ounces spaghetti
2 tablespoons margarine, melted
2 tablespoons flour
½ teaspoon salt
½ teaspoon pepper
⅛ teaspoon cayenne pepper, optional
1 cup milk
1 cup sour cream
1 cup cottage cheese
2 cups cooked bite-size chicken pieces
4 ounces mushrooms, optional
2 tablespoons minced onion
4 tablespoons chopped fresh parsley
1 cup fresh or frozen green peas, optional
1 cup fresh or frozen sliced carrots, optional
Bread crumbs, optional
Grated Parmesan cheese, optional

Bring chicken broth and water to a boil in a large pot. Cook pasta until done. Remove from heat and drain thoroughly. Place in a well-greased 9 x 13-inch glass baking dish. Combine remaining ingredients, except crumbs and Parmesan, adding one ingredient at a time and mixing well after each addition. Pour over spaghetti and bake in a preheated 350° oven for 1 hour, sprinkling with bread crumbs and/or Parmesan near the end of cooking time, if desired. To cook in microwave, heat 15 to 20 minutes, rotating during cooking. **Serves 8.**

Variation: *Low or no-fat ingredients work well in this dish. May substitute turkey for chicken.*

Mediterranean Chicken

¾ cup flour
1 teaspoon salt
¼ teaspoon freshly ground pepper
10 chicken breast halves
5 tablespoons butter, divided
3 tablespoons olive oil, divided
1 teaspoon oregano
1 large clove garlic, minced
2 cups dry red wine
1 (12-ounce) can frozen orange juice
  concentrate, thawed
10 large mushrooms, sliced
2 large red onions, sliced
2 large green bell peppers, sliced
Cooked wild rice

Preheat oven to 375°. Combine flour, salt and pepper on a plate. Dredge chicken in flour mixture and shake off excess. Add oregano and garlic to 8 tablespoons butter and 4 tablespoons olive oil and melt in a large skillet over medium-high heat. Brown chicken on all sides. Remove chicken with a slotted spoon to a 4-quart casserole dish. Mix wine and orange juice concentrate and add to skillet. Bring to a boil, reduce heat and simmer, uncovered, 2 to 3 minutes. Pour over chicken. Cover and bake 30 minutes. Melt remaining butter with remaining oil in same skillet over medium-high heat. Sauté onion, mushrooms and green pepper until soft, 3 to 4 minutes. Spoon over chicken and bake, uncovered, 30 minutes more, basting every 10 minutes until tender and well-glazed. Serve with wild rice. **Serves 10.**

Grilled Turkey Steaks

1 bone-in turkey breast
1 cup reduced sodium soy sauce
½ cup vegetable oil
2 tablespoons ground ginger
1 tablespoon sesame oil
5 cloves garlic, crushed

Best to buy frozen turkey breast and have butcher cut breast in half lengthwise then crosswise into 1-inch chops with bone left in. Combine remaining ingredients in a small bowl. Pour into a large zip lock bag. Add chops, seal and refrigerate overnight. Remove turkey and grill over medium heat, covered, about 20 minutes, turning once.

Sound Bites

Chervil, parsley, marjoram, and tarragon are herbs that are compatible with poultry.

Sound Bites

Chicken stock freezes well for a long period of time.

Mexican Chicken

4 boneless, skinless chicken breasts,
   cooked and shredded
Butter
1 large onion, chopped
½ cup mayonnaise
1 can diced tomatoes with green chiles
1 (10¾-ounce) can cream of chicken soup
1 (10¾-ounce) can cream of mushroom soup
1 (18-ounce) jar pasteurized process cheese sauce
1 to 2 cups crushed salted tortilla chips

Place chicken in a 9 x 13-inch glass baking dish. Melt butter in a large skillet over medium-high heat. Sauté onions until translucent. Add remaining ingredients, except chips, to skillet and heat, stirring, until blended. Pour over chicken and bake in a preheated 325° oven for 20 minutes. Top with chips and bake an additional 10 minutes. **Serves 4.**

Mushroom-Garlic Chicken with Artichokes

6 skinless, boneless chicken breast halves,
   pounded to ¼-inch thickness
Salt and freshly ground black pepper
3 tablespoons butter or margarine
8 cloves garlic, crushed
1 tablespoon olive oil
¼ pound mushrooms, sliced
1 (14-ounce) can artichoke hearts, drained
   and quartered
2 tablespoons dry Marsala
1 tablespoon lemon juice
Cooked rice or pasta

Season chicken with salt and pepper to taste. Melt butter over medium heat in a large skillet. Add half of garlic and sauté 1 minute. Add chicken and cook until lightly browned, about 3 minutes per side. Remove to a warm serving platter. Add olive oil and remaining garlic to skillet. Cook 1 minute. Add mushrooms and sauté until tender, about 3 minutes. Add artichokes and cook until heated through, about 1 minute. Add Marsala and lemon juice. Bring to a boil and cook, stirring constantly, until mixture thickens, about 5 minutes. Pour over chicken. Serve with rice or pasta. **Serves 6.**

Poppy Seed Chicken

8 cooked chicken breasts or
1 cooked chicken, cut-up
2 (10¾-ounce) cans cream of chicken soup
½ cup sour cream
1 tube round, buttery crackers, crumbled
(about 35 crackers)

Topping:
1 tube round, buttery crackers, crumbled
(about 35 crackers)
2 tablespoons poppy seeds
½ cup margarine, melted

Combine chicken, soup, sour cream and cracker crumbs in a large bowl. Mix well and pour into a greased casserole dish. Make topping by combining remaining cracker crumbs and poppy seeds. Sprinkle over casserole and drizzle with margarine. Bake in preheated 350° oven until crumbs are brown and mixture is bubbling, about 30 minutes. **Serves 8.**

Sweet and Sour Chicken Breasts

1¼ pounds boneless, skinless chicken breasts
1 tablespoon vegetable oil
¼ cup sugar
¼ cup white or red wine vinegar
¼ cup ketchup
¼ cup soy sauce
¼ teaspoon Asian hot sauce or to taste, optional
1¼ teaspoons cornstarch
1 tablespoon water
Hot cooked rice

Trim visible fat from chicken and cut chicken into 1-inch cubes. Heat oil in wok or sauté pan over medium heat. Add chicken and sauté, stirring, 1 minute. Cover and cook 3 more minutes, stirring once or twice. Thoroughly mix sugar, vinegar, ketchup, soy sauce and hot sauce in a small bowl. Add to chicken and mix well. Bring to a simmer. Cover and cook over low heat until chicken is tender, 5 minutes. Blend cornstarch and water in a small cup. Add to simmering sauce in center of pan, then quickly stir into remaining sauce. Heat until bubbling. Serve hot over rice. **Serves 4.**

Sound Bites

For a brown crust on roasted chicken, rub mayonnaise generously over skin before cooking.

Sound Bites

Rub chicken with a good brandy before roasting along with other seasonings for extra flavor.

Southern Chicken Pot Pie

4 tablespoons butter
¼ cup chopped scallions
2 tablespoons chopped fresh parsley
2 cups water
4 teaspoons instant chicken broth granules
3 to 4 tablespoons flour
2 tablespoons sugar
1 cup half and half
2 large potatoes, cut in 1-inch cubes and cooked
1½ cups diced carrots, cooked
1 (10-ounce) package frozen tiny peas, cooked
1½ pounds cooked, cubed chicken breasts
2 unbaked 9-inch pie crusts

Melt butter in a large skillet over medium-high heat. Sauté scallions and parsley until scallions are softened. Add water and chicken broth and stir until granules are dissolved. Gradually stir in flour and cook, stirring constantly, until sauce is thickened. Add sugar and half and half. Place cooked vegetables and chicken in bottom of a pie crust. Cover with sauce. Place second crust over top, crimp edges together with a fork and cut slits in center. Bake in preheated 350° oven until crust is brown, 35 to 45 minutes.

Wild Rice and Chicken

1 (6¾-ounce) box long grain and wild rice
2 tablespoons butter
1 tablespoon flour
1 cup milk
½ cup grated Cheddar cheese
2 tablespoons white wine or lemon juice
2 cups diced cooked chicken

Prepare rice according to package directions and place in a lightly greased 1½-quart casserole. Melt butter in a medium saucepan over medium heat. Blend in flour. Gradually add milk and cook over low heat, stirring constantly, until sauce is thickened and smooth. Add cheese and wine and heat, stirring, until cheese is melted. Add chicken. Pour sauce over rice and mix well. Bake in preheated 350° oven until hot and bubbly, about 20 minutes.
Serves 6.

Viva La Chicken

6 large chicken breasts
1 (10¾-ounce) can cream of chicken soup
1 (10¾-ounce) can cream of mushroom soup
1 (12-ounce) can evaporated milk
1 (6-ounce) can sliced black olives, drained
1 (10-ounce) can green enchilada sauce
1 (4-ounce) can diced green chiles, drained
1 large onion, chopped
16 corn tortillas, cut into 1-inch strips
1 pound Monterey Jack cheese, grated

*Boil chicken until done. Remove from broth, reserving broth, and cool. Cut into bite-size pieces. Combine 1 cup reserved broth, the soups, milk, olives, enchilada sauce, green chiles and onion in a large bowl. Layer a third of tortilla strips in the bottom of a 4-quart casserole dish which has been coated with nonstick vegetable spray. Spread half of chicken over tortillas. Spoon half of sauce over chicken. Repeat layering. Top with remaining tortilla strips. Sprinkle with cheese, cover and refrigerate overnight. Bake in preheated 350° oven for 1½ hours, until cheese is melted and casserole is bubbling. **Serves 10 to 12.***

Sound Bites

To turn a chicken while cooking, use two wooden spoons rather than a fork, so that the flesh will not be pierced.

Chicken Liver Stroganoff

1 pound chicken livers
½ cup flour
1 teaspoon salt
½ cup vegetable oil
2 large onions, thinly sliced, separated into rings
1 teaspoon lemon pepper
1 teaspoon black pepper
1 teaspoon parsley
½ cup hot water
1 cup sour cream
Toasted bread points or cooked noodles

*Dredge livers in a mixture of flour and salt. Heat oil in a large skillet over medium heat. Add livers and cook until evenly brown on all sides. Add onion rings and cook, stirring constantly, until well-browned. Drain excess oil from skillet. Add lemon pepper, parsley and hot water. Simmer, uncovered, for 5 minutes. Add sour cream and heat thoroughly. Serve immediately on toast points or over noodles. **Serves 4.***

Sound Bites

To enhance the flavor of the rice – after peeling the shrimp, boil the shells in water for 5-10 minutes. Discard the shells and use the water to cook rice.

Seafood Risotto

7 to 8 cups chicken broth
2½ cups chopped onion, divided
½ cup melted butter or margarine, divided
¾ cup extra virgin olive oil, divided
1 (1 pound) package Arborio or other short
    grain rice
1 cup dry white wine, divided
3 cloves garlic, minced
3 (6½-ounce) cans chopped clams, undrained
1 cup sliced fresh mushrooms
½ cup chopped fresh parsley
¼ teaspoon dried oregano
½ teaspoon salt
¼ teaspoon freshly ground pepper
1 pound medium fresh shrimp, peeled and
    deveined
⅓ cup freshly grated Parmesan cheese

*Bring chicken broth to a boil in a large saucepan. Cover, reduce heat to low and keep warm. Sauté 1½ cups onion in ¼ cup butter and ½ cup olive oil in a large skillet over medium-high heat, stirring constantly, until tender. Add rice and ½ cup wine. Cook over medium-high heat, stirring constantly, until most of the liquid is absorbed. Add ½ cup reserved chicken broth. Cook, stirring constantly, until most of liquid is absorbed. Continue adding remaining chicken broth, ½ cup at a time, and cook, stirring constantly, until mixture is creamy and rice is tender. Set aside and keep warm. In another large skillet place garlic, remaining 1 cup onion, remaining ¼ cup butter and remaining ¼ cup olive oil. Sauté over medium-high heat, stirring constantly, until tender. Stir in clams, clam liquid, remaining ½ cup wine, mushrooms, parsley, oregano, salt and pepper. Bring to a boil. Reduce heat and simmer, uncovered, 8 minutes. Return to a boil and add shrimp. Reduce heat and simmer, uncovered, 5 minutes. Add shrimp mixture to rice mixture. Cook, uncovered, over medium heat until thoroughly heated, 1 to 2 minutes. Sprinkle with Parmesan and serve immediately. **Serves 4 to 6.***

Shrimp and Artichoke Casserole

1 (14-ounce) can artichoke hearts, drained
1 pound cooked and shelled shrimp
2 tablespoons butter
¼ pound fresh mushrooms, sliced
1½ cups white sauce
¼ cup dry sherry
1 tablespoon Worcestershire sauce
¾ cup grated Parmesan cheese
Salt and pepper
Paprika
Parsley

Place artichoke hearts and shrimp in a buttered casserole dish. Melt butter in a medium skillet over medium-high heat. Sauté mushrooms 6 minutes. Place over shrimp. Combine white sauce, sherry, Worcestershire sauce, and salt and pepper to taste. Pour over mushrooms. Sprinkle with Parmesan and paprika. Bake, uncovered, in pre-heated 375° oven 35 minutes. Garnish with parsley. Serve with rice and a green salad.

Greek Style Shrimp

Wonderful with Feta and Mint Rice, page 170.

3 tablespoons olive oil
½ cup chopped onion
1 (28-ounce) can Italian plum tomatoes,
    drained and chopped
⅓ cup dry white wine
1 teaspoon dried oregano
1 pound uncooked medium shrimp,
    peeled and deveined
Salt and pepper

Heat oil in a large heavy skillet over medium heat. Add onion and sauté until translucent, about 8 minutes. Add tomatoes, wine and oregano. Simmer until thickened, stirring occasionally, about 5 minutes. Add shrimp and stir until opaque, 3 minutes. Season with salt and pepper to taste. **Serves 4 to 6.**

Sound Bites

White Sauce

For gravies, sauces, creamed and scalloped dishes.

2 tablespoons butter

2 tablespoons flour

1 cup milk

¼ teaspoon salt

⅛ teaspoon pepper

Melt butter and blend in flour. Add milk gradually, stirring constantly. Reduce heat and cook 3 minutes longer; add seasonings.

Sound Bites

Be careful not to overcook fish when grilling. Just a few minutes too long and the seafood will be dry and lose its wonderful flavor. Check the fish, if it doesn't flake when pricked with a fork, it isn't done. Check again in one minute.

Spicy Marinated Shrimp

3 pounds cooked shrimp, peeled with tails left intact
1 large red onion, thinly sliced
3 large lemons, thinly sliced
¾ cup olive oil
½ cup finely chopped cilantro
¼ cup white wine vinegar
3 tablespoons fresh lemon juice
3 jalapeños, minced
3 large cloves garlic, minced
¼ teaspoon cayenne pepper
Salt and pepper

Layer shrimp, onion and lemon slices in a large glass bowl. Combine remaining ingredients and pour over all. Cover and refrigerate at least 4 hours before serving.

Sautéed Shrimp with Gorgonzola Sauce

16 large uncooked shrimp, peeled with tails left intact and deveined
Flour for dredging
1 tablespoon butter
2 tablespoons brandy
⅓ cup whipping cream
⅓ cup packed crumbled Gorgonzola cheese (about 1½ ounces)
⅓ cup grated Parmesan cheese (about 1 ounce)
1½ teaspoons minced fresh marjoram or ½ teaspoon dried, crumbled

*Dredge shrimp in flour and shake off excess. Melt butter in heavy large skillet over high heat. Add shrimp and sauté 1 minute. Add brandy and cook 30 seconds. Add cream, Gorgonzola, Parmesan and marjoram and boil until shrimp are cooked through and sauce thickens, stirring frequently and turning shrimp with tongs, 3 minutes. Divide shrimp between plates and top with sauce. **Serves 2.***

Spicy Grilled Shrimp

½ cup soy sauce
½ cup light olive oil
5 tablespoons Cajun seasoning mix
¼ cup sesame oil
¼ cup fresh lemon juice
2 tablespoons minced fresh ginger
2 teaspoons dry mustard
2 teaspoons hot pepper sauce
32 uncooked large shrimp, peeled with
    tails left intact, deveined

*Whisk together all ingredients except shrimp in a large bowl. Add shrimp and stir to coat. Let stand 30 minutes. Heat barbecue grill to medium-high. Remove shrimp from marinade and grill until pink and cooked through, about 2 minutes per side. Transfer to platter to serve. **Serves 8.***

Sound Bites

Thin, tender filets
such as flounder,
perch, or trout
should be cooked
in packets of foil
and not directly
on the oiled grids.

Shrimp Scampi

¼ cup butter
½ onion, finely chopped
2 cloves garlic, minced
¼ teaspoon dried tarragon
1 tablespoon fresh lemon juice
¼ teaspoon steak sauce
¼ teaspoon Worcestershire sauce
⅛ teaspoon hot pepper sauce
1 pound shrimp, peeled and deveined
1 tablespoon chopped fresh parsley
Hot cooked fettuccine

*Melt butter in heavy skillet over medium-high heat. Add onion and garlic and sauté for 3 to 4 minutes. Add tarragon, lemon juice, steak sauce, Worcestershire sauce and hot pepper sauce. Bring to a boil. Add shrimp and cook, stirring constantly, until shrimp are cooked through, 5 to 6 minutes. Sprinkle with parsley and serve over fettuccine. **Serves 2.***

French Quarter Barbecued Shrimp

3 slices bacon, chopped
1½ cups margarine, melted
2 tablespoons Dijon mustard
1½ teaspoons chili powder
½ teaspoon dried basil, crumbled
½ teaspoon dried thyme, crumbled
2 teaspoons coarsely ground black pepper
½ teaspoon dried oregano, crumbled
2 cloves garlic, minced
1½ tablespoons chopped onion
1 tablespoon liquid crab boil
½ teaspoon hot pepper sauce
1½ pounds uncooked, unshelled shrimp

Fry bacon until crisp. Add remaining ingredients except shrimp and bring to a boil, stirring to blend. Place shrimp in a baking dish and top with sauce. Bake in preheated 375° oven for 20 minutes. Serve with French bread to soak up sauce.

Shrimp Creole

1 tablespoon margarine
½ cup chopped onion
½ cup chopped celery
½ cup chopped green bell pepper
1 tablespoon chopped parsley
1 large can tomato sauce
½ cup water or dry white wine
1 tablespoon ketchup
Dash of nutmeg
1 pound peeled, deveined shrimp
Cooked rice

*Melt butter in a heavy saucepan. Sauté onion, celery and green pepper until soft. Add parsley, tomato sauce, ½ cup water, ketchup and nutmeg. Bring to a boil, reduce heat and simmer 20 minutes. Add shrimp and continue cooking until shrimp is cooked through, 6 to 8 minutes. Serve over rice. **Serves 4.***

Scampi Dijonnaise with Garlic Tomato Pasta

3 tablespoons olive oil
11 cloves garlic, minced
2 shallots, minced
24 cleaned jumbo shrimp
½ cup Cabernet Sauvignon
¼ cup lemon juice
2 tablespoons Dijon mustard
½ cup fresh minced basil
1 tablespoon unsalted butter
Salt and pepper

Garlic Tomato Pasta:
8 ounces linguine
3 tablespoons olive oil
2 cloves garlic, minced
3 medium tomatoes, quartered
½ cup fresh chopped parsley

Heat olive oil in a large skillet over medium-high heat. Combine garlic and shallots. Sauté half of garlic mixture for 1 minute. Add shrimp and cook on one side, shaking mixture so it won't stick or burn. Turn shrimp and add remaining garlic mixture. Cook for 1 minute. Pour in wine and continue cooking for 2 minutes. Remove shrimp with a slotted spoon to a dish. Add lemon, mustard and basil to skillet and simmer until sauce is thickened. Whisk in butter and add salt and pepper to taste. Toss in shrimp.

*For pasta, cook pasta according to package directions. Heat oil in a sauté pan and sauté garlic for 1 to 2 minutes. Add tomatoes and continue cooking for 1 to 2 minutes. Add parsley and toss with linguine. Make a bed of linguine on serving platter. Top with shrimp and sauce. **Serves 4 to 6.***

Sound Bites

Number of raw, unshelled shrimp per pound:
Jumbo, 18-20
Large, 21-25
Medium, 26-35
Small, over 35

Sound Bites

Thick fish steaks (1 to 1½ inches) should be placed at least 6 inches from the coals. Those thinner than 1 inch can be placed 4 inches from the coals.

Southern Shrimp Creole

¼ cup vegetable oil
¼ cup flour
1½ cups chopped onion
1 cup chopped celery
¾ cup chopped green onions
1 large green bell pepper, seeded and chopped
2 cloves garlic, minced
1 (28-ounce) can Italian-style tomatoes, undrained and chopped
1 (8-ounce) can tomato sauce
1 (6-ounce) can tomato paste
½ cup red wine
1½ teaspoons salt
1 teaspoon freshly ground pepper
½ teaspoon cayenne pepper
2 bay leaves
1 tablespoon fresh lemon juice
2 teaspoons Worcestershire sauce
Dash of hot pepper sauce
3 to 4 pounds medium fresh shrimp, peeled and deveined
1 tablespoon chopped fresh parsley (optional)
Hot cooked rice

*Combine oil and flour in a large Dutch oven. Cook over medium heat, stirring constantly, until roux is caramel-colored, about 15 minutes. Add onion, celery, green onions, green pepper and garlic. Cook, stirring frequently, until tender, about 15 minutes. Stir in tomatoes and remaining ingredients except shrimp, parsley and rice. Bring to a boil. Cover, reduce heat, and simmer 1 hour, stirring occasionally. Add shrimp and simmer until shrimp turn pink, about 10 minutes. Remove and discard bay leaves. Stir in parsley. Serve over rice. **Serves 8 to 10.***

Crab Meat Imperial

¼ cup butter
1 tablespoon grated onion
¼ cup sifted flour
1 cup milk
½ cup dry white wine
½ cup sherry
1 teaspoon salt
Dash of hot pepper sauce
1 (4-ounce) can sliced mushrooms, drained
1 egg yolk, beaten
1 pound crab meat (check for shells)
Hot cooked rice

Melt butter in a heavy saucepan over medium-high heat. Sauté onion until translucent. Blend in flour, but do not brown. Gradually add milk, wine and sherry. Cook, stirring constantly, until thickened. Add salt, pepper sauce and mushrooms. Remove from heat when bubbles appear. Quickly stir in egg yolk and crab meat. Serve over rice. **Serves 6.**

Crab Superior

2 tablespoons butter
2 tablespoons chopped onion
2 tablespoons chopped green bell pepper
3 tablespoons flour
¾ cup milk
½ teaspoon salt
¼ teaspoon pepper
Dash of hot pepper sauce
1 teaspoon lemon juice
½ teaspoon tarragon vinegar
1 pound crab meat (check for shells)
Buttered bread crumbs

Melt butter in a heavy saucepan over medium-high heat. Sauté onion and bell pepper until onion is translucent. Stir in flour and blend well. Add milk gradually. Cook over low heat, stirring constantly, until mixture thickens. Remove from heat. Combine salt, pepper, hot pepper sauce, lemon juice, vinegar and crab meat in a bowl. Mix with sauce and pour into a casserole dish. Cover with buttered bread crumbs and bake in preheated 375° oven for 25 minutes. **Serves 4.**

Sound Bites

To boil shrimp – (Shrimp may be cleaned and deveined before or after cooking.) Drop shrimp into boiling salted water to cover, using 1 tablespoon salt per 1 quart water. (If desired, add sliced onion, parsley sprigs and whole peppercorns.) Simmer, covered until shrimp are pink. Drain and refrigerate.

Sound Bites

Mix ¼ cup of sugar and one cup of water and bring to boil while cooking fish or strong smelling foods. This helps to eliminate the odor.

Scallops and Shrimp in Brandy Sauce

¼ cup olive oil
1 large clove garlic, pressed
1 pound sea scallops
1 pound large shrimp, peeled and deveined
1 teaspoon salt
½ teaspoon white pepper
1 teaspoon drained tiny capers
2 teaspoons minced parsley
½ teaspoon crushed red pepper flakes
¼ cup brandy
3 tablespoons fresh lemon juice
Sliced black olives for garnish

Sauté olive oil and garlic in a large skillet over medium-high heat for 1 minute. Add shrimp and scallops and sauté, stirring, 2 minutes. Sprinkle with salt and pepper. Combine capers, parsley and red pepper flakes and sprinkle over skillet. Sauté one minute. Add brandy and lemon juice. Increase heat and cook, stirring, until shrimp are pink and scallops are done. Garnish with olives and serve immediately. **Serves 6 to 8.**

Cornmeal Crusted Salmon with Green Peppercorn–Dijon Sauce

2 (6-ounce) skinless salmon fillets
Salt and pepper
2 tablespoons cornmeal
1 tablespoon flour
2 teaspoons corn oil
3½ teaspoons Dijon mustard
½ teaspoon drained green peppercorns in brine, chopped
¼ cup plain yogurt
3 tablespoons low fat sour cream

Season salmon with salt and pepper. Combine cornmeal and flour on a pie plate and dredge salmon in mixture. Heat oil in a heavy medium skillet over medium-high heat. Sauté salmon until just firm to touch and coating is brown, about 4 minutes per side. Transfer salmon to a plate. Wipe out skillet with a paper towel. Add mustard and peppercorns to skillet. Whisk over medium heat 30 seconds. Reduce heat to low and add yogurt and sour cream. Whisk until just heated through, about 30 seconds. Do not boil. Spoon sauce into center of 2 plates, dividing equally. Top with salmon. **Serves 2.**

Fresh Baked Salmon

¼ cup butter, softened
3 tablespoons minced fresh parsley
2 tablespoons fresh lemon juice
1 clove garlic, minced
1 teaspoon salt
½ teaspoon dried basil, crumbled
½ teaspoon pepper
2 to 2½ pounds salmon fillet or steak

Combine all ingredients except salmon. Spread on salmon and bake on a foil-lined broiler pan in a pre-heated 350° oven 25 to 30 minutes. **Serves 8.**

Salmon Cakes with Lemon-Herb Mayonnaise

2 cups loosely packed crumbled cooked salmon
½ cup cornflake crumbs
2 green onions, chopped
¼ cup finely chopped celery
¼ cup mayonnaise
2 tablespoons chopped fresh thyme or
    2 teaspoons dried, crumbled
Dash of Worcestershire sauce
Salt and pepper
1 large egg
2 tablespoons butter

Lemon-Herb Mayonnaise:
¾ cup mayonnaise
1 tablespoon fresh lemon juice
1 tablespoon prepared horseradish
2½ teaspoons chopped fresh thyme or
    1 teaspoon dried

Combine salmon, cornflake crumbs, green onions, celery, mayonnaise, thyme and Worcestershire sauce in a medium bowl. Stir gently to blend. Season with salt and pepper to taste. Mix in egg and shape into 6 patties, about ¾-inch thick.

For the Mayonnaise: *Combine all ingredients in a small bowl. Season to taste with salt and pepper. (Salmon cakes and sauce can be prepared 1 day ahead. Wrap separately and refrigerate.)*

When ready to cook, melt butter in heavy large skillet over medium-low heat. Add salmon cakes and sauté until brown and cooked through, about 5 minutes per side. Transfer to platter and serve with sauce. **Serves 6.**

Sound Bites

Fish that are good
for grilling and
broiling –

Bass

Black Striped Bass
 (Rockfish)

Cod

Crappie

Flounder

Grouper

Mackerel

Pompano

Porgy

Redfish

Red Snapper

Scrod

Sole

Salmon

Swordfish

Trout

Southern Seafood Stew

½ pound bacon, diced
2 carrots, finely diced
3 onions, thinly sliced
4 cloves garlic, crushed or minced
3 cups fresh or canned plum tomatoes
1 pound red potatoes, halved
1 cup clam juice
½ cup Champagne
½ teaspoon dried thyme
Pinch of sugar
2 cups chicken stock
Salt and pepper to taste
½ pound smoked sausages, sliced
2 dozen clams (fresh or canned)
1 pound medium shrimp, peeled
½ pound white fish, cut in small pieces
¼ teaspoon cayenne pepper (optional)

Sauté bacon, carrots, onions and garlic in a large Dutch oven over medium-high heat until grease is rendered and vegetables are softened. Drain half of drippings from pot. Add tomatoes, potatoes, clam juice and Champagne. Sprinkle in thyme and sugar. Bring to a boil, reduce heat and simmer 30 minutes. Add stock and correct seasoning. Bring to a low boil. Add remaining ingredients and simmer until seafood is cooked through. **Serves 8.**

Basil-Marinated Swordfish

½ cup olive oil
½ cup vegetable oil
3 tablespoons Dijon mustard
3 tablespoons fresh lemon juice
3 large cloves garlic, minced
1½ cups chopped fresh basil leaves
8 (8-ounce) swordfish steaks, 1-inch thick
Lemon wedges
Fresh basil sprigs

Whisk both oils, mustard, lemon juice and garlic in a large bowl. Stir in basil. Arrange swordfish steaks in single layer in shallow glass baking dish. Pour marinade over. Cover and refrigerate 3 hours, turning occasionally. Heat barbecue grill to medium-high. Remove fish from marinade and grill until cooked through, about 7 minutes per side. Transfer to plates and garnish with lemon wedges and basil sprigs. **Serves 8.**

Grilled Swordfish with Fresh Tomato-Herb Salsa

4 large fresh plum tomatoes
¼ cup chopped fresh basil
2 tablespoons chopped fresh marjoram
1 shallot, minced
2 tablespoons balsamic vinegar
1 tablespoon olive oil
4 (6-ounce) swordfish steaks, ¾ to 1-inch thick
Olive oil
Cracked black peppercorns
Salt

Bring medium saucepan of water to a boil. Add tomatoes and blanch 30 seconds. Drain. Transfer to a medium bowl and cover with cold water. Cool and peel tomatoes. Cut in half and squeeze out juices. Chop tomatoes and transfer to a bowl. Add herbs, shallot, vinegar and 1 tablespoon olive oil. Season with salt and pepper. Heat barbecue grill to medium-high or preheat broiler. Brush fish with oil. Sprinkle with generous amount of peppercorns and salt. Grill until just cooked through, about 7 minutes per side. Transfer fish to plates. Spoon tomato salsa over and serve. **Serves 4.**

Sound Bites

To poach: Boil water seasoned with salt, lemon juice, bay leaf and herbs in a large oval pan. Water should be deep enough to cover the fish. Simmer for 10 minutes per inch of thickness.

Sole with Tarragon and Red Peppercorn Sauce

¾ cup dry red wine, divided
½ cup plus 2 tablespoons bottled clam juice, divided
¼ cup tarragon white wine vinegar
2 shallots, minced
1 generous teaspoon red peppercorns, minced
¼ cup whipping cream
9 (4-ounce) sole fillets
Salt and pepper
2 fresh tarragon sprigs
½ cup unsalted butter, cut into pieces, room temperature
3 tablespoons minced fresh tarragon
Additional red peppercorns

Combine ½ cup red wine, ¼ cup plus 2 tablespoons clam juice, vinegar, shallots and peppercorns in a heavy medium saucepan. Boil until reduced to ¼ cup, about 12 minutes. Remove from heat and stir in cream. Season sole lightly with salt and pepper. Fold each fillet in half crosswise, forming rough triangles. Place in heavy large skillet. Add remaining wine and clam juice. Add enough cold water to skillet to just cover sole. Add tarragon sprigs. Cover tightly. Bring to a gentle simmer. Remove from heat. Turn sole over, cover and let stand until fish is just opaque in center, about 5 minutes. Using slotted spoon, remove fish from skillet and drain. Arrange on platter and cover to keep warm. Boil sauce until thickened slightly, 2 minutes. Remove from heat. Add butter and whisk until smooth. Add minced tarragon. Season with salt and pepper. Spoon over sole and garnish with additional peppercorns.
Serves 6.

Snapper with Lime Butter Sauce

¾ cup dry white wine
3 tablespoons fresh lime juice
2 tablespoons chopped shallots
1 cup whipping cream
6 (8-ounce) snapper fillets
Salt and pepper
Flour
7 tablespoons butter, divided
2 papayas, peeled, seeded and diced
2 avocados, peeled and thinly sliced

*Combine wine, lime juice and shallots in a heavy medium saucepan. Bring to a boil and boil until liquid is reduced to ¼ cup, stirring occasionally, about 5 minutes. Add cream and boil until thickened to sauce consistency, about 5 minutes. Strain into small saucepan. (Can be made one day ahead. Cover and refrigerate.) Season fish with salt and pepper. Dredge fish in flour and shake off excess. Melt 3 tablespoons butter in heavy large skillet over medium-high heat. Add fish in batches and cook until brown and cooked through, about 4 minutes per side. Transfer to plates and tent with foil to keep warm. Bring sauce to simmer. Whisk in remaining butter. Spoon sauce over fish. Garnish with papaya and avocado and serve. **Serves 6.***

Red Snapper with Mint and Garlic

¼ cup olive oil
2 tablespoons minced garlic
1 tablespoon balsamic vinegar or red wine vinegar
2 teaspoons minced fresh mint
1 teaspoon salt
1 teaspoon pepper
1 pound red snapper or orange roughy fillets

*Heat barbecue grill to medium-high or preheat broiler. Combine oil, garlic, vinegar, mint, salt and pepper in a small bowl. Place fish on a baking sheet and brush both sides generously with mint mixture. Place fish on grill or in broiler and cook until cooked through, about 3 minutes per side, brushing frequently with mint mixture. Divide fish between plates and serve immediately. **Serves 2.***

Scallops in Saffron Chardonnay Sauce

3 tablespoons finely chopped shallots
6 tablespoons unsalted butter, divided
1½ cups fish stock
1 cup Chardonnay
1 cup whipping cream
¼ to ½ teaspoon saffron threads, crumbled
Grated rind and juice of ½ orange
Small pinch dried red chili pepper flakes
Salt and white pepper
1½ pounds whole fresh sea scallops

*Sauté shallots in 2 tablespoons butter in a heavy sauce-pan over medium-high heat until translucent. Add fish stock and wine and boil until reduced by half. Add cream and reduce by half again, or until mixture coats back of spoon. Strain and return to saucepan. Add saffron, orange zest and juice, red pepper flakes and salt and pepper to taste. Keep sauce warm. Sauté scallops in remaining butter until warmed through and just opaque. Using a slotted spoon, divide scallops onto warmed serving plates and top with warm sauce. **Serves 4 as a main course, 6 as a first course.***

Rémoulade Sauce

2 cloves garlic, minced
1 small onion, grated
1 cup mayonnaise
½ cup chili sauce
½ cup ketchup
½ cup vegetable oil
1 teaspoon black pepper
Dash paprika
Dash of hot pepper sauce
1 tablespoon Worcestershire sauce
1 tablespoon water
1 tablespoon vinegar
1 teaspoon prepared mustard

Blend all ingredients in a blender. Serve over cold boiled shrimp atop shredded lettuce or grilled fish.

Lemon Dill Marinade for Fish

2 tablespoons dill weed
1 teaspoon garlic powder
¼ teaspoon Beau Monde seasoning
4 tablespoons olive oil
2 tablespoons tarragon vinegar
Juice of 2 lemons

Combine all ingredients and pour over fish. Cover and refrigerate 2 hours. Excellent for salmon.

Bordelaise Sauce

4 tablespoons butter
2 shallots, chopped
2 cloves garlic, chopped
2 onions, thickly sliced
4 carrots, thinly sliced
2 sprigs parsley
2 whole cloves
12 black peppercorns
1 bay leaf
4 tablespoons flour
2 (10½-ounce) cans beef bouillon
1 teaspoon salt
¼ teaspoon pepper
¼ cup dry red wine
2 tablespoons snipped fresh parsley

Melt butter in a large skillet over medium-high heat. Sauté shallots, garlic, onion, carrots, parsley sprigs, cloves, peppercorns and bay leaf until onion is golden and tender. Reduce heat to low and blend in flour. Cook, stirring constantly, until flour is light brown and sauce is thickened. Gradually add bouillon and simmer until slightly thickened and smooth, stirring often. Strain sauce into a bowl, pressing solids against sieve. Add salt, pepper, wine and snipped parsley. Cover and chill until ready to use. Reheat slowly in a double boiler. Best served over beef.

Sound Bites

One lemon yields
four tablespoons
of lemon juice.
Squeeze lemon
through a strainer
of cheesecloth to
obtain clear
lemon juice.

Jezebel Sauce

1 (1.2-ounce) can dry mustard
1 (4-ounce) jar prepared horseradish
1 (16-ounce) jar pineapple preserves
1 (16-ounce) jar apple jelly

Stir mustard and horseradish together in a medium bowl until a paste is formed. Add preserves and jelly and mix by hand until thoroughly blended. Cover and refrigerate until ready to use. This sauce will keep in refrigerator for several months. Serve over cream cheese as an appetizer or as a sauce for pork or lamb.

Brown Barbecue Chicken Marinade

2 cups red wine vinegar
4 tablespoons salt
8 ounces vegetable oil
½ bottle hot pepper sauce
3 tablespoons Worcestershire sauce
¼ teaspoon garlic powder

Combine all ingredients. Brush on chicken while grilling.
Yield: sufficient sauce for 6 chickens.

John Willingham's All-Purpose Marinade

Use to marinate meat, poultry and vegetables. Or use it to baste or as a dip. It's also tasty added to Bloody Marys, Virgin Marys and bullshots. And it's great in salad dressings.

1 cup cider vinegar
½ cup freshly squeezed orange juice, unstrained
½ cup freshly squeezed lemon juice
2 to 3 thin slices lemon peel
1 tablespoon packed dark brown sugar
1 tablespoon lemon pepper
1 tablespoon freshly ground black pepper
1 teaspoon hot pepper sauce
½ teaspoon garlic powder

Combine all ingredients in a glass bowl. Use immediately or cover and refrigerate up to 24 hours.

Red Pepper Mayonnaise

1 cup mayonnaise
1 teaspoon tarragon vinegar
1 roasted red pepper, peeled and seeded

Puree all ingredients in a blender or food processor until smooth. Great with pork or beef tenderloin.

Lime Jalapeño Mayonnaise

1 cup mayonnaise
½ teaspoon grated lime rind
2 teaspoons fresh lime juice
1 jalapeño pepper, seeded and chopped

Combine all ingredients in a small bowl. Cover and refrigerate at least 8 hours. Wonderful with sliced beef tenderloin sandwiches.

Apricot Barbecue Glaze

2 large apricots
3 tablespoons dark brown sugar
¼ cup Worcestershire sauce
¼ cup light soy sauce
1 tablespoon grated fresh ginger or
   1½ teaspoons ginger powder
Few drops of hot pepper sauce
2 tablespoons tomato paste
1 clove garlic
Freshly ground black pepper

Place apricots in a small saucepan with enough water to cover. Bring to a simmer and simmer 2 minutes. Drain off water. When cool enough to handle, slip skins from apricots, halve and pit them. Place in a blender or food processor with remaining ingredients. Purée. Pour over lamb, pork or chicken before grilling.

Sound Bites

Meat that has been marinated will cook more quickly.

Red Bell Pepper Sauce

3 red bell peppers
2 tablespoons butter
2 tablespoons olive oil
⅓ cup sliced mushrooms
3 large cloves garlic, minced
2 tablespoons finely chopped onion
½ cup canned vegetable broth
2 tablespoons whipping cream
1 tablespoon chopped fresh basil
Salt and pepper

Char peppers over gas flame or under broiler until blackened on all sides. Seal in paper bag and let stand 10 minutes. Peel and discard charred skin and seeds. Chop remaining pepper. Melt butter with oil in heavy large skillet over medium heat. Add mushrooms, garlic and onion and sauté until tender, about 4 minutes. Puree peppers, mushroom mixture and broth in blender. Transfer to saucepan. Simmer 5 minutes. Stir in cream and basil. Season with salt and pepper. (Can be made one day ahead and chilled. Rewarm before serving.) Delicious on grilled chicken. **Yield: 1⅔ cups.**

Tenderloin Mushroom Sauce

½ cup butter
3 tablespoons flour
¼ teaspoon seasoned salt
¼ teaspoon lemon pepper
1 (10-ounce) can beef consomme
1 pound fresh mushrooms, sliced

Melt butter over low heat in a large saucepan. Gradually stir in flour and seasonings. Cook, stirring constantly, until flour is golden. Gradually add consomme and blend well. Bring to a boil, stirring frequently, then reduce heat and add mushrooms. Cook until mushrooms are tender. Serve with beef tenderloin.

Korean Sesame Marinade

1½ cups soy sauce
¼ cup packed brown sugar
2 tablespoons dark Asian sesame oil
1 tablespoon maple syrup
1 tablespoon sugar
5 cloves garlic, finely chopped
3 tablespoons sliced green onions
2 teaspoons grated fresh ginger
½ teaspoon cracked black pepper

Combine all ingredients. Pour over chicken and marinate 45 minutes to 1 hour.

Lime Marinade for Fish or Pork

⅔ cup strained lime juice
⅔ cup olive oil
1 tablespoon prepared horseradish
2 shallots, finely chopped
1 tablespoon crushed fresh thyme leaves or
  1 teaspoon dried, crumbled
1½ teaspoons salt
¼ teaspoon pepper
2 teaspoons Worcestershire sauce
3 tablespoons rum

Combine all ingredients. Pour over tuna steaks or pork tenderloin and marinate 3 hours, turning once.

Seafood Sauce

1½ cups mayonnaise
2 teaspoons grated onion
1 teaspoon Worcestershire sauce
2 tablespoons lemon juice
2 tablespoons grated green bell pepper

Combine all ingredients, cover and refrigerate. Serve over favorite seafood or as a dip for boiled shrimp.

Sound Bites

Ginger Root is available year-round in the produce department of your supermarket. Look for roots with unshriveled skins and few knobs. Wrap loosely and refrigerate. The root may also be frozen and peeled and sliced as needed.

Pasta & Rice

Pasta & Rice

Have You Heard ...

...about the Pink Palace

A palace in a river town? Why not! "The King" lived here, a Pyramid rounds out the skyline, and it annually "snows down south" (describing the cotton fields before harvest). It is no surprise, then, that Clarence Saunders, founder of the Piggly Wiggly stores, in 1922 began building his "Pink Palace" in east Memphis. Personally designed by Saunders, he demanded that his dream home utilize only Southern workmanship and contractors; the pink marble used on the facade was brought in by rail from Georgia. Most of Memphis passed by the construction site on Central Avenue, hoping to see the indoor swimming pool, the ballroom, the bowling alley and the private lake, golf course and airplane landing strip. Eight bedrooms with adjoining bathrooms were part of the 32-room design totaling 36,500 square feet.

Misfortune struck as Saunders, after spending close to a million dollars on the estate, had financial problems on Wall Street and lost his dream home. The grounds were divided into Chickasaw Gardens subdivision and the mansion was a gift to the city for use as a museum. Saunders' home was known as the Memphis Museum of Natural History and Industrial Arts, emphasizing education, natural history and industrial arts with occasional exhibits from other parts of the country and the world. A modern building for museum displays was added in 1976, and the home was closed. In 1996, much to the delight of any Memphian who had trooped through the old museum on a school field trip or showed it off to curious visitors, the Pink Palace Mansion reopened, presenting exhibits in the East and West wings that highlight citizens and their contributions to Memphis, the South and our country, as well as the heritage of the region. The reopening of this home, including its grand lobby with historic murals, an unforgettable polar bear, and accounts of the life of Ed Crump, former mayor and head of the political "Memphis Machine", has made this much-loved building accessible, once again, to Memphians. The Museum's newest addition which includes an IMAX theatre and a modern exhibition hall adds to the history and aura of a remarkable building.

Grisanti's Elfo's Special Buttered Spaghetti with Shrimp and Mushrooms

4 ounces thin spaghetti
½ cup butter
1 small garlic clove
4 jumbo raw shrimp, diced
3 large mushrooms, diced
3 tablespoons Romano cheese
½ teaspoon salt
Freshly ground pepper to taste

*Cook thin spaghetti in rapidly boiling salted water for 10 minutes. Stir occasionally. Drain, rinse with cold water and set aside. Heat butter in a large skillet. Add garlic, shrimp and mushrooms. Cook slowly in the hot butter for 5 minutes. Add the spaghetti to the skillet. Sprinkle with Romano cheese, salt and pepper. Using a large spoon, turn spaghetti over from edge of skillet to center, being careful not to cut it. Continue until spaghetti is very hot, but do not let the butter brown. Turn out onto a warm serving dish and serve with grated Romano cheese. **Serves 2.***

Penne Pasta with Tomatoes, Herbs and Gorgonzola Cheese

4 teaspoons olive oil
1 large onion, diced
4 large cloves garlic, minced
1 (28-ounce) can diced tomatoes or 4 to 6 peeled, seeded and diced golden tomatoes
Salt and freshly ground pepper
8 ounces Gorgonzola cheese
1 pound penne pasta, cooked according to package directions
½ cup chopped herbs (in winter use a mixture of sage, parsley, thyme and rosemary; in summer fresh basil)

*Sauté onion in olive oil in a large saucepan over medium-high heat until translucent. Add garlic and sauté one minute more. Add tomatoes and cook until most of liquid is reduced, 8 to 10 minutes. Salt and pepper to taste and reduce heat to low. Crumble half of cheese finely and the other half into larger pieces. Add to tomato mixture and stir until sauce has become somewhat creamy. Pour over hot cooked pasta and sprinkle with herbs. **Serves 4 to 6.***

Sound Information

The Memphis Oral School for the Deaf has an Assistive Learning Devices Demonstration Center which enables individuals with hearing loss and their families to learn more about the latest technology in alerting and signaling equipment for the phone, door bell, alarms and television.

Penne with Vodka and Tomato Cream Sauce

1 tablespoon butter
1 tablespoon olive oil
1 small onion, chopped
1 (28-ounce) can Italian plum tomatoes,
    drained, seeded and chopped
1 cup whipping cream or low-fat sour cream
¼ cup vodka
¼ to ½ teaspoon crushed red pepper flakes
Salt and pepper
1 pound penne pasta
Grated Parmesan cheese
Minced fresh chives

Melt butter with oil in heavy large saucepan over medium heat. Add onion and sauté until translucent, about 8 minutes. Add tomatoes and cook until almost no liquid remains in pan, stirring frequently, about 25 minutes. Add cream, vodka and red pepper and boil until thickened to sauce consistency, about 2 minutes. Season to taste with salt and pepper. (Sauce can be prepared 1 day ahead. Cover and refrigerate.)

Cook pasta in large pot of boiling salt water until just tender but still firm to bite, stirring occasionally. Drain well and transfer to a large bowl. Bring sauce to simmer. Pour over pasta and toss well. Sprinkle with Parmesan and chives and serve. **Serves 4.**

Brie Pasta

⅛ cup olive oil
½ pound brie cheese, rind removed and
    cut into small pieces
16 ounces bowtie or penne pasta, cooked
    and drained
2 cups chopped ripe tomatoes
2 tablespoons fresh chopped basil or
    2 teaspoons dried, crumbled

Combine olive oil and brie in a small saucepan over very low heat. Cook, stirring constantly, until brie is melted. Pour over pasta and stir well. Add tomatoes and basil and toss. Serve hot.

Pasta Frittata with Goat Cheese and Tomato

8 ounces angel hair pasta, cooked according
   to package directions
8 large eggs, lightly beaten
4 large cloves garlic, minced
Salt and pepper
2 tablespoons olive oil
6 ounces soft fresh goat cheese
2 cups chopped, peeled, seeded
   tomatoes, drained
2 tablespoons balsamic vinegar or
   1 tablespoon red wine vinegar
¼ cup chopped fresh basil or
   1 tablespoon dried, crumbled
3 tablespoons grated Parmesan cheese

*Preheat broiler. Combine pasta, eggs and garlic in a bowl. Season with salt and pepper. Heat oil in 12-inch cast-iron skillet or broiler-proof nonstick skillet over medium-high heat. Add pasta mixture and spread evenly. Reduce heat to medium and cook 6 minutes. Cover and cook until mixture is set, about 4 minutes. Transfer skillet to broiler and broil until top is golden, about 3 minutes. Sprinkle with goat cheese and broil until cheese softens, about 2 minutes. Slide frittata out onto platter. Combine tomatoes, vinegar and basil. Season to taste with salt and pepper. Top frittata with tomato mixture and sprinkle with Parmesan cheese. **Serves 8.***

Angel Hair Pasta with Pine Nuts and Basil

¾ cup olive oil
½ cup pine nuts, crushed
2 (2¼-ounce) cans sliced ripe olives, drained
18 cloves garlic, crushed (about 1 small head)
2 tablespoons chopped fresh basil
1 (16-ounce) package angel hair pasta,
   cooked according to package directions
¼ cup freshly grated Parmesan cheese

*Combine olive oil, pine nuts, ripe olives, garlic and basil in a skillet. Cook over medium heat until thoroughly heated. Place drained pasta in a bowl and toss with pine nut mixture. Sprinkle with cheese. **Serves 8.***

Pasta with Sun-Dried Tomatoes

¼ cup sun-dried tomato bits
1 (7-ounce) package angel hair pasta
¼ cup plus 2 tablespoons extra virgin olive oil
⅓ cup chopped fresh parsley
1 tablespoon tomato paste
1 clove garlic, minced
½ teaspoon salt
¼ teaspoon crushed red pepper
⅛ teaspoon pepper
Freshly grated Parmesan cheese

Place tomato in a small bowl and cover with hot water. Let stand 15 minutes then drain. Cook pasta according to package directions and drain. Place in a Dutch oven and add sun-dried tomato and remaining ingredients except cheese. Cook over medium-low heat until heated, stirring occasionally. Remove to a serving platter and sprinkle with cheese. **Serves 4.**

Black Bean Pasta

Great vegetarian, low fat dish!

1 large onion, sliced
1 small red bell pepper, cut into strips
1 small yellow bell pepper, cut into strips
4 ounces fresh mushrooms, sliced
2 tablespoons olive oil
1 (16-ounce) can whole tomatoes, undrained
1 (15-ounce) can black beans, drained and rinsed
1 (15½-ounce) can kidney beans, undrained
1 (3½-ounce) jar capers, undrained
¼ cup sliced ripe olives
¼ teaspoon dried rosemary
¼ teaspoon dried basil
¼ teaspoon pepper
1 pound hot, cooked angel hair pasta
Grated Parmesan Cheese

Sauté onion, bell peppers and mushrooms in olive oil in a large skillet over medium-high heat, stirring constantly, until tender. Add tomatoes and remaining ingredients except pasta and Parmesan. Bring to a boil, reduce heat and simmer 30 minutes. Serve over pasta and sprinkle with cheese. **Serves 6.**

Bowtie Pasta with Broccoli, Fontina Cream and Crispy Prosciutto

4 ounces prosciutto, sliced and julienned
½ pound bowtie pasta, cooked
2 cups whipping cream
1 cup grated fontina cheese
2 cups steamed broccoli florets
1 tablespoon chopped garlic
Freshly ground black pepper
Grated Romano cheese

Sauté prosciutto in large pan until crisp. Remove prosciutto and set aside. Heat cream in a large sauté pan. Add fontina cheese, garlic and freshly ground black pepper to taste. Bring to a slow boil. Add broccoli and pasta. Toss until pasta is heated thoroughly. Serve pasta topped with crispy prosciutto and grated Romano cheese. **Serves 4.**

Penne Pasta with Sausage Cheese Sauce

1 pound mild Italian sausage
½ pound mushrooms, sliced or diced
1 medium onion, diced
1½ cups whipping cream
¾ cup chicken broth
1 (10-ounce) package frozen tiny peas, thawed
⅔ cup mascarpone or cream cheese
¾ cup freshly grated Parmesan cheese
1 pound penne pasta

Remove sausage from casings and cook in a Dutch oven until no longer pink, breaking large pieces with a wooden spoon. Remove from pan with a slotted spoon and drain. Add mushrooms to Dutch oven and cook until liquid has evaporated. Remove with a slotted spoon and add to sausage. Sauté onions in drippings until transparent, about 5 to 6 minutes, stirring occasionally. Add cream, bring to a boil and cook 5 minutes. Add broth and cook, stirring occasionally, until reduced to a thin sauce consistency, 8 to 10 minutes. Return sausage and mushrooms to sauce. Add peas and mascarpone and cook until peas are tender, about 5 minutes. Cook pasta according to package directions until just al dente. Drain well and add to sauce. Toss over heat until pasta is well-coated. Sprinkle with Parmesan and serve. **Serves 6 to 8.**

Sound Bites

Cut pasta, such as rigatoni, penne, shells or spiral pasta are best suited for the robust and chunky sauces traditionally made of meats or vegetables so that the sauce is caught in the tube or wraps around the spiral. Long pasta such as spaghetti, fettuccine and linguine are best when topped with olive oil, cream, tomatoes or seafood based sauces.

Shrimp and Goat Cheese Vermicelli

1 pound peeled and deveined medium shrimp
Pinch of sweet red pepper flakes or
⅓ cup chopped red bell pepper
¼ cup plus 2 tablespoons olive oil, divided
½ teaspoon crushed dried basil
⅔ cup crumbled goat cheese or feta cheese
½ teaspoon crushed garlic
2 (14½-ounce) cans diced tomatoes, undrained
¼ cup dry white wine
10 leaves fresh basil, chopped or
¾ teaspoon dried
3 sprigs fresh oregano, chopped or
½ teaspoon dried
¼ teaspoon salt
¼ teaspoon freshly ground pepper
4 to 6 oil-packed sun-dried tomatoes,
drained and slivered
8 ounces vermicelli, cooked and drained

Sauté shrimp, red pepper flakes and basil in 2 tablespoons olive oil in a large skillet over medium heat, stirring constantly, until shrimp turn pink, about 2 minutes. Arrange shrimp mixture in an ungreased 9 x 13-inch baking dish. Sprinkle with cheese. Add remaining oil and garlic to skillet. Sauté over medium-low heat. Add tomatoes and cook 1 minute. Stir in wine and remaining ingredients, except pasta, and simmer, uncovered, for 10 minutes, stirring occasionally. Spoon over shrimp and cheese. Bake, uncovered, in preheated 400° oven for 10 minutes. Serve over pasta.

Italian Sausage Alfredo

½ cup butter (do not substitute)
1 (16-ounce) container sour cream
1½ cups white zinfandel wine
1 quart heavy cream
1 pound Italian sausage, cooked and drained
Sliced mushrooms, optional
Cooked fettuccine
12 ounces freshly grated Parmesan cheese

Heat butter and sour cream in a large saucepan until butter is melted. Add wine and cream. Bring to a boil and cook until thickened and reduced by half. Add sausage and mushrooms, if desired. Pour over pasta and toss to coat. Sprinkle with grated Parmesan before serving.

Linguine with Clam Sauce

4 tablespoons butter
1 clove garlic, minced
1 small onion, finely chopped
4 cans minced clams, undrained
½ teaspoon crushed red pepper
½ teaspoon salt
½ teaspoon oregano
½ cup grated Parmesan cheese
1 pound linguine pasta
Lemon wedges

Melt butter in a skillet over medium-high heat. Sauté garlic for 2 minutes. Add onion and cook until soft. Add clams with juice, salt, oregano, and red pepper. Cook until heated through. Cook linguine according to package directions and drain. Place in a large bowl and top with sauce and grated Parmesan cheese. Serve garnished with lemon wedges.

Penne with Basil Seafood Sauce

¼ cup olive oil
½ pound bay scallops
10 ounces uncooked shrimp, peeled and deveined
4 cloves garlic, minced
1⅓ pounds tomatoes, seeded and chopped
1 cup chopped fresh basil or
   1 tablespoon dried, divided
¾ cup bottled clam juice
½ cup whipping cream
½ pound penne, fresh cooked
Salt and pepper

Heat oil in heavy large skillet over medium heat. Add scallops and shrimp and sauté until just cooked through, about 3 minutes. Transfer to a bowl with a slotted spoon. Add garlic to skillet and sauté 1 minute. Add tomatoes and half of basil. Simmer until sauce thickens, about 10 minutes. Increase heat to medium-high and add clam juice and cream. Simmer until thickened to sauce consistency, about 6 minutes. Add penne, seafood and remaining basil and toss. Season with salt and pepper to taste.
Serves 4.

Three-Green Pasta with Scallops and Pesto Sauce

1 pound asparagus, trimmed and cut into
   1½-inch pieces
½ pound fresh green beans, trimmed and
   cut into 1½-inch pieces
1 pound fettuccine
3 tablespoons butter, divided
1 (10-ounce) package frozen peas, thawed
Salt and pepper
2 pounds sea scallops, each one quartered
1½ cups purchased pesto sauce
¾ cup whipping cream
2 tablespoons fresh lemon juice

*Bring large pot of salted water to boil. Add asparagus and green beans and cook until just crisp-tender, about 5 minutes. Transfer to a bowl, using strainer. Add fettuccine to water and boil until just tender but still firm to the bite, stirring occasionally. Melt 1½ tablespoons butter in large heavy skillet over medium-high heat. Add asparagus, green beans and peas. Season with salt and pepper. Stir until heated through and coated with butter, about 1 minute. Return to bowl. Melt remaining butter in same skillet. Add scallops, season with salt and pepper and sauté until just cooked through, about 1 minute. Remove from heat. Drain pasta and add to skillet. Add vegetables, scallops, pesto, cream and lemon juice and stir over low heat until pasta is coated with sauce. Season to taste with salt and pepper and serve. **Serves 8.***

Spinach and Artichoke Stuffed Manicotti

2 (10-ounce) packages frozen chopped spinach
¼ cup margarine
½ onion, chopped
1 (14-ounce) can artichoke hearts, drained
    and chopped
1 cup shredded Monterey Jack cheese
Salt and pepper
8 manicotti shells, cooked and drained
Favorite Italian sauce

Cook spinach according to package directions and drain well, squeezing out excess liquid and blotting with paper towels. Melt margarine in medium skillet and sauté onions until translucent. Add spinach and artichoke hearts and simmer 15 minutes. Add cheese and stir until melted. Season with salt and pepper to taste. Stuff manicotti with spinach mixture and place in buttered casserole dish. Top with Italian sauce and bake in preheated 350° oven until bubbly, about 30 minutes.

Italian Sauce

2 onions, diced
¼ cup vegetable oil
8 cloves garlic, minced
¼ cup chopped fresh parsley
    or 1 tablespoon dried
1 pound ground beef
2 (6-ounce) cans tomato paste
2½ to 3 cups water
2 teaspoons Italian seasoning
1 to 2 tablespoons sugar
1 teaspoon salt
¼ teaspoon pepper

Sauté onion in oil in a Dutch oven over medium-high heat until soft. Add garlic and parsley and sauté 1 minute more. Add ground beef and brown, draining off excess fat. Add tomato paste and water and stir until combined. Add remaining ingredients. Bring to a boil, reduce heat and simmer 3 hours. Add more sugar if bitter.

Sound Bites

Fresh pasta – must be refrigerated and used or frozen within a short time. It also cooks very quickly and must be watched over carefully. The price of fresh pasta is usually considerably higher per pound than that of dried pasta.

Dried pasta – has a long shelf life and should be cooked according to package directions, although we recommend cooking "al dente", which loosely translates to "to the bite" or "to the tooth".

Spinach Manicotti

1 pound fresh spinach
Salt and pepper
¼ cup finely minced onion
¼ cup unsalted butter, divided
½ cup finely diced prosciutto
1½ cups freshly grated Parmesan cheese, divided
¼ teaspoon freshly grated nutmeg
Manicotti shells, cooked and drained

Béchamel Sauce:
2 cups milk
3 tablespoons unsalted butter
3 tablespoons flour
½ teaspoon salt

Trim stems and any discolored leaves from spinach and rinse well several times in cold water. Place in a saucepan with just the water that clings to it and sprinkle with ½ teaspoon salt. Toss over medium heat until wilted, then cover and cook, stirring occasionally, until tender, 10 to 15 minutes. Drain and squeeze out as much liquid as possible in a dish towel. Chop.

For Béchamel Sauce: *Heat milk in a small saucepan to a bare simmer. Melt butter over low heat in a heavy saucepan. Add flour, stirring constantly. Cook for 2 to 3 minutes, but do not brown. Remove from heat and gradually whisk in milk. Return to heat, add salt and cook, stirring constantly, until sauce is thickened. Simmer about 5 minutes, stirring frequently. Keep warm.*

Heat 2 tablespoons butter in a small skillet over medium heat. Sauté onions, stirring occasionally, until tender. Add prosciutto and stir until just heated through. Add spinach and cook, stirring constantly, until all butter is absorbed. Transfer to a mixing bowl and add 1 cup Parmesan cheese, nutmeg and ⅓ cup béchamel. Mix thoroughly and season to taste with salt and pepper. Preheat oven to 450°. Butter a 9 x 13-inch baking pan and spread 2 tablespoons béchamel over bottom in a thin layer. Stuff manicotti shells with 1 tablespoon spinach mixture and place in dish, arranging in a single layer. Spread remaining béchamel evenly over shells, being sure to cover the ends. Sprinkle with remaining Parmesan and dot with slivers of remaining butter. Bake until heated through, about 5 minutes, then run under broiler until just golden brown and crusty. Serve immediately. **Serves 6.**

Classic Lasagna

1 pound Italian sausage
1 clove garlic, minced
1 tablespoon fresh basil leaves
1½ teaspoons salt
1 (1 pound) can tomatoes
2 (6-ounce) cans tomato paste
2 eggs, lightly beaten
3 cups fresh ricotta or cream-style cottage cheese
½ cup grated Parmesan or Romano cheese
2 tablespoons parsley flakes
1 teaspoon salt
½ teaspoon pepper
10 ounces lasagna noodles, cooked and drained
1 pound mozzarella cheese, thinly sliced

*Brown sausage in a skillet over low heat. Drain excess fat. Add garlic, basil, salt, tomatoes, and tomato paste. Bring to a boil, reduce heat and simmer, uncovered, for 30 minutes, stirring occasionally. In a separate bowl, combine eggs, ricotta, parsley, salt and pepper. Mix well. Layer half of noodles in a 9 x 13-inch baking dish. Spread with half of ricotta cheese mixture. Top with half sliced mozzarella cheese. Spoon half of tomato sauce over cheese. Repeat layers. Bake in preheated 375° oven for 30 minutes. Let stand 10 minutes before serving. May be assembled early and refrigerated, covered. Increase baking time to 45 minutes if chilled. **Serves 8 to 10.**

Sound Information

AIM-HI is Achieving Independence thru Mainstreaming the Hearing Impaired and is the cooperative program between the Memphis Oral School for the Deaf and Lausanne Collegiate School, Memphis. MOSD students "graduate", and enroll at Lausanne, usually in the first grade. A MOSD teacher is on staff at Lausanne to provide classroom teaching some of the day; much of the time is spent with all the children in the class doing school work.

Seafood Lasagna Rolls

15 ounces ricotta cheese
4 ounces mozzarella cheese, shredded
¼ cup grated Parmesan cheese
1 (10-ounce) package frozen chopped spinach,
  thawed and drained
1 pound cooked shrimp, shelled and deveined
1 pound crab meat
Salt and pepper
12 lasagna noodles, cooked and drained

Sauce:
4 tablespoons butter
3 tablespoons flour
3 cups half and half
⅓ cup chopped onion
¼ cup sherry, optional
1 heaping tablespoon chopped fresh basil
  or 1 teaspoon dried, crumbled
1 heaping tablespoon chopped fresh oregano
  or 1 teaspoon dried, crumbled
Salt and pepper

Combine cheeses, spinach, cooked shrimp and crab in a large bowl. Season to taste with salt and pepper. Lay noodles on work surface. Spread an even layer of spinach filling on each. Roll up jelly-roll style and place in a 9 x 11-inch baking pan which has been coated with nonstick spray.

For Sauce: *Melt butter in a medium saucepan. Whisk in flour until smooth. Add remaining ingredients, bring to a boil, then lower heat and simmer until reduced and thickened. Pour over lasagna rolls and bake in preheated 350° oven for 20 to 25 minutes.* **Serves 12.**

Cheese Enchiladas

1 large onion, chopped
2 large cloves garlic, crushed
1 tablespoon chili powder
½ cup plus 2 tablespoons vegetable oil, divided
1 (28-ounce) can whole tomatoes, undrained
1 teaspoon ground cumin
1 teaspoon dried oregano
½ teaspoon salt
⅛ teaspoon pepper
1½ cups shredded Cheddar cheese
   (about 6 ounces)
1½ cups shredded Monterey Jack cheese
   (about 6 ounces)
1 (9-ounce) package 6 or 7-inch corn tortillas

*Sauté onion, garlic and chili powder in 2 tablespoons oil in a 3-quart saucepan over medium-high heat until onion is tender, about 5 minutes. Add tomatoes, cumin, oregano, salt and pepper. Break up tomatoes with a fork. Bring to a boil, reduce heat, and simmer, uncovered until sauce thickens, about 30 minutes. Combine cheeses in a small bowl. Heat remaining oil in an 8-inch skillet. Dip each tortilla lightly into hot oil to soften. Drain on paper towels. Dip each tortilla into tomato sauce to coat both sides. Spoon 2 tablespoons cheese mixture on each tortilla. Roll tortilla around cheese and place seam-side down in un-greased 9 x 13-inch baking dish. Pour remaining tomato sauce over enchiladas. Sprinkle with remaining cheese and bake, uncovered, in preheated 350° oven until cheese is melted and enchiladas are hot, about 20 minutes. **Serves 6.***

Feta and Mint Rice

Perfect with Greek-style Shrimp, see page 135.

3 tablespoons olive oil
½ cup chopped onion
1½ cups long-grain rice
3 cups chicken broth
1 cup crumbled Feta cheese
5 to 6 tablespoons chopped fresh mint
Salt and pepper

Heat oil in large heavy saucepan over medium heat. Add onion and sauté until translucent. Add rice and stir 1 minute. Add broth and bring to a boil. Reduce heat to low, cover and cook until broth is absorbed, about 20 minutes. Fluff rice with a fork. Add Feta and mint and mix with fork. Season to taste with salt and pepper. **Serves 4 to 6.**

Green Chile Rice

3 cups sour cream
½ cup chopped canned sweet or mild green
   chiles, partially drained
½ cup chopped canned hot green chiles,
   partially drained
Salt and pepper
3 cups cooked rice
¾ pound Monterey Jack cheese, grated
½ cup grated Cheddar cheese

Combine sour cream, chiles, salt and pepper. Add cooked rice and stir. Place half of rice mixture in bottom of a buttered 2-quart casserole dish; top with half of Monterey Jack cheese. Repeat. Sprinkle with Cheddar cheese and bake, uncovered, in preheated 350° oven until cheese is melted and bubbly, about 25 minutes. Can be made ahead and refrigerated. Increase cooking time if chilled. **Serves 6 to 8.**

Red Beans and Rice

3 (16-ounce) cans red or kidney beans
¼ cup chopped onion
1 clove garlic, chopped
1 bay leaf
4 tablespoons Worcestershire sauce
½ teaspoon black pepper
½ teaspoon salt
¼ teaspoon hot pepper sauce, optional
Pinch of ground thyme
1 pound Cajun-style smoked sausage,
    browned and drained
6 cups hot cooked rice

Place all ingredients except sausage and rice in a large saucepan. Bring to a boil, reduce heat and cover. Simmer 1½ hours, stirring occasionally. Add cooked sausage and simmer 30 more minutes. Serve over hot rice. **Serves 6.**

Seasoned Rice

2 cups uncooked converted rice
2½ cups chicken stock
1½ tablespoons finely chopped onion
1½ tablespoons finely chopped celery
1½ tablespoons finely chopped green bell pepper
1½ tablespoons finely chopped red bell pepper
1½ tablespoons unsalted butter or margarine, melted
½ teaspoon salt
⅛ teaspoon garlic powder
A pinch of each: white pepper, cayenne
    pepper and black pepper

Combine all ingredients in a greased 9 x 5-inch loaf pan. Mix well and seal pan tightly with aluminum foil. Bake in preheated 350° oven until rice is tender, about 1 hour and 10 minutes. **Serves 6.**

Sound Bites

*To cook rice in advance –
Steam or boil rice, drain well if it was boiled, and fluff with a fork. Allow rice to cool, then put in a shallow ovenproof dish. Cover with foil, and refrigerate. When ready to serve, transfer with foil to a preheated 325° oven. Bake for 30 minutes. Remove foil, fluff rice with a fork, add butter and seasonings.*

Red Hot Rice

2¼ cups chicken broth
¼ cup tomato sauce
2 tablespoons dry sherry
1 tablespoon oyster sauce
2 teaspoons sesame oil
½ teaspoon sugar
1 teaspoon Chinese chili sauce
½ teaspoon minced garlic
1 tablespoon finely minced fresh ginger
2 tablespoons unsalted butter
1½ cups uncooked long-grain rice, washed
    and drained
½ cup raisins
5 to 6 dried Shiitake mushrooms, soaked in hot
    water for 20 minutes, stemmed and minced
⅓ cup minced green onions
¼ cup pine nuts, toasted

*Combine chicken broth, tomato sauce, sherry, oyster
sauce, sesame oil, sugar and chili sauce in a medium
bowl. Heat garlic, ginger and butter in a large saucepan
over medium-high heat. Cook until butter sizzles. Add rice
and continue cooking 5 minutes, stirring constantly. Add
raisins, mushrooms and chicken broth mixture. Heat to
boiling, stirring frequently. Reduce heat, cover and simmer until all liquid is absorbed, 18 to 24 minutes. Remove
cover and stir in green onions and pine nuts. Serve immediately. **Serves 6 to 8.**

Wild Rice

3 tablespoons butter
½ cup uncooked wild rice, washed and drained
¼ cup sliced almonds
2 tablespoons minced green onions
½ cup sliced fresh mushrooms
2 chicken bouillon cubes
1½ cups water

*Melt butter in a large skillet. Sauté rice, almonds, onion
and mushrooms for 7 minutes. Place in a 2-quart casserole
dish. Combine bouillon cubes and water in a 2-cup measure. Microwave on high until boiling and cubes are dissolved. Pour over rice mixture and cover. Bake in preheated 325° oven for 1½ hours.*

Saffron Rice with Peppers

2 cups fish or chicken broth
2 cups dry white wine
2 cups uncooked long-grain white rice
½ teaspoon powdered saffron
¼ cup olive oil
1 red bell pepper, seeded and chopped
½ cup chopped shallots
1 tablespoon minced garlic
¼ cup chopped fresh basil
½ teaspoon salt

Garnish:
Thinly sliced red bell pepper
Fresh basil leaves or fresh parsley sprigs

Preheat oven to 400°. Heat fish broth and wine to boiling in a large saucepan over high heat. Add rice and saffron. Reduce heat to medium-low and cover. Simmer until rice is tender and most of liquid is absorbed, 15 to 20 minutes. Heat olive oil in a medium skillet over medium heat. Sauté bell pepper and shallots until shallots are translucent, about 5 minutes. Add garlic, basil and salt. Stir and remove from heat. Combine with rice mixture. Press firmly into a lightly oiled 6-cup ovenproof ring mold. (May be prepared to this point up to 1 day in advance. Cover and chill. Bring to room temperature before proceeding.) Bake 10 minutes. Release mold onto a large serving platter and garnish with bell pepper slices and basil or parsley.
Serves 6 to 8.

Variation: Dish may be prepared entirely in saucepan. Serve after combining bell pepper mixture and rice.

Wild Rice Casserole

1 (6-ounce) package instant wild rice
1 (4-ounce) can mushrooms, drained
2 teaspoons prepared mustard
½ teaspoon salt
2½ cups water
1 (10-ounce) package frozen spinach
¾ cup chopped onions
1 tablespoon butter or margarine
1 (8-ounce) package cream cheese, cubed

*Mix wild rice, mushrooms, mustard and salt in a 2-quart lidded casserole dish; set aside. Bring water, spinach, onions and butter to boil in a saucepan. Cook until spinach is thawed. Pour over rice mixture and cover tightly. Bake in preheated 375° oven for 35 minutes. Uncover and stir in cream cheese. Bake, uncovered, an additional 10 to 15 minutes. **Serves 6.***

Pine Nut and Orange Wild Rice

1 cup golden raisins
½ cup water
1 (6-ounce) package long-grain and wild rice
½ cup pine nuts, toasted
2 tablespoons chopped fresh parsley
2 to 4 tablespoons extra virgin olive oil
2 tablespoons grated orange rind
2 tablespoons orange juice
¼ teaspoon freshly ground pepper
Freshly grated Parmesan cheese

*Combine raisins and water in a small saucepan. Bring to a boil, cover, reduce heat and simmer 3 minutes. Remove from heat and let cool. Drain. Cook rice according to package directions. Combine with raisins and remaining ingredients except Parmesan cheese in a medium bowl. Stir well. Sprinkle with Parmesan cheese and serve immediately. **Serves 6 to 8.***

Southwestern Wild Rice

6 cups water
1½ cups uncooked wild rice, thoroughly rinsed
½ cup uncooked long-grain white rice,
  thoroughly rinsed
1 pound hot bulk pork sausage
1 pound mild bulk pork sausage
¼ cup white vinegar
¼ cup chili powder
½ cup packed, chopped fresh cilantro
Salt

Heat water to boiling in a large saucepan. Add wild rice, reduce heat to medium-low, cover and simmer 45 minutes. Add white rice, cover and cook until just tender, 15 to 20 minutes. Drain well. Preheat oven to 350°. Brown sausage over high heat, stirring frequently. Pour off drippings. Add vinegar and stir to loosen browned bits in bottom of pan. Add chili powder. Remove to a large bowl and add rice mixture and cilantro. Mix lightly with a fork, and season with salt to taste. Spoon into a buttered large shallow baking dish. (May be prepared to this point and kept covered in refrigerator up to 2 days before finishing.) Bake uncovered until hot in center and lightly browned on top, about 25 minutes. Increase baking time to 40 minutes if chilled. **Serves 6 to 8 as main dish, 12 as side dish.**

Sound Bites

After rice is cooked do not leave it in the pan for more than 10 minutes or it will become gummy.

Vegetables & Side Dishes

Vegetables & Side Dishes

ETTA GRIGSBY PARTEE
1884 — 1911

Have You Heard ...

...about Elmwood Cemetery

The grave markers will tell you stories that could only be true – no one could invent all that is on the granite in the 80 acres of Elmwood Cemetery, 825 S. Dudley. Two miles outside the city limits when established in 1852, 30 years after Memphis was founded, the grounds were donated by a prominent family as the city's first cemetery. (Today it is Memphis' oldest, active cemetery; the Victorian cottage used as the Elmwood office is listed in the National Register of Historic Places; and the Tennessee Historical Commission placed a plaque on the grounds recognizing the illustrious who are buried there.) This historic cemetery is the final resting place of numerous public officials including E.H. "Boss" Crump, controversial Mayor of Memphis, four United States senators and two Tennessee governors, one being Isham G. Harris who was in office at the beginning of the Civil War. They are buried alongside other such notables as Herman Arnold, who orchestrated the familiar song "Dixie"; Robert Church, the South's first black millionaire; Annie Cook, a "madam who became a martyr" during the 1878 yellow fever epidemic; Virginia Moon, a Southern spy; Patrick Henry's eldest daughter; 14 Confederate generals and one Union officer.

The Confederate monument, on a slight crest, catches the eye as does the large stone angel carved in a prayerful stance memorializing victims of yellow fever (by 1878, over 900 entries listed the fever as cause of death). Unusual markers are throughout Elmwood with the tallest and costliest being the W.C. Thomas family's solid, pink granite spire which took 200 men and 4 derricks to erect at the cost of a half million dollars. Elmwood Cemetery reflects the history of one city and region. To walk its grounds is to note customs and events of the past and to appreciate the affection and pride the many families had for their loved ones.

Greek Style Green Beans

1 medium onion, chopped
1 clove garlic, chopped
½ cup olive oil
Salt and pepper to taste
1 teaspoon dry dill or 2 tablespoon fresh dill
1 (8-ounce) can tomato sauce
¼ cup water
1½ pound fresh green beans or
    2 10-ounce boxes frozen green beans

Sauté onion and garlic in olive oil on medium low heat until translucent. Add salt, pepper and dill. Add tomato sauce, water and green beans. Cover and cook until tender approximately 1 hour. **Serves 4 to 6.**

Jim's Place East

Asparagus Amandine

2 tablespoons butter or margarine
¼ cup sliced almonds
Dash of garlic or onion powder
1 (12-ounce) can asparagus spears, drained
Parsley, optional

Melt butter in a large skillet. Add almonds and garlic powder. Cook over low heat until almonds are toasted. Push almonds to one side and add asparagus. Cover and heat. Spoon almond butter over asparagus and top with parsley, if desired.

Texas Beans and Rice

1 (28-ounce) can pork and beans
1 (8-ounce) can stewed tomatoes
½ cup salsa
1 cup beer
1 cup instant rice

Combine beans, salsa, beer and tomatoes in a large saucepan. Bring to a boil, reduce heat and simmer, uncovered, 30 minutes. Stir in rice, cover and cook until rice is done, about 5 minutes. **Serves 6 to 8.**

Great with barbecued ribs.

Sound Information

Mainstreaming is the integration of the hearing impaired child into the community as early, as easily and as effectively as possible. Mainstream support services and on site speech therapy is available to hearing impaired students in regular classroom settings.

Baked Beans

1 (28-ounce) can pork and beans
1 large clove garlic, minced
¼ to ⅓ cup finely chopped onion
¼ cup ketchup
¼ teaspoon dry mustard
1 tablespoon Worcestershire sauce, or more to taste
2 tablespoons brown sugar
2 tablespoons maple syrup
3 to 4 slices bacon, uncooked

Combine all ingredients except bacon. Pour into a greased 3-quart glass baking dish. Top with uncooked bacon slices and bake in preheated 325° oven for 2 hours. **Serves 4 to 6.**

Broccoli with Almonds

2 pounds fresh broccoli
1 teaspoon salt
1 beef bouillon cube
¾ cup hot water
1 cup half and half
¼ cup butter or margarine
¼ cup flour
2 tablespoons sherry
2 tablespoons lemon juice
⅛ teaspoon pepper
2 teaspoons monosodium glutamate
½ cup shredded Cheddar cheese
¼ cup slivered almonds

Remove large leaves from broccoli. Cut tough ends off stalks and wash broccoli thoroughly. Separate into spears. Cook broccoli, covered, in a small amount of boiling salted water until crisp-tender, about 10 minutes. Drain well and place in an 8 x 12-inch baking dish which has been coated with nonstick vegetable spray. Dissolve bouillon cube in hot water and stir in cream. Melt butter in a heavy saucepan over low heat. Blend in flour, stirring until smooth. Cook 1 minute, stirring constantly. Gradually add bouillon mixture. Cook over medium heat, stirring, until thick and bubbly. Stir in sherry, lemon juice, pepper and monosodium glutamate. Pour sauce over broccoli and sprinkle with cheese and almonds. Bake in preheated 375° oven for 25 to 30 minutes. **Serves 6.**

Broccoli Mold

2 (10-ounce) packages frozen chopped broccoli
3 tablespoons butter
3 tablespoons flour
¼ cup chicken broth
1 cup sour cream
⅓ cup minced green onions, tops included
3 eggs, lightly beaten
¾ cup grated Swiss cheese
½ cup slivered almonds, toasted
1 teaspoon salt
½ teaspoon pepper
½ to 1 teaspoon nutmeg

Cook broccoli in 1 cup boiling salted water until barely tender. Drain thoroughly and finely chop by hand. Heat butter in a skillet and blend in flour until smooth. Gradually add chicken broth and sour cream. Add green onions and cook over low heat, stirring constantly, until thick. Stir in eggs and cook 1 minute, stirring constantly. Add cheese and heat until melted. Add remaining ingredients. Pour into an oiled 1-quart ring mold or 8 (5-ounce) custard cups. Bake in a hot water bath in a preheated 350° oven until a knife inserted in center comes out clean, about 50 minutes for the ring mold or 30 minutes for the custard cups. May be made ahead and frozen before baking. If baking when frozen, increase baking time about 30 minutes.

Beautiful filled with sautéed mushrooms.

Honey-Bourbon Carrots

2 pounds large carrots, peeled
1⅓ cups water
6 tablespoons butter
6 tablespoons bourbon
6 tablespoons honey

Slice carrots diagonally into ¼-inch pieces. Place in a large heavy skillet and add remaining ingredients. Cook over medium-high heat until carrots are tender and liquid is reduced to a glaze, stirring occasionally, about 20 minutes. Season to taste with salt and pepper. **Serves 8.**

Sound Bites

In selecting broccoli at the market, look for the bunches that have slender stems and tight, dark green flower buds. If the flower buds are the least bit yellow, the broccoli is past its prime.

Broccoli Soufflé

3 tablespoons butter
3 tablespoons flour
1 teaspoon salt
1 cup milk
⅛ teaspoon nutmeg
1 teaspoon lemon juice
1 (10-ounce) package frozen chopped broccoli, cooked according to package directions
4 eggs, separated

*Melt butter in a saucepan over medium heat. Add flour and salt and cook until bubbly, stirring constantly. Add milk and cook until thick, stirring frequently. Add nutmeg, lemon juice and drained broccoli. Remove from heat and cool slightly. Beat egg yolks and add to broccoli mixture. Cool completely. Beat egg whites until stiff. Fold into broccoli mixture and pour into a buttered 1½-quart casserole dish. Place in a hot water bath and bake, uncovered, in a preheated 325° oven until firm. **Serves 6 to 8.***

Alsatian Dilled Cabbage

4 tablespoons butter
½ cup chopped onion
1 small head cabbage (about 2½ pounds), cut into ½-inch dice
½ teaspoon salt
4 teaspoons chopped fresh dill or 1½ teaspoons dried
1 tablespoon flour
1 cup sour cream
1 tablespoon mild vinegar
1 teaspoon sugar

*Melt butter in a large deep pan and sauté onion until softened and light gold in color. Add cabbage, salt and dill and stir to mix. Cover pan and cook over medium heat until cabbage is just tender-crisp. Do not overcook. Remove from heat. Stir flour into sour cream. Return cabbage to medium heat and add sour cream mixture. Cook, stirring, until cabbage is glazed, about 3 to 5 minutes. Add vinegar and sugar, stir to blend and serve immediately. **Serves 6.***

Baked Carrot and Apple Casserole

6 Delicious apples, peeled, cored and thinly sliced
2 cups cooked, sliced carrot
⅓ cup firmly packed brown sugar
2 tablespoons flour
¾ cup orange juice

Place half of apples in a greased 2-quart casserole dish. Top with half of carrots. Combine brown sugar and flour. Sprinkle half over carrots. Repeat layers. Pour orange juice over top and bake, uncovered, in preheated 350° oven for 45 minutes.

Honey Orange Butternut Squash

2 pounds butternut squash, peeled, seeded
    and cut into ¾-inch pieces
2 tablespoons butter
4 teaspoons honey
½ teaspoon grated orange zest
4 tablespoons orange juice
Salt and pepper

*Steam squash until just tender, but not soft, 5 to 6 minutes. Place butter, honey, orange zest and orange juice in a skillet. Heat, stirring, until butter is melted. Add squash and salt and pepper to taste. Cook over low heat, stirring, until squash is well-coated, about 2 minutes. **Serves 4.***

Easy Corn Casserole

1 (11-ounce) can whole kernel corn, undrained
1 (16-ounce) can cream-style corn
½ cup margarine, melted
1 cup sour cream
2 eggs, lightly beaten
1 box corn muffin mix
1 cup shredded Cheddar cheese

Combine both cans of corn, margarine, sour cream and eggs in a large mixing bowl. Add muffin mix and stir just to moisten. Pour into a greased 9-inch baking dish and bake in preheated 350° oven for 30 to 40 minutes. Sprinkle with cheese and bake an additional 10 to 15 minutes.

Sound Bites

Bread crumbs
can be made
by placing stale
bread in a
blender and
chopping
until fine. Store
in freezer
for use in
recipes when
needed.

Garlic Green Bean Casserole

2 tablespoon bacon drippings
2 cans French-style green beans
2 cloves garlic
1 (10¾-ounce) can cream of mushroom soup
¾ cup grated Cheddar cheese
1 teaspoon chili powder
1 teaspoon paprika
½ cup cracker crumbs
1 to 2 tablespoons butter

*Place bacon drippings, green beans and garlic in a large saucepan. Boil for 30 minutes. Remove beans with a slotted spoon and place in a greased 2-quart baking dish. Reserve bean stock. Heat soup in a medium saucepan. Stir in ¾ cup reserved bean stock. Add cheese and cook until melted, stirring frequently. Add chili powder and paprika. Pour over beans. Sprinkle with cracker crumbs and dot with butter. Bake in preheated 325° oven for 40 to 50 minutes. **Serves 4 to 6.***

Cheese Grits Casserole

1 teaspoon salt
3½ cups water
1 cup quick-cooking grits (not instant)
1 (6-ounce) roll garlic cheese
2 eggs, well beaten
¼ cup milk
¼ cup butter
Salt and pepper

Add salt to water in a large saucepan. Bring to a boil and gradually stir in grits. Cover pan, reduce heat to medium and cook until thickened, 5 to 7 minutes, stirring occasionally. Add cheese and stir until melted. Add a small amount of cheese mixture to eggs and blend. Gradually add eggs to saucepan, stirring constantly. Add milk and butter and season to taste with salt and pepper. Pour into a greased 1-quart casserole dish and bake in preheated 350° oven until set, about 1 hour. Let stand 5 minutes after removing from oven.

Nutty Celery Casserole

3 cups sliced celery
1 (10¾-ounce) can cream of chicken soup
1 (8-ounce) can sliced water chestnuts, drained
1 (6-ounce) package slivered almonds
½ cup butter or margarine
32 round, buttery crackers, crumbled

*Boil celery for 7 minutes and drain well. Combine celery, soup and water chestnuts and pour into a greased 9 x 13-inch glass baking dish. Melt butter in a large skillet and sauté almonds until lightly browned. Add cracker crumbs and stir to combine. Sprinkle over celery mixture and bake in preheated 350° oven for 30 minutes. **Serves 8 to 10.***

Corn Pudding

4 large eggs
1 (28-ounce) package frozen whole kernel
   corn, thawed and divided
3 cups milk
⅓ cup minced red bell pepper
½ cup minced onion
1 teaspoon salt
10 drops hot pepper sauce

*Preheat oven to 325°. Place eggs and 2 cups corn in a food processor. Pulse until almost smooth. Heat milk in a large saucepan just until boiling. Add remaining corn, bell pepper, onion, salt and hot pepper sauce. Remove from heat and stir in egg mixture. Pour into a lightly greased shallow 2-quart baking dish. Bake, uncovered, just until firm to the touch, about 45 minutes. Serve immediately. **Serves 12.***

Zesty Corn Casserole

½ cup margarine
1 large onion, chopped
1 (16-ounce) can diced tomatoes with chili peppers
1 (16-ounce) can yellow whole kernel corn, drained
1 (16-ounce) can white shoe peg corn, drained
1 (16-ounce) can yellow cream-style corn

*Melt margarine in a large saucepan over medium heat. Sauté onion until translucent. Add remaining ingredients. Remove from heat, cover and refrigerate at least 8 hours. Bake in preheated 325° oven for 2 hours. **Serves 8.***

Sound Bites

To keep cauliflower white while cooking, add a little milk to the water.

Coyote Corn

2 tablespoons butter
2½ cups fresh or frozen corn kernels
3 to 4 sun-dried tomatoes, soaked in hot
    water 15 minutes, drained and chopped
3 tablespoons finely chopped fresh basil
⅓ cup chopped green onions, including tops
Salt and freshly ground black pepper

Heat butter in a medium skillet over medium-high heat until foam subsides. Add corn and sun-dried tomatoes and cook, stirring frequently, about 4 minutes. Place in serving bowl and add basil and green onions. Season with salt and pepper to taste. Toss to combine and serve warm or at room temperature. **Serves 4.**

Broccoli Stuffed Onions

3 medium Spanish onions or 6 medium Vidalia
    onions, peeled and halved
1 package chopped broccoli, thawed
½ cup Parmesan cheese
⅓ cup mayonnaise
2 teaspoons lemon juice
2 tablespoons butter
2 tablespoons flour
1 teaspoon salt
1 cup milk
1 (3-ounce) package cream cheese, softened

Parboil onions in salted water for 10 to 12 minutes. Drain. When cool enough to handle, remove centers, leaving a ¾-inch shell. Chop enough onion centers to equal 1 cup. Combine with broccoli, Parmesan cheese, mayonnaise and lemon juice in a small bowl. Mix thoroughly and spoon into onion halves. Place in a 9 x 13-inch baking dish which has been coated with nonstick vegetable spray. Melt butter in a small saucepan over medium heat. Blend in flour and salt and stir until smooth. Add milk and cook until thickened, stirring constantly. Remove from heat and blend in cream cheese. Spoon over onion halves. Bake, uncovered, in preheated 375° oven for 20 minutes.

Zippy Green Beans

These beans are a fantastic change from the traditional green bean casserole.

¾ pound bacon
2 medium onions, chopped
1½ cans diced tomatoes with chili peppers
5 cans French-style green beans, drained

*Fry bacon in a Dutch oven until crisp. Remove and drain. Pour off some of drippings and sauté onion in remaining drippings. Add tomatoes and beans. Crumble bacon and stir into beans. Bring to a boil, reduce heat and simmer 30 minutes. **Serves 14.***

Okra Fritters

¼ cup cornmeal
¼ cup flour
½ cup finely chopped onion
½ cup evaporated milk
1 large egg, lightly beaten
3 tablespoons chopped fresh parsley
2 tablespoons grated Parmesan cheese
½ teaspoon salt
¼ teaspoon cayenne pepper
2 cups sliced fresh okra (about ⅔ pound) or
   2 cups frozen sliced okra, thawed
Vegetable oil for frying
Salt, optional

*Combine cornmeal, flour, onion, milk, egg, parsley, cheese, salt and pepper in a large bowl. Stir in okra. Pour oil to a depth of 2 inches in a Dutch oven. Heat to 350°. Drop okra mixture by tablespoonfuls into oil and cook until golden brown, turning once. Drain on paper towels and sprinkle with salt, if desired. Serve immediately. **Serves 4 to 6.***

Sound Bites

Freezing Okra – Wash and dry fresh okra. Slice to desired thickness. Toss okra in 1 beaten egg and add enough cornmeal to coat well. Place on cookie sheets in freezer until frozen. Turn into zip lock freezer bags and freeze for up to 6 months.

Mushroom Casserole

2 cups soft French bread crumbs, divided
½ cup butter, melted and divided
1 pound fresh mushrooms, sliced
Salt and pepper
⅓ cup white wine

Combine one-third of crumbs with one-third of butter in a small bowl and set aside. Alternate layers of mushrooms, remaining crumbs and remaining butter in a buttered 1½-quart casserole. Sprinkle salt and pepper between layers. Drizzle wine over all and bake, covered, in preheated 325° oven for 25 minutes. Sprinkle with reserved crumbs and bake an additional 10 minutes, uncovered, until crumbs are toasted.

Bleu Cheese and Cheddar Potato Gratin

¼ cup butter
¼ cup flour
1 cup whipping cream
1 cup milk
½ teaspoon ground white pepper
½ teaspoon salt
¼ teaspoon paprika
1 tablespoon dried parsley
½ cup crumbled bleu cheese
2 teaspoons minced garlic
1 cup thinly sliced onion, separated into rings
2 pounds white potatoes, peeled and thinly sliced
1 can artichoke hearts, drained and quartered
1 cup shredded Cheddar cheese

*Melt butter in a heavy saucepan over low heat. Add flour and stir until smooth. Cook, stirring constantly for 1 minute. Gradually add cream and milk. Cook over medium heat, stirring constantly, until mixture is thickened and bubbly. Stir in salt, white pepper, paprika and parsley. Sprinkle bleu cheese and garlic in a lightly greased 9 x 13-inch baking dish. Top with half of onion rings. Arrange half of potatoes over onion rings. Layer half of artichoke quarters over potatoes and top with half of sauce. Repeat layers. Bake, covered, in preheated 350° oven for 1 hour. Sprinkle evenly with Cheddar cheese and bake, uncovered, until potatoes are tender, about 15 minutes. Let stand 10 minutes before serving. **Serves 8 to 10.***

Fried Onion Mum

3 cups cornstarch
1½ cups flour
2 teaspoons garlic salt
2 teaspoons paprika
1 teaspoon salt
1 teaspoon pepper
24 ounces beer
Vegetable oil for frying
6 onions

Seasoned Flour:
2 cups flour
4 teaspoons paprika
2 teaspoons garlic powder
¼ teaspoon cayenne pepper
½ teaspoon black pepper

Chili Sauce:
1 pint mayonnaise
1 pint sour cream
½ cup bottled chili sauce
½ teaspoon cayenne pepper

Combine cornstarch, flour, garlic salt, paprika, salt and pepper in a large bowl. Stir in beer and blend well. Set aside. Begin heating oil in a deep fat fryer. While oil is heating, cut a ¾-inch slice off top of each onion and remove skin. Slice onions vertically in quarters to ½ inch from base. Slice vertically 4 more times and gently spread slices apart to form flower petals. Remove a few petals from center to make room for dipping sauce. Combine seasoned flour ingredients in a narrow bowl. Dip onions in flour and shake off excess. Mix beer batter again. Dip onions in batter to coat. Gently lower onions into hot oil and deep fry until golden, about 1½ minutes. Turn and brown on other side. Drain, inverted, on paper towels. Combine chili sauce ingredients. Place onions upright and serve hot with sauce.

Sound Bites

Store chopped onions in a screw top jar in the refrigerator. They will keep for several days.

Bacony Deviled Eggs

12 large eggs, hard-cooked, peeled and halved
½ cup mayonnaise
¼ cup sour cream
1 tablespoon Dijon mustard
1 tablespoon prepared white horseradish
½ pound bacon, cooked crisp, drained and
　crumbled fine
4 scallions, finely chopped
Salt and pepper

Place egg yolks in a small bowl and mash with back of a spoon. Add mayonnaise, sour cream, mustard and horseradish and stir until smooth. Add bacon and scallions. Salt and pepper to taste. Pipe or spoon back into whites and chill. **Serves 2 dozen.**

Divine Spinach Casserole

3 (10-ounce) packages frozen chopped spinach
4 tablespoons butter
2 tablespoons flour
2 tablespoons chopped onion
½ cup evaporated milk
6 ounces jalapeño cheese
1 teaspoon Worcestershire sauce
½ cup cracker crumbs
Butter

Cook spinach according to package directions. Drain well, reserving liquid. Melt butter over medium heat in a large saucepan. Add flour and stir until well blended. Add onion and cook until soft. Stir in milk and reserved liquid. Cook, stirring frequently, until thickened. Add cheese and Worcestershire sauce and stir until cheese is melted. Combine sauce and spinach and place in a buttered casserole. Top with cracker crumbs and dot with butter. Bake in preheated 350° oven for 30 minutes. **Serves 8.**

Italian Potatoes in Foil

Baking potatoes
Garlic powder
Salt and pepper
Paprika
Parsley Flakes
Oregano
Grated Parmesan cheese
Butter

Prepare 1 potato per person. Slice potato into strips and place on a square piece of foil. Season to taste with garlic powder, salt, pepper, paprika, parsley and oregano. Top each potato with 3 pats of butter and sprinkle generously with Parmesan cheese. Wrap tightly in individual packets and bake in preheated 350° oven for 1½ hours.

Cheesy Potatoes

5 to 7 boiled medium potatoes, peeled
   and quartered
¼ cup chopped onion
4 cups shredded Colby cheese
3 cups shredded Monterey Jack cheese
Crumbs from 4 slices bread
½ cup butter

Place potatoes in a 9 x 13-inch glass baking dish which has been coated with nonstick vegetable spray. Sprinkle with onion and cheeses. Cover with crumbs and dot with butter. Bake, uncovered, in preheated 350° oven for 30 minutes. **Serves 10.**

Easy Elegant Spinach

4 (10-ounce) packages frozen chopped spinach
2 pints sour cream
1 envelope dry onion soup mix
2 (5-ounce) cans water chestnuts, drained
   and chopped

Cook spinach according to package directions. Drain well, pressing out liquid with a spoon. Combine with remaining ingredients and place in a 2-quart casserole which has been coated with nonstick vegetable spray. Bake in pre-heated 350° oven for 30 to 40 minutes. **Serves 12.**

New Potatoes with Basil Cream Sauce

2 pounds unpeeled new potatoes, sliced
2 tablespoons dry white wine
2 tablespoons finely chopped shallot
1½ cups whipping cream
¼ cup chopped fresh basil
¼ teaspoon salt
⅛ teaspoon white pepper

Cook potatoes in boiling salted water to cover 10 to 15 minutes. Drain carefully, leaving skins intact. Keep warm. Combine wine and shallot in a large saucepan. Bring to a boil and cook 1 minute. Add whipping cream and return to a boil. Reduce heat and simmer 20 minutes, stirring occasionally. Stir in basil, salt and pepper. Arrange potatoes on a serving plate. Top with sauce and serve immediately. **Serves 8.**

Spinach Rockefeller

2 (10-ounce) packages frozen chopped spinach
1 (14-ounce) can artichoke hearts, drained
    and quartered
1 (8-ounce) carton sour cream
¾ cup cracker crumbs
½ cup butter
¼ cup chopped onion
2 eggs, beaten
½ teaspoon garlic powder
½ teaspoon Parmesan cheese
½ teaspoon pepper
½ teaspoon salt
¼ teaspoon monosodium glutamate
⅛ teaspoon thyme
3 dashes hot pepper sauce

Cook spinach 5 minutes and drain well. Combine with remaining ingredients and pour into a greased casserole. Sprinkle with additional Parmesan cheese and dot with butter. Bake in preheated 350° oven for 30 minutes.

Spinach and Mushroom Casserole

2 (10-ounce) packages frozen chopped spinach
2 tablespoons butter
½ pound fresh mushrooms, sliced
1 teaspoon salt, divided
4 slices American cheese, diced
1 (5⅓-ounce) can evaporated milk
¼ teaspoon garlic salt

Cook spinach according to package directions. Drain well, pressing out liquid with a spoon. Melt butter in a skillet and sauté mushrooms until lightly browned. Sprinkle with ½ teaspoon salt. Melt cheese in milk in a heavy saucepan over low heat. Add remaining salt. Turn spinach into a shallow baking dish and sprinkle with garlic salt. Stir in cheese mixture. Top with mushrooms and drippings. Bake, uncovered, in a preheated 350° oven for 20 minutes.
Serves 4.

Salechi

2 tablespoons water
¾ tablespoon olive oil
2 (10-ounce) packages frozen chopped spinach
¼ teaspoon oregano
¼ teaspoon basil
¼ teaspoon garlic powder
8 ounces mozzarella cheese, grated
1 (3½-ounce) package sliced pepperoni
1 to 3 cups bread crumbs
5 large mushrooms, sliced
1 tomato, sliced, optional
½ to 1 cup Parmesan cheese

Combine water and oil in a large saucepan. Bring to a boil and add spinach and seasonings. Reduce heat and cook until spinach is thawed. Drain thoroughly and spread a third in bottom of a 1-quart casserole which has been coated with nonstick vegetable spray. Top with a third of the mozzarella, a third of the pepperoni, a layer of bread crumbs and a third of the mushrooms. Repeat two more times. Cover with sliced tomatoes, if desired, and sprinkle with Parmesan cheese. Bake in preheated 325° oven for 20 to 30 minutes.

Sound Bites

A lettuce leaf added to canned vegetables when heating will add a fresh vegetable taste.

Sound Bites

Baked potatoes
in a hurry –
Boil in salted
water 10 minutes
before popping
into a very
hot oven.

Herbed Twice-Baked Potatoes

2% milk works well.

6 medium potatoes, baked
½ cup butter, softened
1 package garlic herb pasta sauce mix
½ cup milk
1 cup shredded Cheddar cheese, divided

Cut small oval slice from each potato and scoop out pulp, being careful to leave skins intact. Mash pulp with butter. Combine sauce mix with milk and add to mashed potatoes, mixing well. Add ⅔ cup cheese and blend well. Spoon into potato skins. Place in a shallow baking dish and sprinkle with remaining cheese. Bake, uncovered, in preheated 400° oven until heated through, about 15 minutes. **Serves 6.**

Oven-Roasted Ratatouille

2 medium zucchini
1 small eggplant
Salt and freshly ground black pepper
1 pound cherry tomatoes, skinned
1 small red bell pepper
1 small yellow bell pepper
1 medium onion
2 large cloves garlic, minced
1 handful fresh basil leaves
¼ cup olive oil

Cut zucchini and eggplant into a 1-inch dice, leaving skin on. Sprinkle with 2 teaspoons salt and pack into a colander. Cover with a plate small enough to fit into colander and top with a heavy weight. Leave for an hour to allow bitter juices to drain. After an hour, squeeze out any remaining juice and dry vegetables thoroughly with paper towels. Preheat oven on its highest setting. Seed and cut bell peppers into 1-inch squares. Chop onion in 1-inch squares. Arrange all of the vegetables in a 12 x 16-inch shallow roasting pan. Sprinkle with garlic. Tear up basil leaves roughly and mix with olive oil. Drizzle oil over vegetables, making sure each one has a good coating. Season with salt and pepper. Roast on highest shelf in oven until vegetables are roasted and tinged brown at edges, 30 to 40 minutes. Remove and serve immediately. **Serves 4.**

Spinach Soufflé

6 eggs, beaten
6 tablespoons flour
2 (10-ounce) packages frozen chopped spinach,
    thawed and drained
½ cup butter, melted
1 (16-ounce) container cottage cheese
2 cups shredded Cheddar cheese

Whisk together eggs and flour until well blended. Add remaining ingredients and place in a greased 9 x 13-inch baking dish. Bake, uncovered, in preheated 350° oven until top is brown and soufflé is set, about 30 minutes.

Fresh Peach–Squash Casserole

2½ cups sliced yellow crookneck or
    zucchini squash
1 cup sliced fresh peaches
2 tablespoons brown sugar
Salt to taste
2½ tablespoons butter

*Layer squash and peaches in a buttered 2-quart casserole. Continue alternating layers until all have been used. Sprinkle with brown sugar and salt and dot with butter. Cover and bake in preheated 350° oven for 45 minutes to one hour. **Serves 4.***

Squash and Pepper Sauté

2 medium yellow squash, sliced
2 medium zucchini, sliced
1 medium red bell pepper, julienned
¼ cup olive oil
1 envelope Italian salad dressing mix
3 tablespoons red wine vinegar

*Stir-fry vegetables in oil in a wok or iron skillet over medium-high heat until crisp-tender, about 3 to 5 minutes. Sprinkle with dressing mix and toss. Stir in vinegar and mix well. **Serves 6.***

Sound Bites

Put dried beans in a bowl of cold water and discard any that float to the surface, which is an indication of insect or mold damage.

Sound Information

The Memphis Oral
School for the
Deaf is located at
711 Jefferson,
Memphis,
in the
Boling Center,
at the
University of
Tennessee.

Fried Green Tomatoes

½ cup milk
1 egg, lightly beaten
½ cup cornmeal
½ cup flour
Salt and freshly ground pepper
4 medium green tomatoes, thickly sliced
4 tablespoons bacon drippings or vegetable oil
   (do not use butter)

Combine milk and egg in a shallow dish, blending well. Combine cornmeal, flour, salt and pepper to taste on a plate. Dip tomato slices in milk mixture, then dredge in seasoned flour. Shake off excess. Fry tomatoes in hot bacon drippings or oil in a heavy iron skillet, turning to brown both sides. Drain on paper towels and serve warm.

Tomatoes Stuffed with Bacon and Cheese

4 large beefsteak tomatoes
8 slices bacon
1 medium onion, chopped
4 tablespoons minced fresh parsley
1 tablespoon chopped fresh basil or
   1 teaspoon dried
Salt and fresh ground pepper to taste
4 ounces Monterey Jack cheese, freshly grated
Chopped parsley for garnish

*Preheat oven to 350°. Slice top off each tomato. Remove pulp carefully, leaving shell intact. Reserve pulp. Invert shells to drain. Fry bacon until crisp and drain, reserving 2 tablespoons bacon drippings. Crumble bacon. Sauté onion and tomato pulp in reserved bacon dripping until most of liquid is evaporated. Remove from heat and add parsley, basil, salt, pepper, bacon and cheese. Fill tomato shells with mixture and place in a baking dish. Bake, uncovered, for 20 to 30 minutes. Do not overcook or shells will fall apart. Sprinkle with parsley before serving. **Serves 4.***

Tomato Pie

1 9-inch pie crust, unbaked
6 Roma tomatoes, sliced
½ cup diced sweet onion
1 cup mayonnaise
1 cup shredded sharp Cheddar cheese
1 cup shredded mozzarella cheese
1 tablespoon chopped fresh basil
Few drops of hot pepper sauce
1 teaspoon Creole seasoning

Bake pie crust in preheated 400° oven for 5 to 10 minutes. Layer tomatoes and onions in crust. Combine remaining ingredients and spoon over tomatoes. Reduce oven temperature to 350° and bake pie for 45 minutes. Serve warm or cold. **Serves 6.**

Sound Bites

To peel tomatoes easily – pour boiling water over tomatoes and let stand for 60 seconds.

Zucchini Soufflé

2 pounds zucchini
8 ounces hot pepper cheese, grated
3 eggs, beaten

Grate zucchini and squeeze out moisture with paper towels. Combine zucchini, eggs and cheese in a medium bowl. Pour into a greased 2-quart casserole and bake, uncovered, in preheated 350° oven until set in center, about 30 minutes. **Serves 4.**

Apricot Casserole

Good with pork or chicken.

4 ounces round buttery crackers, crushed
5 (17-ounce) cans apricot halves, drained
⅔ cup firmly packed light brown sugar
½ cup butter, melted

Alternate layers of crumbs, apricots and sugar in a buttered casserole dish. Pour butter over top and bake in preheated 300° oven for 30 to 45 minutes.

"Great" Baked Fruit Compote

Excellent as a dessert or a side dish with poultry or beef.

1 (1 pound, 13-ounce) can peach halves
1 (1 pound, 14-ounce) can pitted apricots
1 (1 pound, 14-ounce) can pineapple chunks
1 (1 pound, 13-ounce) can pear halves
2 (1 pound) cans pitted Bing cherries
Brown sugar
Cinnamon
Lemon juice
Butter
Cream sherry
⅓ cup cornstarch

Drain fruit thoroughly, reserving syrups. Layer each fruit in a large casserole dish, sprinkling each layer with a generous amount of brown sugar, then cinnamon, lemon juice, dots of butter and cream sherry. Bake in preheated 350° oven for 45 minutes. Combine ¾ cup of reserved juice with cornstarch. Mix thoroughly and pour over baked fruit. Return to oven for an additional 15 minutes. Serve hot. May be prepared in advance and reheated in a 350° oven for 15 minutes. **Serves 12.**

Casserole Zucchini

2 large zucchini, chopped
½ cup olive oil
1 clove garlic, minced
Salt and pepper
Oregano
½ cup bread crumbs
½ cup grated Parmesan cheese

Place zucchini in a shallow baking dish and drizzle with oil. Sprinkle with garlic. Combine salt, pepper, oregano and bread crumbs. Spread over zucchini and sprinkle with cheese. Bake in preheated 350° oven for 30 minutes. **Serves 4.**

Almond Zucchini

4 to 5 small zucchini (about 1 pound),
    cut into ¼-inch slices
2 tablespoons butter
2 tablespoons sliced almonds
2 tablespoons minced fresh parsley

*Place zucchini in a 2-quart microwave-safe casserole and cover. Microwave on high just until fork-tender, 4 to 6 minutes, stirring twice. Place butter and almonds in a 2-cup measure and microwave on high until butter melts and nuts soften, 45 seconds to 1 minute. Pour over zucchini and sprinkle with parsley. **Serves 4.***

Cheesy Pineapple Casserole

1 (20-ounce) can pineapple chunks
    or crushed pineapple
½ cup sugar
3 tablespoons flour
1 cup cubed pasteurized process cheese
    spread or grated sharp Cheddar cheese
½ cup margarine, melted
½ cup crushed round buttery crackers

*Drain pineapple, reserving 3 tablespoons juice. Combine sugar and flour and add reserved juice. Place pineapple and cheese in a large bowl and top with sugar mixture. Mix until well-coated. Spoon into a 9 x 12-inch casserole dish. Combine margarine and cracker crumbs and mix well. Sprinkle over pineapple and bake in preheated 350° oven until crumbs are browned, 20 to 30 minutes. **Serves 10.***

Desserts

Desserts

Have You Heard ...

... about The Orpheum Theatre

Cats, cats, and more cats, a ghost, and Cary Grant all belong to the history of the fabulous show house known as The Orpheum Theatre. Just before the turn of the century, the Grand Opera House was built at the corner of Main and Beale Street. Known across the country as one of the finest in presenting vaudeville, the Grand became part of the Orpheum Circuit, and thus took its name. In 1923 a fire started during an exotic dance by Blossom Seeley, destroying the building. The present building, twice as large as the old theatre, was built in 1928 for $1.6 million and has seen the great stars of the stage and screen perform to thrilled audiences. (The ghost story revolves around the legend that a young girl, playing near the rebuilding construction of The Orpheum, was accidentally killed and then made the theatre her home.)

George Burns and Gracie Allen brought many laughs to Memphis, just as Harry Houdini brought "oohs" and "aahs" with his daring escape tricks – all on a stage lavishly decorated with brocade draperies, lighted by crystal sconces and chandeliers. The Wurlitzer pipe organ made a lasting impression on all who heard it! The M.A. Lightman family, owners of a chain of movie theatres, purchased the Orpheum in 1940, and many Mid-Southerners saw their favorite Hollywood stars on the large screen at the Malco. When the family decided to sell in the mid 70's, there was much community discussion about the use of the theatre. The Memphis Development Foundation came to the rescue, restoring the much-loved name of Orpheum to the marquee on Main Street as well as bringing in concerts and touring Broadway productions.

After a two-year, $5 million renovation in the early 1980's, the "South's Finest Theatre" offers such favorites as Andrew Lloyd Webber's Cats and in late 1997, The Phantom of the Opera, as well as concerts, opera, ballet and one-man shows (Cary Grant was an overwhelming success in one of his performances before his death). Whether it be a summer evening's screening of Casablanca or a large-scale production of Les Miserables, the splendor of the Orpheum's decor, the awesome lobby staircase, and the original, still-in-use pipe organ all link past entertainment ages with sophisticated technology of the present.

Crème Brûlée

2 cups heavy cream
2 cups half & half
1 cup sugar, divided
9 egg yolks
1 teaspoon vanilla
1 ounce Grand Marnier

Heat cream, half & half, vanilla and ½ cup sugar until near boiling. Whisk egg yolks, ½ cup sugar and Grand Marnier. Whisk hot cream mixture into eggs and skim off foam. Bake in 4 ounce soufflé cups at 350° in a water bath for 45 to 60 minutes until custard sets. **Serves 8.**

Café Society

White Chocolate Mousse

4 ounces white chocolate
1½ tablespoons water
2 egg yolks
½ cup sugar
1 pint whipping cream
Dash of Kirsch
Raspberry sauce

Melt chocolate with water in top of a double boiler. Combine egg yolks and sugar in a small bowl. Slowly add to melted chocolate. Beat cream until stiff. Fold into chocolate mixture and add a dash of Kirsch. Pour into serving dish and chill. Serve on individual plates which have been flooded with raspberry sauce. **Serves 6 to 8.**

Sound Bites

White chocolate has a mild flavor similar to milk chocolate. It can be found in specialty food shops and the baking section of some supermarkets.

Luscious Lemon Tarts

⅓ cup butter, melted
½ cup sugar
Grated rind and juice of 2 lemons
2 eggs, well beaten
1 cup whipping cream, whipped
Mint sprigs or lemon peel twists

Tart Shells:
1⅓ cups flour
½ cup cold butter, cut into 8 pieces
1 teaspoon salt
¼ cup ice water

Blend butter, sugar, lemon rind and juice in top of a double boiler. Cook until thoroughly heated. Add a small amount to eggs and blend well. Pour egg mixture into double boiler and cook until thickened, stirring constantly. Chill.

For Shells: *Place flour, butter and salt in food processor. Process until consistency of coarse meal, 5 to 10 seconds. With machine running, pour ice water through feed tube. Stop processing as soon as dough forms a ball. Remove to a floured surface and roll to ¼-inch thickness. Cut dough and fit into tart pans. Fill with beans or rice before baking to prevent bubbling. Bake in preheated 400° oven until lightly browned, 15 to 20 minutes. Remove beans or rice and cool before filling.*

To assemble, fill shells with lemon filling and top with a tiny dollop of whipped cream. Garnish with a sprig of mint or a lemon peel twist. **Yield: 3 to 4 dozen.**

Grand Marnier Soufflé

6 egg yolks
¾ cup sugar
3 ounces Grand Marnier liqueur
2 cups whipped whipping cream
Chocolate sprinkles

Combine egg yolks and sugar and beat until yolks are thick and lemon-colored. Fold in Grand Marnier. Fold in whipped cream and spoon into serving cups. Freeze at least 2 hours. Garnish with chocolate sprinkles and additional whipped cream.

Lime–Chocolate Delicious

1 (13-ounce) can evaporated milk
1 (3-ounce) package lime gelatin
1¾ cups hot water
¼ cup lime juice
2 teaspoons lemon juice
1 cup sugar
2 cups chocolate wafer crumbs
⅓ cup melted butter
Shaved semisweet chocolate

Chill milk in freezer until icy cold. Dissolve gelatin in hot water, chill until partially set and whip until fluffy. Stir in lime juice, lemon juice and sugar. Whip evaporated milk and fold into gelatin. Combine wafer crumbs and butter. Press into a 9 x 13-inch pan. Pour gelatin mixture into crust, cover and chill. Garnish with shaved chocolate and cut into squares to serve.

Sound Bites

Whipping cream ahead of time – add a touch of unflavored gelatin to keep cream from separating (¼ teaspoon per cup of cream).

Tiramisu

⅔ cup sugar
¼ cup water
4 large egg yolks
½ teaspoon vanilla
9 ounces mascarpone, softened
4 tablespoons dark or light rum
1 cup whipping cream
36 ladyfingers
⅓ cup espresso coffee

Combine sugar and water in a small saucepan. Bring to a boil over medium heat, stirring constantly. Continue to boil, brushing down sides of pan with a brush dipped in cold water, until syrup reaches the soft ball stage, or a candy thermometer registers 210°. Beat egg yolks with an electric mixer until they are combined. Add syrup in a stream and beat until cool. Beat in vanilla. Whisk mascarpone and rum together in another bowl and add to syrup mixture. Beat cream with mixer until it holds soft peaks, then fold into mascarpone mixture. Lay open ladyfingers on a baking sheet and drizzle with espresso. Line the bottom and sides of an 8-cup serving dish with 24 ladyfingers. Pour half of mascarpone mixture over ladyfingers. Top with a layer of 12 ladyfingers and layer remaining cheese mixture into dish. Chill.

Sound Bites

Heavy cream is most often labeled whipping cream in the dairy case of the grocery store.

Natchez Charlotte Russe

2 eggs, separated
½ cup sugar, divided
¼ teaspoon salt
1 cup milk, scalded
1 package unflavored gelatin
3 tablespoons sherry
1 cup whipping cream
Ladyfingers

Beat egg yolks with ¼ cup sugar and salt until sugar is dissolved. Add a small amount of scalded milk to yolks, blend thoroughly, then pour yolk mixture into milk in a saucepan. Cook over low heat, stirring constantly, until custard coats spoon. Strain. Soak gelatin in ¼ cup water for 5 minutes. Add to custard and beat well. Stir in sherry, cover and chill 30 minutes. Beat egg whites with remaining sugar until stiff but not dry. Beat cream until stiff. Fold whites and cream into custard and blend thoroughly. Line dessert dishes with halved ladyfingers. Top with custard and chill. **Serves 8.**

Low-Fat Layered Ice Cream Dessert

16 ounces chocolate syrup
1 can fat free sweetened condensed milk
¾ cup reduced fat margarine, divided
24 reduced fat chocolate sandwich cookies, crushed
½ gallon frozen vanilla yogurt, softened
1 (8-ounce) container fat free frozen whipped topping, thawed
½ cup chopped pecans

Combine syrup, condensed milk and ½ cup margarine in a medium saucepan. Bring to a boil and simmer 5 minutes. Cool completely. Melt remaining margarine and mix with crushed cookies. Spread evenly in bottom of a 9 x 13-inch glass baking dish. Chill in freezer for 30 minutes. Spread softened yogurt over crust and chill 30 more minutes. Top with cooled syrup mixture and chill 30 minutes. Spread with whipped topping and sprinkle with pecans. **Serves 12.**

Coffee Liqueur Mocha Ice Cream Pie

7 ounces sweetened flaked coconut
4 ounces pecans, finely chopped
2 tablespoons flour
½ cup butter, melted
3 pints mocha chip ice cream, softened
Whipped cream
Grated semisweet chocolate
1 cup coffee liqueur, divided

Preheat oven to 375°. Combine coconut, pecans and flour in a small bowl. Blend in butter and press mixture into bottom and up sides of a 10-inch metal pie pan. Bake until golden brown, about 10 minutes. Cool crust. Pack ice cream into crust and freeze until firm. Top with whipped cream and sprinkle with grated chocolate. Cut into wedges and pour 2 tablespoons coffee liqueur over each wedge.

Variation: *Cappuccino ice cream may be used.*

Apple Bavarian Torte

Crust:
½ cup butter, softened
⅓ cup sugar
¼ teaspoon vanilla
1 cup flour

Cheese Mixture:
1 (8-ounce) package cream cheese, softened
¼ cup sugar
1 egg, lightly beaten
½ teaspoon vanilla

Apple Mixture:
6 medium Granny Smith apples, peeled and sliced
⅓ cup sugar
½ teaspoon cinnamon
¼ cup sliced almonds

*Preheat oven to 450°. Combine butter, sugar, vanilla and flour. Press into bottom of a springform pan. Blend cream cheese and sugar in a small bowl. Beat in egg and vanilla. Pour over crust. Toss apples with sugar and cinnamon. Layer over cheese mixture. Bake 10 minutes, then reduce heat to 400°. Continue baking for 25 minutes. Sprinkle with almonds and bake until almonds are lightly browned. Cool before removing collar of pan. **Serves 12.***

Sound Bites

To add extra flavor to a fruit tart or pie, sprinkle a layer of dried coconut over the base before adding filling. This will also help prevent the base from becoming soggy.

Bread Pudding with Maple Pecan or Custard Sauce

1 small loaf French bread, cut into 1-inch cubes
3½ cups half and half
1 cup plus 2 tablespoons sugar
3 eggs
2½ teaspoons grated lemon peel
2 teaspoons vanilla
1 teaspoon freshly grated nutmeg
1½ teaspoons cinnamon
½ teaspoon salt
¾ cup golden raisins, optional

Place bread cubes in a shallow bowl and cover with half and half. Let stand 45 minutes, turning bread occasionally. Preheat oven to 325°. Whisk sugar, egg, lemon peel, vanilla, nutmeg, cinnamon and salt together. Fold into bread mixture. Add raisins, if desired. Turn into a buttered 3-quart baking dish. Bake until knife inserted in center comes out clean, about 80 minutes for a deep dish and 50 minutes for a shallow one. Serve warm with Maple Pecan or Custard Sauce.

Maple Pecan Sauce

1 cup maple syrup
1 teaspoon grated lemon peel
½ teaspoon nutmeg
2 tablespoons butter
½ cup toasted pecans

Heat syrup with lemon peel until very hot, but not boiling. Stir in remaining ingredients. Serve warm.

Custard Sauce:
½ cup butter
8 ounces brown sugar
7 ounces evaporated milk
Pinch of salt
Pinch of baking soda

Combine butter and sugar in a small saucepan. Cook over low heat until butter is melted and sugar is dissolved. Add remaining ingredients and heat until warm.

Cherry Strudel

Filling:
1¼ cups sugar
½ cup firmly packed light brown sugar
1½ tablespoons cornstarch
4 cups pitted, tart, fresh or frozen and
   thawed cherries
⅓ cup water
2 teaspoons grated lemon or orange rind
½ teaspoon vanilla or almond extract
¼ teaspoon allspice
⅛ teaspoon cinnamon

Pastry:
8 sheets phyllo pastry, thawed if frozen
3 tablespoons melted butter, divided

Topping:
1 tablespoon powdered sugar

Combine sugar, brown sugar and cornstarch in a medium saucepan. Stir in cherries, water, lemon rind and vanilla. Cook over medium heat until bubbling and thickened. Reduce heat to low, add allspice and cinnamon, and cook, stirring occasionally, for 15 minutes. Remove from heat and cool completely.

For Pastry: Preheat oven to 400°. Unfold sheets of phyllo so they lie flat. Stack 4 sheets on plastic wrap. Brush top sheet with 1 tablespoon melted butter. Cover remaining sheets with plastic wrap and a damp cloth to prevent them from drying out. Spread half of filling along a short side of top pastry sheet. Starting with short side and using plastic wrap as a guide, roll up pastry jelly-roll style. Fold ends under. Place seam-side down on a greased baking sheet. Brush with ½ tablespoon melted butter. Repeat with remaining phyllo, butter and filling to make second strudel. Bake until golden, 15 to 20 minutes. Transfer baking sheet to a wire rack to cool for 15 minutes. Transfer strudels to a cutting board to cool completely. Sprinkle with powdered sugar.

Special Pumpkin Pie

Preparing a Pumpkin from Scratch:

Cut pumpkin into 2-inch thick slices. Remove all seeds and membrane. Cut slices into 4 to 5-inch long pieces and place in a large pot. Cover with water and bring to a boil. Boil until pumpkin is soft, 25 to 35 minutes. Place in a colander to drain and cool. When cool enough to handle, scrape pulp from skin and process in a food processor until smooth. Refrigerate until ready to use.

> 2 (9-inch) unbaked pie shells
> 1 egg white, beaten
> 1⅓ cups sugar
> ¼ teaspoon salt
> 2 teaspoons cinnamon
> ½ teaspoon nutmeg
> 1 teaspoon ground ginger
> 4 eggs, lightly beaten
> 3⅓ cups milk
> 3 cups fresh pumpkin purée or
>   2 cans pumpkin pie filling

Brush pie shells with beaten egg white and bake in pre-heated 450° oven for 5 minutes. Combine sugar, salt, cinnamon, nutmeg and ginger in a large bowl. Add eggs and blend well. Pour in milk and mix well. Add pumpkin and blend. Pour into pie shells and bake 20 to 25 minutes. Reduce heat to 325° and bake until a table knife inserted in middle of pie comes out clean, about 1 hour more.

Fawn Pie

> 2 tablespoons cornmeal
> 2 tablespoons flour
> 2 cups sugar
> 4 eggs, beaten
> ½ cup melted butter
> 1 small can crushed pineapple, partially drained
> 1 small can coconut
> 1 (9-inch) unbaked pie shell

Combine cornmeal, flour and sugar in a mixing bowl. Add eggs, butter, pineapple and coconut and blend. Pour into pie shell. Bake in preheated 350° oven for 50 to 60 minutes.

German Chocolate Pie

Meringue Crust:
2 egg whites
⅛ teaspoon salt
½ cup sugar
⅛ teaspoon cream of tartar
½ cup finely chopped pecans
½ teaspoon vanilla

Filling:
1 package German sweet chocolate
3 tablespoons hot water
1 teaspoon vanilla
1 cup whipping cream, whipped

Beat egg whites in a medium bowl until foamy. Add salt and continue beating until soft peaks form. Add sugar and cream of tartar gradually, beating until mixture is very stiff. Stir in pecans and vanilla. Turn into a lightly buttered pie pan and form into a nest-like shell, building up a ½-inch edge. Bake in preheated 300° oven for 50 minutes. Remove and cool before filling.

For Filling:** Melt chocolate in top of a double boiler. Add hot water and blend. Cool slightly and stir in vanilla. Fold in whipped cream and turn into cooled meringue shell. Chill 2 hours before serving. **Serves 8.

Sound Bites

Don't have superfine sugar? Place granulated sugar in a food processor with a metal blade and process for a few seconds.

Southern Pecan Pie

3 eggs
1 cup dark corn syrup
½ cup sugar
¼ cup butter, melted
1 teaspoon vanilla
1 cup pecan halves plus enough halves
    to cover top of pie
1 (9-inch) unbaked pie shell
Vanilla ice cream, optional

Beat eggs well in a medium bowl. Add corn syrup, sugar, melted butter and vanilla. Beat until well combined. Arrange 1 cup pecan halves in bottom of pie shell. Top with egg mixture. Arrange additional pecans over top. Bake in preheated 350° oven until set, about 1 hour. Serve with vanilla ice cream, if desired.

Mocha Butter Crunch Pie

Chocolate Walnut Crust:
1 cup flour
⅓ cup firmly packed light brown sugar
¼ teaspoon salt
5 tablespoons well-chilled butter
¾ cup finely chopped walnuts
3 tablespoons finely chopped
    unsweetened chocolate
2½ tablespoons water
1 teaspoon vanilla

Mocha Butter:
1 cup unsalted butter, softened
1 cup firmly packed light brown sugar
4 teaspoons instant coffee powder
2 teaspoons vanilla
3 ounces unsweetened chocolate, melted
4 eggs

Mocha Cream Topping:
2 cups whipping cream
½ cup powdered sugar
2 tablespoons plus 1 teaspoon instant
    coffee powder
Grated semisweet chocolate

For Crust: *Preheat oven to 350°. Combine flour, sugar and salt in a large bowl. Cut in butter until mixture resembles coarse meal. Stir in nuts and chocolate with a fork. Blend in water and vanilla. Press mixture into a 9-inch glass pie plate, covering rim. Bake until golden brown and set, 15 to 20 minutes. Cool completely.*

For Butter: *Cream butter in a large bowl until light and fluffy. Beat in sugar, coffee powder and vanilla until smooth. Stir in melted chocolate. Add eggs one at a time, beating 4 minutes after each addition. Mound into crust, cover and chill several hours.*

Just before serving, whip cream with powdered sugar and coffee powder until stiff peaks form. Spoon into pastry bag fitted with star tip. Pipe large rosettes over pie, covering completely. Garnish with grated semisweet chocolate.

French Silk Pie

Meringue Crust:
2 egg whites
⅛ teaspoon salt
⅛ teaspoon cream of tartar
½ cup sugar
½ cup finely chopped pecans
½ teaspoon vanilla

Filling:
¼ pound sweet cooking chocolate or
   1 small package milk chocolate chips
3 tablespoons water
1 tablespoon brandy
1 cup whipping cream
Shaved chocolate

For Meringue Crust: *Combine egg whites, salt and cream of tartar in a mixing bowl. Beat until foamy. Add sugar 2 tablespoons at a time, beating after each addition until sugar is blended. Continue beating until stiff peaks form. Fold in nuts and vanilla. Spoon into lightly greased 8-inch pie plate, making a nest-like shell with sides ½ inch above edge of pie plate. Bake in preheated 300° oven 50 to 55 minutes. Cool completely.*

For Filling: *Place chocolate and water in a saucepan. Stir over low heat until melted. Cool. Add brandy. Whip cream until soft peaks form. Fold cooled chocolate mixture into cream. Mound in meringue shell and chill for at least 2 hours. Garnish with shaved chocolate.*

Variation: *Swirl 2 teaspoons raspberry purée or warmed raspberry jelly on serving plates and top with pie.*

Heath Bar Ice Cream Surprise

Vanilla or butter brickle ice cream
1 package Heath Bar chips
1 package frozen sweetened raspberries, thawed
   and puréed
Chocolate hard shell ice cream topping, warmed

Scoop small balls of ice cream with an ice cream scoop, working quickly, and roll in Heath Bar chips. Place in muffin tins and freeze until firm. When ready to serve, swirl 2 teaspoons raspberry purée on dessert plate. Place ice cream ball on purée and top with warmed chocolate topping.

Fresh Berry Crumb Pie

Crumb Crust and Topping:
1 cup hazelnuts or almonds (about 4 ounces)
2 cups flour
½ cup sugar
¾ cup chilled butter, cut into small pieces

Filling:
½ cup sugar
1½ tablespoons cornstarch
2 pints fresh berries (blueberries, raspberries
   and/or strawberries)

Preheat oven to 350°. Spread nuts in a medium baking pan and roast, stirring occasionally, until toasted, about 10 minutes. Turn onto a cloth towel and rub off and discard papery skins. Increase oven temperature to 450°. Process nuts in a food processor until finely ground, about 10 seconds. Turn nuts into a large bowl. Add flour and sugar and stir to combine. Cut butter into mixture with a pastry blender or 2 knives until coarse crumbs form. Using fingers, evenly press half of mixture into bottom and up sides of an 8 or 9-inch tart pan.

***For Filling:** Mix sugar and cornstarch in a medium bowl. Gently fold in berries. Spoon into crust, spreading evenly. Sprinkle with remaining crumb mixture and bake until topping is golden and filling is bubbly, about 30 minutes. Transfer to a wire rack to cool for 10 minutes. Serve warm.* **Serves 6.**

Chocolate Cherry Cake

1 package super moist chocolate fudge cake mix
1 can cherry pie filling
2 eggs
1 teaspoon almond extract
1 cup sugar
5 tablespoons butter
⅓ cup milk
1 (6-ounce) package chocolate chips

Place cake mix, pie filling, eggs and almond extract in a medium bowl and mix by hand until blended. Pour into a greased 9 x 13-inch baking pan and bake in preheated 350° oven for 40 minutes. While cake is baking, combine sugar, butter and milk in a small saucepan. Bring to a boil and boil for 1 minute. Reduce heat to low and add chocolate chips. Stir until chips are melted. Pour over hot cake.

Caramel Ice Cream Supreme

½ cup firmly packed dark brown sugar
½ cup quick cooking oatmeal
1 cup chopped pecans
1 cup margarine, melted
2 cups flour
1½ jars caramel sauce
½ gallon vanilla ice cream, softened

Combine brown sugar, oatmeal, pecans, margarine and flour in a large bowl. Mix until a cookie-like dough forms. Spread on a baking sheet and bake in preheated 400° oven for 15 minutes. Crumble with a spoon while still hot. Spread half of crumbs in bottom of 9 x 13-inch baking pan. Top with half of caramel sauce. Spread ice cream over sauce and top with remaining crumbs and sauce. Freeze. Remove from freezer 5 to 10 minutes before serving. **Serves 10 to 12.**

Sound Bites

For a perfect, golden caramel topping on crème brûlée, sprinkle the set custard with a thick layer of superfine sugar, and spray with a fine water mister. Caramelize under a hot broiler.

Chocolate Coffee Liqueur Pound Cake

1 (18½-ounce) box German chocolate
   cake mix, pudding recipe
½ cup sugar
⅓ cup vegetable oil
3 eggs
¾ cup water
¼ cup bourbon
½ cup coffee liqueur
¾ cup double-strength coffee
2 teaspoons cocoa
Dash of vanilla

Icing:
½ cup butter
1 cup sugar
⅓ cup evaporated milk
1½ cups semisweet chocolate chips

Preheat oven to 350°. Combine all cake ingredients in a large bowl and beat for 4 minutes. Bake in a greased Bundt pan for 50 minutes. Cool in pan 10 minutes, then invert onto serving dish.

For Icing: Combine butter, sugar and milk in a heavy saucepan. Bring to a boil, stirring, and heat until butter is melted and sugar is dissolved. Remove from heat, add chips and stir until chips are melted. Pour over cake.

White Chocolate Bread Pudding with White Chocolate Sauce

8 ounces French bread, cut into 1-inch pieces
3½ cups whipping cream, divided
1 cup milk (do not use low-fat or nonfat)
½ cup sugar
18 ounces good-quality white chocolate, coarsely chopped, divided
7 large egg yolks
2 large eggs

*Preheat oven to 275°. Arrange bread cubes on a baking sheet. Bake until light golden and dry, about 10 minutes. Transfer sheet to a rack and cool bread completely. Increase oven temperature to 350°. Combine 3 cups whipping cream, milk and sugar in a heavy large saucepan. Bring to simmer over medium heat, stirring until sugar dissolves. Remove from heat. Add 10 ounces white chocolate (about 1¾ cups) and stir until melted and smooth. Whisk yolks and eggs in large bowl to blend. Gradually whisk in warm chocolate mixture. Place bread cubes in a 2-quart glass baking dish. Add half of chocolate mixture. Press bread cubes into chocolate mixture and let stand 15 minutes. Gently mix in remaining chocolate mixture and cover dish with foil. Bake 45 minutes. Uncover and bake until top is golden brown, about 15 minutes. Transfer to rack and cool slightly. Can be prepared 1 day ahead. Cover and refrigerate. Rewarm covered pudding in 350° oven for 30 minutes before serving. Bring remaining ½ cup cream to simmer in heavy medium saucepan. Remove saucepan from heat and add remaining 8 ounces white chocolate. Stir until melted and smooth. Serve pudding warm with warm sauce. **Serves 6.**

Glazed Lemon Almond Pound Cake

1 cup blanched almonds
1 cup sugar
1 cup unsalted butter, softened
4 large eggs
1 tablespoon freshly grated lemon rind
1 cup flour
1 teaspoon baking powder
¼ teaspoon salt
¼ cup fresh lemon juice

Glaze:
¼ cup fresh lemon juice
2 cups powdered sugar

Garnish:
1 thin-skinned lemon, sliced ⅛-inch thick
¾ cup sugar
Or fresh lemon slices

Place almonds and sugar in food processor and grind very fine. Cream butter in a large bowl of electric mixer. Add almond mixture and beat until mixture is light and fluffy. Add eggs, one at a time, beating well after each addition. Beat in rind. Sift flour, baking powder and salt into another bowl. Add to creamed mixture alternately with lemon juice, beginning and ending with flour mixture. Blend batter after each addition. Pour into a buttered and floured 8-inch round pan with a 2-inch depth. Bake in middle of a preheated 350° oven until a tester comes out clean, about 50 minutes. Transfer pan to a rack and cool 10 minutes. Invert cake onto rack and let cool completely. May be made 3 days in advance, covered and chilled.

For Glaze: *Place lemon juice in a medium bowl. Sift sugar over it gradually, whisking, and whisk until mixture is smooth. Pour over top of cake and smooth with a spatula, letting some glaze drip down sides. Let cake stand until glaze hardens, about 1 hour. Transfer to a cake plate.*

For Garnish: *Place lemon slices in a saucepan and cover with cold water. Bring just to a boil, then drain. Repeat procedure. Turn lemon slices into a bowl. Combine ½ cup water and sugar in a saucepan. Cook over moderately low heat, stirring, until sugar is completely dissolved. Add lemon slices and simmer, partially covered, stirring occasionally, until syrup is very thick and lemon rind is translucent, about 45 minutes. Decorate cake and cake plate with the candied lemon slices or fresh lemon slices. Serve with French vanilla ice cream, if desired.*

Sound Bites

Blanched almonds means the outer skin has been removed. Do this by placing the almonds in a bowl and cover with boiling water; let the almonds sit for 1 minute. Drain, rinse under cold water, and drain again. Pat dry and slip the skin off.

Italian Love Cake

1 package marble fudge cake mix
2 (15-ounce) containers ricotta cheese
4 eggs
¾ cup sugar
1 teaspoon vanilla

Icing:
1 small box instant chocolate pudding
1 cup milk
1 (8-ounce) container frozen whipped topping, thawed

Prepare cake mix according to package directions and pour into a greased 9 x 13-inch baking pan. Combine ricotta, eggs, sugar and vanilla in a large bowl. Blend well and drop by spoonfuls evenly over batter. Bake in pre-heated 350° oven for 1 hour. Remove and cool.

For Icing: Combine pudding mix and milk in a medium bowl. Beat until thickened. Fold in whipped topping and spread over cooled cake. Refrigerate.

Pistachio Layer Cake

1 cup flour
1 cup margarine or butter, softened
1 cup chopped pecans, divided
1 (8-ounce) package cream cheese, softened
⅔ cup powdered sugar
1 container frozen whipped topping, thawed, divided
2 packages instant pistachio pudding
2 cups milk

Combine flour, butter and ½ cup pecans in a small bowl. Spread in bottom of a buttered 9 x 13-inch baking pan. Bake in preheated 350° oven for 10 minutes. Cool. Blend cream cheese and powdered sugar in a medium bowl until smooth. Fold in half of whipped topping. Spread over cooled flour mixture. Combine pudding mix and milk in a medium bowl. Beat until thickened. Pour over cream cheese mixture. Fold remaining nuts into remaining whipped topping and spread over pudding layer. Chill.

Mississippi Mud Cake

1 cup butter
½ cup cocoa
1½ cups flour
Pinch of salt
2 cups sugar
4 eggs, lightly beaten
1½ cups chopped nuts
1 teaspoon vanilla
Marshmallows (miniature)

Frosting:
⅓ cup cocoa
½ cup milk
¼ cup butter
1 (16-ounce) box powdered sugar, sifted

Place butter and cocoa in a heavy saucepan over low heat. Heat until butter is melted. Remove from heat and stir in sugar and eggs. Mix well. Add flour, salt, nuts and vanilla. Pour into a greased 9 x 13-inch baking pan and bake in preheated 350° oven until a toothpick inserted in center comes out clean, 35 to 40 minutes. Sprinkle enough marshmallows to cover warm cake.

For Frosting: *Combine cocoa, milk and butter in a saucepan and heat until butter is melted. Remove from heat and gradually beat in sugar. Continue beating until smooth. Spread over warm cake.*

Sound Bites

If granulated sugar cakes and hardens, put in a pan in moderate preheated oven, turn off the heat and let stand until it softens.

Sound Bites

To help make serving of cakes easier sprinkle the cake platter with sugar before laying down the bottom layer.

Deep South Carrot Cake

3 cups grated carrots
2 cups flour
2 cups sugar
2 teaspoons baking soda
1 teaspoon baking powder
½ teaspoon salt
1 teaspoon cinnamon
4 eggs, well beaten
1½ cups vegetable oil
1 teaspoon vanilla

Cream Cheese Frosting:
1 (16-ounce) package powdered sugar
1 (8-ounce) package cream cheese, softened
½ cup butter, softened
1 teaspoon vanilla
1 cup chopped pecans

Combine carrots, flour, sugar, baking soda, baking powder, salt and cinnamon in a large bowl. Stir in eggs, oil and vanilla and mix well. Spoon batter into 3 greased and floured 9-inch cake pans. Bake in preheated 350° oven until a toothpick inserted in center comes out clean, about 30 minutes. Cool completely before frosting.

For Frosting: Cream powdered sugar, cream cheese, butter and vanilla in a large bowl until well blended. Stir in pecans. Frost between cooled cake layers and spread over top and sides of cake.

Macadamia Fudge Torte

Cake:
1 package devil's food cake mix
1½ teaspoons cinnamon
⅓ cup vegetable oil
1 (16-ounce) can sliced pears in light syrup, drained
2 eggs
⅓ cup finely chopped macadamia nuts
2 teaspoons water

Filling:
⅓ cup low-fat sweetened condensed milk
½ cup semisweet chocolate chips

Sauce:
1 (12¼-ounce) jar caramel ice cream topping
3 tablespoons milk

Combine cake mix, cinnamon and oil in a large bowl. Blend on low speed of mixer until crumbly, about 30 seconds. The mixture will be dry. Place pears in a food processor or blender and purée until smooth. Pour into another large bowl and add 2½ cups of cake mixture and eggs. Beat on low until moistened, then 2 minutes on medium speed. Spread in bottom of a 9 or 10-inch spring-form pan which has been coated with nonstick vegetable spray.

***For Filling:** Combine milk and chips in a small saucepan over medium-low heat. Heat, stirring, until chips are melted. Drop by spoonfuls over pear mixture. Add nuts and water to remaining cake mixture and stir to combine. Sprinkle over filling. Bake in preheated 350° oven until center springs back when touched, 45 to 50 minutes. Let cool in pan for 10 minutes before removing collar. Cool at least 1½ hours before serving.*

To serve, combine caramel sauce and milk in a small saucepan. Heat over low heat until warm. Place a spoonful of sauce on each serving plate and top with torte. Serve with ice cream, if desired.

Classic Coconut Cake

1 tablespoon shortening
½ cup butter
3 eggs
1½ cups sugar
1 cup milk
1½ cups self-rising flour
1 teaspoon vanilla

Icing:
2 cups sugar
2 cups milk
½ cup butter
1 (14-ounce) package shredded coconut

Place shortening and butter in a 9 x 13-inch baking dish. Heat in a preheated 325° oven until melted, watching carefully to prevent burning. Combine eggs, sugar and milk in a large mixing bowl. Gradually add flour and combine well. Stir in vanilla. Pour melted butter mixture into bowl, leaving enough in baking dish to coat. Mix well, then return to dish. Bake until a toothpick inserted in center comes out clean, about 40 minutes.

While cake is baking, combine sugar, milk and butter in a large saucepan. Bring to a boil and stir in coconut. Remove cake from oven and pierce surface at close intervals with a fork. Pour hot icing mixture over cake, spreading coconut evenly. Serve hot or cold, refrigerating any leftovers.

Absolutely Heavenly Amaretto Cake

1 cup butter or margarine, softened
2½ cups sugar
6 large eggs
3 cups sifted cake flour
¼ teaspoon baking soda
½ teaspoon salt
1 (8-ounce) carton sour cream
2 teaspoons almond extract
1 teaspoon lemon extract
1 teaspoon orange extract
1 teaspoon vanilla
¾ cup amaretto, divided
¾ cup orange marmalade
¼ cup plus 2 tablespoons apricot preserves
½ to 1 cup chopped blanched almonds, toasted

Beat butter at medium speed with an electric mixer in a large bowl until soft and creamy, about 2 minutes. Gradually add sugar, beating at medium speed 5 to 7 minutes. Add eggs, one at a time, beating just until yellow disappears. Combine flour, baking soda and salt in a another bowl. Add to butter mixture alternately with sour cream, beginning and ending with flour mixture. Mix at low speed just until blended after each addition. Stir in flavorings and ½ cup amaretto. Pour into a greased and floured 12-cup Bundt pan. Bake in preheated 325° oven until a toothpick inserted in center comes out clean, about 1 hour and 15 minutes. Cool in pan on a wire rack 10 to 15 minutes. Remove from pan and let cool completely on rack.

Combine remaining amaretto, marmalade and preserves in a small saucepan. Cook over medium heat until marmalade and preserves melt, stirring frequently. Drizzle over cake and sprinkle with almonds.

Sound Bites

To make sour cream in a pinch – add 1 teaspoon lemon juice to ⅔ cup light cream. Stir and let stand until thickened.

Sound Bites

When you're making a dessert soufflé, sprinkle sugar over the surface of the buttered mold before you pour in the soufflé batter. This will give it a fine sweet crust.

Chocolate Chip Cheesecake

Crust:
2 cups graham cracker crumbs
¼ cup sugar
6 tablespoons butter, melted

Filling:
2¼ pounds cream cheese, softened
1⅔ cups sugar
5 eggs, room temperature
1 cup Irish cream liqueur
1 tablespoon vanilla
1 cup semisweet chocolate chips, divided

Coffee Cream:
1 cup chilled whipping cream
2 tablespoons sugar
1 teaspoon instant coffee powder
Chocolate curls

Preheat oven to 325°. Coat 9-inch springform pan with nonstick vegetable spray. Combine crumbs and sugar in pan and stir in butter. Press mixture over bottom and 1 inch up sides of pan. Bake until light brown, about 7 minutes. Remove from oven.

For Filling: *Beat cream cheese in large bowl with electric mixer until smooth. Gradually mix in sugar. Add eggs one at a time, beating well after each addition. Blend in liqueur and vanilla. Sprinkle half of chips over crust. Spoon in filling. Sprinkle with remaining chips. Bake until puffed, springy in center and golden brown, about 1 hour and 20 minutes. Cool completely.*

For Coffee Cream: *Beat cream, sugar and coffee powder until peaks form. Spread over cooled cake. Garnish with chocolate curls. Cut into thin slices to serve. **Serves 8.***

Texas Praline Cheesecake

Crust:
1 cup graham cracker crumbs
2 tablespoons sugar
¼ cup butter, melted

Filling:
3 (8-ounce) packages cream cheese, softened
¾ cup sugar
⅓ cup firmly packed brown sugar
2 tablespoons flour
1½ teaspoons vanilla
3 eggs
½ cup bottled caramel topping
½ cup chopped pecans
Additional bottled caramel topping

Praline Topping:
1 tablespoon brown sugar
1 tablespoon butter
1 tablespoon water
½ cup chopped pecans

For Crust: *Combine all ingredients in a small bowl. Spread in bottom of a 9-inch springform pan. Bake in preheated 325° oven for 10 minutes.*

For Filling: *Combine cream cheese, sugar, brown sugar, flour and vanilla in a mixing bowl. Blend until creamy. Add eggs, one at a time, mixing well after each addition. Remove 1 cup of batter to another bowl and add ½ cup caramel topping to it. Spoon half of plain batter over crust. Cover with caramel batter and sprinkle with pecans. Spread remaining plain batter over pecans. Bake in preheated 450° oven for 7 minutes. Reduce temperature to 325° and continue baking until set, 30 to 40 minutes. Cool and chill.*

For Praline Topping: *Melt brown sugar and butter in a small saucepan over medium-low heat. Add water and bring to a boil. Add pecans and cook 2 minutes, stirring constantly. Spread on wax paper and cool until it hardens enough to be removed.*

Brush top of cooled cake with caramel sauce and garnish with praline topping.

Sound Bites

Lemons will yield nearly twice the amount of juice if they are dropped into hot water a few minutes before squeezing.

Almond Sour Cream Cheesecake

Crust:
2 cups graham cracker crumbs
½ cup blanched almonds
⅓ cup sugar
½ cup unsalted butter, softened

Filling:
3 (8-ounce) packages cream cheese, softened
½ cup sugar
2 teaspoons fresh lemon juice
½ teaspoon vanilla
1 teaspoon almond extract
2 tablespoons amaretto
3 eggs

Topping:
1 (8-ounce) container sour cream
1 tablespoon sugar
2 tablespoons amaretto
½ cup slivered blanched almonds, toasted

Preheat oven to 375°. Combine cracker crumbs, almonds and sugar in a food processor. Add butter and process thoroughly. Press into an 8½-inch springform pan, covering bottom and halfway up sides.

For Filling: Combine cream cheese, sugar, and flavorings in a food processor. Cream thoroughly. Add eggs and process until well blended. Pour into crust and bake until top has just begun to crack, 45 to 50 minutes. Remove from oven and cool for several minutes. Reduce oven temperature to 350°.

For Topping: Stir sour cream, sugar and amaretto together in a bowl. Spoon over cheesecake. Return to oven and bake 20 more minutes. Sprinkle with toasted almonds and cool completely. Refrigerate 4 hours before serving. **Serves 8 to 10.**

Fresh Apple Cake with Butter Sauce

2 cups sugar
½ cup vegetable oil
2 eggs
4 to 5 Granny Smith apples, peeled and chopped
2 cups flour
1 teaspoon baking soda
1 teaspoon cinnamon

Butter Sauce:
½ cup butter
1 cup sugar
½ cup whipping cream
1½ teaspoons vanilla

Preheat oven to 350°. Combine sugar, oil and eggs in a large bowl. Stir in apples. Add dry ingredients and mix to blend. Pour into a greased 9 x 13-inch baking pan. Bake until a toothpick inserted in center comes out clean, about 45 minutes.

For sauce, combine all ingredients in top of a double boiler. Cook, stirring frequently, until thickened. Serve warm with cake.

Lemon Ginger Cookies

2 cups firmly packed light brown sugar
1 cup shortening
2 teaspoons lemon extract
2 eggs
3 cups flour
2 teaspoons baking soda
2 teaspoons cream of tartar
¼ teaspoon ginger
½ teaspoon cinnamon
1 teaspoon salt
Sugar

Cream together brown sugar, shortening, extract and eggs in a large mixing bowl. Combine flour, baking soda, cream of tartar, ginger, cinnamon and salt in another bowl. Gradually beat into sugar mixture and blend well. The batter will be stiff. Form into balls and roll in sugar. (Use red or green sugar at Christmas time.) Place on baking sheets and bake in preheated 375° oven for 10 to 12 minutes. **Yield: 10½ dozen cookies.**

Best White Chocolate Butterscotch Cookies

2½ cups flour
1 teaspoon baking soda
¼ teaspoon salt
1 cup unsalted butter, softened
1½ cups firmly packed dark brown sugar
2 large eggs
1 tablespoon light molasses
2 teaspoons vanilla
1 cup chopped pecans
¾ cup butterscotch pieces
¾ cup white chocolate pieces

Preheat oven to 300°. Combine flour, baking soda and salt in a medium bowl. Beat butter and brown sugar together in a large bowl until smooth and creamy. Add eggs, molasses and vanilla and beat well for 1 minute. Gradually beat in flour mixture on low speed. Stir in remaining ingredients. Drop dough by rounded tablespoons 2 inches apart on ungreased baking sheets. Bake until set, 17 to 18 minutes. Transfer cookies to a wire rack to cool. **Yield: 3 to 4 dozen cookies.**

Italian Anise Cookies

9 eggs, room temperature
2¼ cups sugar
1 tablespoon almond extract
1½ ounces anise liqueur
4 cups flour
2 teaspoons anise seed
Grated lemon rind

Beat eggs in a large bowl until well blended. Gradually add sugar and mix well. Add almond extract and anise and blend well. Gradually add flour. Continue beating until thoroughly mixed. Add anise seed and lemon rind. Turn into a 9 x 13-inch baking pan which has been coated with nonstick spray. Bake in preheated 375° oven until golden brown, 20 to 30 minutes. Cool, then cut down length of pan. Cut again into 2-inch slices.

Butter Pecan Turtle Cookies

Crust:
2 cups flour
1 cup firmly packed brown sugar
½ cup butter, softened
1 cup whole pecans

Caramel Layer:
⅔ cup butter
½ cup firmly packed brown sugar
1 cup milk chocolate chips

Preheat oven to 350°. Combine flour, brown sugar and butter in a mixing bowl. Beat at medium speed for 2 to 3 minutes, scraping often, until well mixed and particles are fine. Pat firmly into ungreased 9 x 13-inch baking pan. Sprinkle evenly with pecans.

Combine butter and brown sugar in a heavy medium saucepan. Cook over medium heat, stirring constantly, until entire surface of mixture begins to boil. Boil 30 seconds to 1 minute, stirring constantly. Pour over pecans. Bake in center of oven until caramel layer is bubbly and crust is golden brown. Remove from oven and sprinkle with chips. Swirl chips as they melt, leaving some whole. Cool and cut into bars.

Sound Bites

If baking sheets are greased too heavily or cookie dough is warm, the cookies will spread; work with cold dough.

Salted Nut Bars

3 cups flour
1½ cups firmly packed brown sugar
½ teaspoon salt
1 cup plus 2 tablespoons butter or margarine, softened, divided
2 cups chopped mixed nuts
½ cup light corn syrup
1 teaspoon water
6 ounces butterscotch chips

Preheat oven to 350°. Mix flour, brown sugar, salt and 1 cup butter in a large bowl. Blend well and press into an ungreased 11 x 17-inch jelly roll pan. Bake for 10 to 12 minutes. Sprinkle with nuts. Place remaining butter and remaining ingredients in a saucepan. Bring to a boil, and boil 2 minutes, stirring constantly. Pour over nuts. Bake an additional 10 to 12 minutes. Cool and cut into bars.
Yield: 4 dozen bars.

Pecan Pie Bars

Better than pecan pie!

1¼ cups butter, softened, divided
1½ cups sugar, divided
3 cups flour
½ teaspoon salt
4 eggs, lightly beaten
1½ cups light or dark corn syrup
2 teaspoons vanilla
2½ cups coarsely chopped pecans

Beat 1 cup butter and ½ cup sugar in large bowl of mixer at medium speed until creamy. Blend in flour and salt at low speed until mixture resembles coarse crumbs. Press dough firmly onto bottom of a lightly greased 10½ x 15½-inch jelly roll pan. Bake in preheated 350° oven until light golden on edges, about 25 minutes. Melt remaining butter in a small saucepan. Whisk eggs, corn syrup, remaining sugar, melted butter and vanilla in a large bowl until well blended. Stir in pecans and pour mixture evenly over hot crust. Bake until filling is firm around edges, about 25 more minutes. Remove to a wire rack and let cool in pan. When completely cool, cut into bars. **Yield: 5 dozen bars.**

Easy Microwave Toffee

¾ to 1 cup finely chopped pecans, divided
½ cup butter
1 cup sugar
½ teaspoon salt
¼ cup water
¾ to 1 cup milk chocolate chips

Grease a 9-inch circle on a cookie sheet. Sprinkle ½ cup pecans evenly over circle. Grease top 2 inches of a 2½-quart glass bowl with butter. Place remaining butter in bowl. Add sugar, salt and water. Do not stir. Microwave on high until mixture just begins to turn light brown, 9 to 11 minutes. Remove from microwave and pour over pecan circle. Sprinkle with chocolate chips and let stand 1 minute. Spread chips over sugar mixture and sprinkle with remaining pecans. Chill until firm. Break into bite-size pieces and store in airtight containers. **Yield: 1 pound candy.**

Toffee-Topped Bars

2 cups firmly packed brown sugar
2 cups flour
½ cup butter or margarine, softened
1 teaspoon baking powder
½ teaspoon salt
1 teaspoon vanilla
1 cup milk
1 egg
1 cup semisweet chocolate chips
½ cup chopped walnuts
½ cup unsweetened flaked coconut, optional

Preheat oven to 350°. Combine brown sugar and flour in a large mixing bowl. Cut in the butter with a pastry cutter or 2 knives until mixture resembles coarse crumbs. Remove 1 cup of mixture and set aside. Add baking powder and salt to mixture in large bowl. Lightly beat in vanilla, milk and egg with a fork. Continue beating until a smooth batter forms. Pour into a lightly greased 9 x 13-inch baking pan. Combine chocolate chips and nuts in a small bowl. Fold in coconut, if desired. Sprinkle reserved crumb mixture over batter. Sprinkle with chip and walnut mixture. Spread topping evenly with a long flat spatula. Bake until a toothpick inserted in center comes out clean, about 35 minutes. Transfer to a wire rack and cool in pan completely before slicing. Cut into 24 bars with a serrated knife. Store in airtight container for up to 5 days. **Yield: 2 dozen bars.**

Scottish Shortbread Triangles

5½ to 6 cups flour, divided
1¼ cups sugar
2 cups cold butter
Sugar

Preheat oven to 325°. Sift 5 cups flour and sugar together in a large bowl three times. Cut butter into flour mixture until mixture resembles coarse meal. Turn onto floured board and knead well, adding ½ to 1 cup additional flour until dough begins to crack. Roll out ⅜-inch thick and cut into 3-inch triangles. Place on a buttered baking sheet which has been covered with buttered parchment paper. Bake until golden, about 20 minutes. Do not overbake. Remove from oven to a wire rack and sprinkle with sugar. **Yield: about 100 cookies.**

Sound Bites

Make sure oven is fully heated before baking – preheat at least 15 minutes. Using an oven thermometer can be helpful, as the precise temperature is crucial when baking.

Coffee Liqueur Squares

Crust:
1½ cups graham cracker crumbs
1 cup chopped pecans
3 tablespoons coffee liqueur

Filling:
½ cup melted butter
¼ cup sugar
⅓ cup cocoa
1 egg
½ teaspoon vanilla

Frosting:
6 tablespoons butter or margarine, softened
1¾ cups powdered sugar
1 tablespoon whipping cream
3 tablespoons coffee liqueur

Combine all crust ingredients and press into bottom of a greased 8-inch square baking pan. Combine filling ingredients in a heavy saucepan. Cook over low heat, stirring, until thick, 3 to 4 minutes. Pour over crust. Cover and chill in refrigerator.

For Frosting: *Combine all ingredients in a small mixing bowl. Beat on medium to high speed for 3 to 4 minutes, until smooth. Spread over chilled chocolate mixture. Chill until set. Cut into small squares to serve.*

Sweetheart Fudge

3 cups sugar
⅔ cup cocoa
⅛ teaspoon salt
1½ cups milk
¼ cup butter or margarine
1 teaspoon vanilla

Combine sugar, cocoa, salt and milk in a heavy saucepan. Bring to a rapid boil over medium heat, stirring constantly. Stop stirring when it starts to boil. Cook without stirring until candy thermometer reaches 210° (the soft ball stage). Remove from heat and add butter and vanilla without stirring. Cool to 110°, then beat with a spoon until fudge thickens and begins to lose its gloss. Immediately spread into a buttered 8-inch square pan. Cool and cut into 1-inch squares. **Yield: about 5 dozen pieces.**

Louisiana Sin-de-Bars

Crust:
½ cup butter
½ cup sugar
5 tablespoons cocoa
1 teaspoon vanilla
1 egg, beaten
1½ cups graham cracker crumbs
1 cup chopped walnuts

Filling:
2 cups powdered sugar
½ cup butter, softened
3 tablespoons powdered instant vanilla pudding
2 tablespoons milk

Icing:
1 (6-ounce) package semisweet chocolate chips
1 tablespoon butter

For Crust: *Combine butter, sugar, cocoa and vanilla in a medium saucepan. Cook over medium heat, stirring, until sugar is dissolved. Add egg and mix well. Add crumbs and nuts. Press into a greased 9 x 12-inch pan, cover and chill.*

For Filling: *Combine all filling ingredients in a large bowl and beat until thickened. Pour over crust. Place chips and butter in a small saucepan. Cook over low heat, stirring, until chips are melted. Spread over filling. Cool 30 minutes, cut into serving pieces and refrigerate until ready to serve.*

Coconut Diamonds with Lemon Icing

Sound Bites

To toast nuts –

In a skillet:
Toast almonds,
whole, sliced,
or slivered in
1 tablespoon of
melted butter for
each cup of nuts
over the lowest
possible heat. Toss
continuously to
prevent burning.
Depending on the
size of the pieces,
almonds will take
anywhere from
30 to 35 minutes
to toast.

In the oven:
Preheat the oven
to 300°. Toast the
nuts on a baking
sheet until nicely
browned.
Almonds may
take as long as
1 hour; check the
pine nuts after
30 minutes.

Dough:
½ cup butter, softened
½ cup firmly packed brown sugar
½ teaspoon salt
1 cup flour

Filling:
2 eggs
1 teaspoon vanilla
1 cup firmly packed brown sugar
2 tablespoons flour
½ teaspoon salt
1 (3½-ounce) can flaked coconut
1 cup chopped walnuts

Lemon Icing:
3 tablespoons margarine, softened
1 to 1½ cups powdered sugar
Splash of lemon juice

For Crust: *Cream together butter, brown sugar and salt in a small mixing bowl. Stir in flour. Pat dough into ungreased 9 x 13-inch pan and bake in preheated 350° oven until golden brown, 10 to 12 minutes.*

For Filling: *While crust is baking, beat eggs in a large bowl. Add vanilla and mix. Gradually add brown sugar, beating just until blended. Add flour and salt. Stir in coconut and nuts. Spread over baked crust. Return to oven and bake until a toothpick inserted in center comes out clean, 20 to 25 minutes. Cool.*

For Icing: *Combine all ingredients in a small bowl. Beat until smooth. Spread over cooled filling and cut into squares.*

Candy Bar Brownies

4 large eggs, lightly beaten
2 cups sugar
¾ cup butter, melted
2 teaspoons vanilla
1½ cups flour
½ teaspoon baking powder
¼ teaspoon salt
⅓ cup cocoa
4 (2.07-ounce) Snickers or other chocolate coated caramel-peanut nougat bars, coarsely chopped
3 (1.55-ounce) milk chocolate bars, finely chopped

*Combine eggs, sugar, butter and vanilla in a large bowl. Blend well. Combine flour, baking powder, salt and cocoa in another bowl. Stir into sugar mixture. Fold in chopped nougat bars. Spoon into a greased and floured 9 x 13-inch baking pan. Sprinkle with chopped milk chocolate. Bake in preheated 350° oven for 30 to 35 minutes. Do not overbake. Cool and cut into squares. The brownies will be chewy. **Yield: 2½ dozen.***

Sound Information

Mission Statement
of the Memphis
Oral School for the
Deaf:
to provide early
identification,
amplification, and
intervention, thus
enabling the deaf,
and hearing
impaired children
to develop their
maximum
potential;
to provide young
deaf and hearing
impaired children
with the opportunity
to learn to use any
degree of residual
hearing they may
have in the
development of
speech and
language; to assist
these children in
becoming a part
of, rather than
apart from, a world
of sound.

Crème de Menthe Brownies

1 cup sugar
½ cup butter, softened
4 eggs, beaten
1 cup flour
½ teaspoon salt
1 (6-ounce) can chocolate syrup
1 teaspoon vanilla

Filling:
2 cups powdered sugar
½ cup butter, softened
2 tablespoons crème de menthe

Glaze:
1 (6-ounce) package chocolate chips
1 tablespoon butter

Preheat oven to 350°. Cream sugar and butter in a medium bowl. Add eggs and blend well. Add flour, salt, syrup and vanilla. Mix well. Pour into a greased 9 x 13-inch pan and bake 20 to 25 minutes. Remove to a wire rack and cool.

Beat filling ingredients in a small bowl until smooth and well blended. Spread over brownies. Melt glaze ingredients in a small saucepan over low heat, stirring. Remove from heat and let cool until a spreading consistency. Spread over mint layer and chill. Cut into squares to serve.

Chocolate Truffles

1 (6-ounce) package semisweet chocolate chips
¼ cup butter
3 tablespoons whipping cream
1 egg yolk, beaten
3 tablespoons liqueur
1½ pounds dipping chocolate
2 tablespoons shortening
Candy sprinkles or chopped nuts

Place chocolate chips, butter and whipping cream in a heavy medium saucepan. Cook over low heat, stirring constantly, until chips are melted. Continue cooking and stirring until mixture is smooth and glossy, about 5 minutes. Remove from heat. Stir a little of chocolate mixture into egg yolk and blend. Return to pan and cook over medium heat, stirring, until it begins to thicken, about 4 minutes. Transfer to a mixing bowl and stir in liqueur. Cover and refrigerate for 1 hour, stirring every 15 minutes. Beat with a mixer until fluffy, then chill 10 more minutes. Drop by teaspoonfuls onto a wax paper-lined baking sheet. Chill 20 minutes. Melt dipping chocolate and shortening together over low heat in a medium saucepan. Dip chilled candy into mixture quickly and place on wax paper-lined cookie sheet. Decorate with sprinkles or nuts. May roll truffles in cocoa or powdered sugar if desired, instead of dipping.

Kids in the Kitchen

Kitchen Safety–

Young children require careful supervision in the kitchen.
Sharp knives, hot pans and electrical appliances can be dangerous
if used or handled incorrectly. Children should be properly supervised
and instructed in the correct use of kitchen utensils and appliances.

Kids in the Kitchen

Have You Heard ...

...about The Memphis Oral School for the Deaf (MOSD)

"If you knew all the joy I feel in being able to speak to you today, I think you would have some idea of the value of speech to the deaf."

—Helen Keller 1896

The Memphis Oral School for the Deaf (MOSD), a non-profit, nationally recognized program, serves deaf and hearing-impaired children in Memphis and the Mid-South. Founded in 1959, the school is accredited by the Tennessee State Department of Education and is affiliated with the Alexander Graham Bell Association for the Deaf as well as OPTION, an international organization of auditory-oral schools. As its name implies, the MOSD utilizes "oral" instructional methods for the purpose of developing speech and language skills. No sign language is used. The common goals for every young student at the school are to LISTEN, to LEARN and to SPEAK.

"When we first learned about our son's deafness, the audiologist informed us of the Memphis Oral School and its success in helping deaf children learn to speak. After our initial meeting at the school, our hopes and dreams were once again alive that our son would be able to communicate verbally. For the three years that our son attended MOSD, and during his continued speech/language therapy from the school, we have been blessed to see our son verbally progress beyond our expectations. We will never forget the day we were told that our son was ready to be mainstreamed. That goal was achieved in less time than anticipated. Strange as it may seem, we were sad to leave the school and its warm and protective environment."

—MOSD graduate's parent

It is known that 95% of all deaf children have some degree of residual or usable hearing. Through early identification, amplification and intervention, the MOSD expert faculty is able to teach these children to listen and to speak. For the remaining 5% of deaf children who do not evidence any residual hearing, there now exists cochlear implant surgery which brings sound to these deaf children for the first time in their lives. A number of MOSD students have benefited from this procedure.

"We see such wonderful progress in our grandson since he is back in school. For the first time, he sounded out 'I love you' to me. Needless to say, it brought tears to my eyes and joy to my heart. I thank God every day for your wonderful school and the amazing work you do with our children."

—MOSD student's grandparent

Jason's French Toast

1 egg
½ teaspoon sugar
¼ teaspoon cinnamon
1 slice bread
Powdered sugar
Syrup

Beat egg in a cereal bowl. Add sugar and cinnamon and mix well. Dip bread in egg mixture, turning until well coated. Place bread on a microwave-safe plate. Pour remaining egg mixture on top. Microwave 1 minute on high. Sprinkle with powdered sugar and top with syrup.

Homemade Donuts

1 (10-count) package refrigerated
    buttermilk biscuits
Shortening
1 cup powdered sugar
2 tablespoons milk

*Flatten each biscuit and cut a hole in the middle with your thumb. Melt enough shortening in a deep frying pan to reach a depth of 3 inches. Heat over medium to medium-low heat. Drop donuts and dough from holes into hot grease and cook until brown on both sides. Remove to a draining rack. Combine powdered sugar and milk to make a glaze. Drizzle over slightly cooled donuts. Serve hot. **Yield: 10 donuts.***

Note: *This recipe should only be prepared with adult supervision.*

Granola-Cinnamon Toast Spread

¾ cup granola
½ cup peanut butter
½ teaspoon cinnamon
8 slices toast

Mix granola, peanut butter and cinnamon in a small bowl with a wooden spoon. Spread 2 tablespoons on each slice of toast. Another method of preparation is to spread 2 tablespoons on untoasted bread and broil 3 inches from heat until spread is bubbly and light brown, about 2 minutes.

Sound Bites

I bought Jason a kid's microwave cookbook when he was 11 years old. He decided the original recipe needed sugar, cinnamon and powdered sugar. I still have the cookbook with his handwritten notes. I hope to pass it on to his child some day.
– Jason's Mom

Miss Cindy's Candle Salad

Sliced canned pineapple
Lettuce leaves
Bananas
Whole maraschino cherries

Place a pineapple slice on lettuce leaves on an individual serving plate to form the candle holder. Cut banana in half horizontally. Place half of banana, cut-side down, in pineapple to make the candle. Fasten a cherry on top of the banana with a toothpick to make the flame.

Celery Boats

Celery stalks
Peanut butter
Cheese spread
Cheddar or American cheese slices

Wash celery stalks and cut into 3 to 4-inch lengths. Fill centers with choice of peanut butter or cheese spread. Cut cheese slices into triangles and attach to celery with toothpicks to form sails.

Macaroni and Cheese Pizza

1 (7¼-ounce) macaroni and cheese dinner
2 eggs
1 (8-ounce) can tomato sauce
1 (4-ounce) can sliced mushrooms, drained
¼ cup chopped onion
¼ cup chopped green bell pepper
1 teaspoon oregano
1 teaspoon basil
1 cup pepperoni slices
4 ounces shredded mozzarella cheese

Prepare macaroni and cheese according to package directions. Add eggs and mix well. Spread on well-greased 12-inch pizza pan. Bake in preheated 375° oven for 10 minutes. Combine tomato sauce, mushrooms, onion, green pepper and seasonings. Spoon over macaroni mixture. Top with pepperoni and sprinkle with cheese. Bake 10 more minutes. **Serves 4.**

Blender Applesauce by MOSD Kids

3 apples
¼ cup honey
Cinnamon to taste
2 tablespoons water

Peel and core apples; cut into small pieces. Place apples in blender with remaining ingredients and blend until smooth. **Serves 4 to 6.**

MOSD Grape Juice Jelly

2 cups bottled grape juice
4 cups sugar
1 (3-ounce) package liquid fruit pectin
2 tablespoons water

Combine all ingredients and stir until sugar is dissolved. Pour into a lidded container, seal and allow it to remain at room temperature overnight. Refrigerate the following day. For firmer jelly, chill several days before serving. Jelly will keep in refrigerator up to 3 weeks.

Tasty Hamburger Patties

1½ pounds ground beef
1½ cups Kix cereal, crushed
1 egg
¼ cup milk
1 small onion, finely chopped
1 tablespoon prepared horseradish
1 tablespoon ketchup
1½ teaspoons salt
⅛ teaspoon pepper

Combine all ingredients in a large bowl. Shape into 6 patties, about 1 inch thick.

To broil, preheat broiler. Broil 3 inches from heat until desired doneness, 5 to 7 minutes per side for medium.

To charcoal broil, place on grill about 4 inches from medium hot coals. Cook until desired doneness, 7 to 8 minutes per side for medium. **Yield: 6.**

Sound Bites

Creative Dough

Very soft and easy to work with. My 3 year old grand-daughter loves this.

1 cup flour

2 teaspoons cream of tartar

1 cup water

1 tablespoon vegetable oil

1 teaspoon vanilla, if you like

About 15 drops of your favorite food color.

Cook all ingredients over medium heat, stirring real hard, about 4 minutes or until mixture forms a ball.

Remove from saucepan and let stand on counter 5 minutes.

Knead dough about 30 seconds or until it is smooth and blended. Cool completely. Store in airtight container in refrigerator.

John Willingham's Bologna Sandwich

This sandwich is without question my very — well, almost my very favorite of all my favorite sandwiches. Don't push down on the top of the sandwich once you close it — it will respond much like a greased watermelon: the harder you squeeze the harder it is to hold it in the proper position. Be sure to have lots of napkins, and a bag of potato chips completes the culinary experience. Trust me! Try this mother of all sandwiches!

- 1 hamburger bun
- 1 tablespoon mayonnaise
- 1 tablespoon creamy peanut butter
- 2 slices bologna
- 1 thin slice tomato (about ¼-inch thick)
- 1 slice onion (about ¼-inch thick)
- 1 slice Cheddar cheese or longhorn cheese

Spread one half of the hamburger bun with mayonnaise and the other with peanut butter. Lay a slice of bologna on each. Lay the tomato slice on one side and the onion slice on the other. Lay the cheese over the onion. Close the sandwich and serve immediately.

Mock Turtle Soup

- 2 medium potatoes
- 3 stalks celery
- 1 small onion
- 2 carrots
- Salt
- 2 cups water
- 2 tablespoons grated Cheddar cheese
- 3 cups milk

Wash vegetables and cut into bite-size pieces. Place in a large saucepan with salt to taste and the water. Bring to a boil, reduce heat, cover and simmer until tender, about 35 minutes. Add cheese and stir to melt. Add milk and a little more water if soup is too thick. Heat on low until warm and serve. **Serves 3 to 4.**

Meal in a Coffee Can

Great dad and kid camping out dinner. Our son loved to go on overnight canoe trips and cook beside the river.

Butter
1 (1 pound) empty coffee can
Hamburger patty
1 baking apple, cored
2 peppermint or cinnamon sticks
2 tablespoons sugar
1 potato, cubed
1 carrot, cut in strips
1 small onion, chopped
Salt and pepper to taste

Place a pat of butter in bottom of coffee can. Top with hamburger patty. Stuff apple with candy, a pat of butter and sugar. Wrap securely in foil. Place on top of patty. Place vegetables around apple. Season to taste with salt and pepper. Seal can with foil and bury in hot coals for 1 to 2 hours. **Serves 1.**

Hot Doggies

4 hot dogs
¼ cup apricot preserves
1 tablespoon prepared mustard

Puncture hot dogs with fork. Cut each hot dog into 8 pieces and place on microwaveable plate. Combine preserves and mustard. Pour over hot dogs. Microwave on high 2 minutes. Serve hot with toothpicks. **Serves 4.**

MOSD – Miss Kristen's Mudpies

1 (8-ounce) container frozen whipped topping, thawed
Shaved chocolate bars or chocolate sandwich cookie crumbs
1 small package gummy worms

Combine topping and chocolate in a medium bowl. Fold in worms. Serve in cups or bowls.

Sound Bites

Finger Paint

⅓ cup cornstarch

3 tablespoons sugar

2 cups cold water

Food color

Mix cornstarch, sugar and water in 1-quart saucepan.

Cook and stir over medium heat about 5 minutes or until thickened; remove from heat.

Divide the mixture into separate cups or containers. Tint mixture in each container with a different food color. Stir several times until cool. Store in airtight container. (The paint works best if you use it the same day you make it.)

Banana Split Brownie Pizza

1 (20-ounce) package brownie mix
12 ounces cream cheese, softened
⅔ cup sugar
1 (8-ounce) can crushed pineapple, drained
1 medium banana, sliced
6 to 8 fresh strawberries, halved
½ cup chopped nuts
Chocolate syrup
Frozen whipped topping, thawed

Prepare brownie mix according to package directions. Spread on a pizza pan which has been lined with parchment paper and bake as directed. Cool. Combine cream cheese and sugar and beat until smooth. Spread over cooled brownie crust. Top with pineapple. Arrange banana slices and strawberries over pineapple and sprinkle with nuts. Drizzle with syrup and garnish with whipped topping.

Sparkled Painted Sugar Cookies

1 cup butter or margarine, softened
2 cups sugar
2 eggs
2 teaspoons vanilla extract
4 cups flour, sifted
2 teaspoons baking powder
½ teaspoon salt
1 pint whipping cream, divided
Assorted food coloring

Cream butter and sugar in a large bowl until light and fluffy. Add eggs one at a time, mixing well after each addition. Add vanilla. Sift flour, baking powder and salt together in another bowl. Add to butter mixture and blend well. Shape dough into a ball, wrap in plastic wrap and refrigerate one hour. Dust work surface with flour and sugar. Place dough on prepared surface and roll to ¼-inch thickness. Cut into shapes with cookie cutters and lift with spatula to place on cookie sheet. Bake in a preheated 375° oven until lightly browned, 10 to 12 minutes. Cool completely before frosting. Pour cream into as many small bowls as needed for desired colors. Add food coloring to get colors you want. Paint over cookies with a clean paint brush. **Yield: 2 dozen cookies.**

Peanut Butter Pizza

½ cup margarine or butter, softened
½ cup peanut butter
½ cup firmly packed brown sugar
⅓ cup sugar
1 egg
1 teaspoon vanilla
1 cup flour
½ cup semisweet chocolate chips
½ cup peanut butter chips
¾ cup tiny marshmallows
⅔ cup peanuts
½ cup miniature candy-coated semisweet
    chocolate pieces

Cream margarine and peanut butter in a medium bowl with mixer on medium to high speed for 30 seconds. Beat in sugars, egg and vanilla on low speed until well blended. Gradually add flour. Spread dough evenly on an ungreased 12 or 13-inch pizza pan. Bake in preheated 350° oven until golden, 15 to 18 minutes. Remove from oven and sprinkle with chocolate and peanut butter chips. Let stand 1 to 2 minutes, until softened. Spread melted pieces over crust with a spatula. Top with remaining ingredients. Return to oven and bake until marshmallows are golden, about 5 minutes. Cool in pan on wire rack. **Serves 12.**

Sound Bites

*Peanut Butter
Pizza is fun to
make
when a
friend comes
to play.*

Twinkie Cake

1 box Twinkies
1 can sweetened condensed milk
2 to 3 bananas, sliced
1 (15-ounce) can crushed pineapple, undrained
1 (12-ounce) container frozen whipped topping,
    thawed
½ cup chopped nuts
½ cup shredded coconut
1 small jar cherries

Layer Twinkies in a 9 x 13-inch baking pan. Pour condensed milk over them. Arrange banana slices over milk. Spread pineapple, with juice, over top. Cover with whipped topping and garnish with nuts, coconut and cherries. Refrigerate.

Looks-Like-a-Big-Burger Cake

1 box golden pound cake mix
2 tablespoons cocoa
2 tablespoons red fruit preserves
1 tablespoon sesame seed

Frosting:
½ cup margarine
1 cup firmly packed brown sugar
¼ cup milk
2 cups powdered sugar

Preheat oven to 300°. Prepare cake mix according to package directions. Pour batter into a 1½-quart casserole dish which has been coated with nonstick vegetable spray and dusted with flour. Bake until a toothpick inserted in center comes out clean, 1 hour to 1 hour and 15 minutes. Cool on wire rack 10 minutes. Invert onto a cutting board and continue cooling.

For Frosting: Fill an 8-inch square pan about a third of way to top with cold water and ice cubes. Melt margarine in a 2-quart saucepan over low heat. Stir in brown sugar. Cook 2 minutes, stirring occasionally. Add milk and heat to a rolling boil, stirring constantly. Remove from heat. Set saucepan in the pan of cold water. Gradually stir in powdered sugar. Beat with a wooden spoon until thick enough to spread.

To Assemble Cake: Cut cake in 3 layers horizontally. Frost bottom layer with frosting. Remove ⅓ cup of remaining frosting and place in a small bowl. Add cocoa and stir to combine. If frosting seems too stiff, add ½ teaspoon water. Place middle section of cake over bottom layer and frost with chocolate frosting. Drizzle sides with preserves to look like ketchup. Place rounded layer on top and frost top layer only with remaining frosting. Sprinkle with sesame seeds.

Easy Chocolate Pie

1 large milk chocolate bar
1 (8-ounce) container frozen whipped topping, thawed
1 prepared graham cracker crust

Melt candy bar in top of double boiler. Remove from heat and cool. Fold in topping and pour into crust. It's ready to eat! **Serves 6.**

Tyler's Favorite Cherry Crunch

1 (15-ounce) can cherry pie filling
1 teaspoon lemon juice
1 box white cake mix
½ cup butter or margarine, softened
1 cup chopped nuts
Vanilla ice cream

Spread pie filling in bottom of an 8-inch square baking pan. Drizzle with lemon juice. Combine dry cake mix, butter and nuts. Spread over filling. Bake in preheated 350° oven for 45 minutes. Serve with ice cream on top.

Microwave Peanut Brittle

1 cup sugar
½ cup white corn syrup
1 cup roasted, salted peanuts
1 teaspoon butter or margarine
1 teaspoon vanilla
1 teaspoon baking soda

Combine sugar and syrup in a 1½-quart casserole dish. Microwave on high 4 minutes. Stir in peanuts and microwave on high until light brown, about 4 minutes. Add butter and vanilla and blend well. Microwave on high 1½ minutes more. Peanuts should be lightly browned and syrup very hot. Add baking soda and stir gently until light and foamy. Pour onto lightly greased baking sheet and let cool 30 minutes to 1 hour. When cool, break into small pieces and store in an airtight container. **Makes 1 pound.**

Microwave Caramel Corn

1 cup firmly packed light brown sugar
½ cup butter
¼ cup white corn syrup
½ teaspoon salt
½ teaspoon baking soda
3 to 4 quarts popped popcorn

Combine brown sugar, butter, syrup and salt in a 2-quart glass bowl. Microwave on high until boiling, then cook on high 2 minutes more. Remove from microwave and add baking soda. Stir until thick and fluffy. Place popped corn in a brown paper bag. Pour syrup over corn, close bag and shake well.

Surprise Cupcakes

1 chocolate cake mix
1 egg, beaten
⅓ cup sugar
⅛ teaspoon salt
1 (8-ounce) package cream cheese, softened
1 (6-ounce) package chocolate chips

Prepare cake according to package directions. Fill greased and floured muffin tins half full. Combine remaining ingredients and blend well. Place 1 teaspoon of mixture in each muffin cup. Bake as directed on package.

Cracker Brittle

40 saltine crackers
1 cup butter or margarine
1 (12-ounce) package semisweet chocolate chips
¼ to ½ cup chopped pecans, optional

Line a baking sheet with foil and cover with crackers. Melt butter in a small sauce pan over medium high heat. Stir in sugar and boil for 3 minutes. Pour over crackers. Bake in preheated 400° oven for 5 minutes. Sprinkle with chips and let stand 5 minutes. Spread softened chips with a knife. Sprinkle with pecans, if desired. Refrigerate until firm, then break apart or peel off foil and cut into squares.

Hot Chocolate

⅓ cup sugar
⅓ cup cocoa
¼ teaspoon salt
½ teaspoon cinnamon
1½ cups half and half
4½ cups milk
Cinnamon sticks

Combine sugar, cocoa, salt and cinnamon in a saucepan. Stir in half and half and milk. Cook over low heat, stirring constantly, until thoroughly heated. Whip hot chocolate with an electric mixer or rotary beater until foamy. Pour into mugs and serve with cinnamon stick stirrer.

Firecracker Soda

1 (6-ounce) can frozen grape juice concentrate,
  thawed
4 cups lemon-lime soda
1 pint vanilla ice cream

Pour concentrate into a pitcher. Stir in soda with a mixing spoon. Place 2 scoops ice cream in each serving glass, using an ice cream scoop. Pour grape drink over ice cream and serve immediately, with a straw, if desired. **Serves 4 to 6.**

Orange Juice Shake

½ cup milk
½ cup orange juice
2 cups vanilla ice cream
½ teaspoon finely grated orange peel
1 teaspoon vanilla

Combine all ingredients in a blender and process until smooth. Pour into chilled glasses. **Serves 3.**

Orange Peanut Butter Milk Shake

½ cup smooth peanut butter
¾ cup orange sherbet
1 cup milk
Dash of cinnamon

Combine all ingredients in a blender and process until smooth. Top each serving with an additional scoop of sherbet.

Strawberry Lemonade

1 quart fresh strawberries, washed and hulled
¾ cup fresh lemon juice
⅓ cup sugar
3½ cups club soda, chilled
Fresh strawberries and lemon slices for garnish

Place strawberries in a blender and blend until smooth. Combine lemon juice and sugar in a large pitcher and stir until sugar is dissolved. Add strawberries and stir well. Stir in club soda just before serving. Garnish with strawberries and lemon slices. **Yield: 7 cups.**

Sound Information

In 1986, the FDA authorized cochlear implantation for totally deaf children. The cochlear implant by-passes the damaged area of the inner ear, and provides direct electrical stimulation to the auditory nerve. This provides hearing sensation, in varying degrees, to those deaf children who do not benefit from conventional hearing aids. For many of these children, they are experiencing partial hearing for the FIRST time in their lives. In 1995-96, 31.3% of the MOSD students had cochlear implants. In the state of Tennessee, 4.6% of deaf children had implants compared to 3.2% in the entire country!

Subsidium "Treats"

-recipe by **MOSD** children and staff

3 cups	*LOVE*
2 cups	*DEDICATED EFFORTS*
3 tablespoons	*TALENT*
A dash of	*PERSONALITY*

Mix and combine well.

*This recipe makes for the best volunteer "treats" in Memphis . . . **SUBSIDIUM!***

Meals & Menus

Have You Heard ...

...about Main Street Memphis

*E*very town has its share of funny street and neighborhood names. In Memphis, the first commercial area north of Market Street was called The Pinch. Davey Crockett recognized this area's importance and campaigned from a flatboat in the part of the Mississippi River known as Catfish Bay. Visit the Pinch today and you will find the Pyramid, which is an internationally known arena, the home court of the University of Memphis Tigers, and the site of many concerts and exhibitions. Also in the district are enjoyable restaurants and antique shops but no flatboats, just the Trolley. Main and Front Streets are easy enough to understand and their historic places are important to the city's development.

The Cotton Row began on Front at Gayoso. Farmers from all over the country used to make their deals in these dingy warehouses. It is said that a good cotton man is "half artist, half business man, and a pinch of gambler thrown in for good measure." Cotton was called "white gold", and was the dominant economic factor in this region for years. On the corner of Front and Poplar is a marker commemorating Casey Jones' famous last run which began at this point. His Cannonball Number 382 and its wreck are immortalized in a famous poem. Government offices, retail and grocery stores, hotels, professional offices, and a park, Court Square – these were and are Main Street, Memphis.

Before the city began its eastward expansion toward Germantown, Collierville and Bartlett, everyone conducted all their business on Main including shopping, doctor's appointments, movie viewing (and, in the early days of vaudeville, live theatre at the Orpheum), and any business with city, state or federal governments. Staying downtown all day was not unheard of. Many husbands/fathers who worked in downtown office buildings would then be met by their family to enjoy dining before returning home. The Center City Commission is currently focusing attention on rejuvenation of this area of Memphis as restaurants, hotels, the Trolley and Peabody Place join the Pyramid, The Orpheum and Beale Street as places to enjoy over and over again.

Bridal Shower Brunch

Almond Punch, page 32
Sausage and Spinach Casserole, page 45
Curried Fruit or Fresh Fruit
Raspberry Bran Muffins, page 49
Cheese Grits, page 184
Ham and Biscuits
Lemon Bread, page 53

Concert in the Park Picnic

Spicy Marinated Shrimp, page 136
Tomato Crostini, page 18
Bowtie Pasta with
Broccoli and Prosciutto, page 161
Sesame Pork with
Ginger Sauce, page 22
Assorted Rolls
Créme de Menthe Brownies, page 236

College Tailgate Party

Beer
Marinated Cheese, page 21
Chicken Tortilla Pinwheels, page 20
Assorted vegetables with dip
Party Chicken Pasta, page 61
Tailgate Picnic Sandwich, page 95
Candy Bar Brownies, page 235

Valentine Dinner for Two

Champagne or wine
Oysters on the half shell
Spinach Salad with Strawberries, page 73
Filet Mignon with Red Wine Sauce, page 109
Asparagus Amandine, page 179
Herbed Twice-Baked Potatoes, page 194
*White Chocolate Mousse with
Raspberry Sauce, page 203*

Supper Club Dinner

Apricot Brandy Slush, page 35
Pesto Cheesecake with Assorted Crackers, page 23
Mushroom Bisque, page 87
Green Salad with
Honey-Lime Dressing, page 80
Green Chile Rice, page 170
Baked Carrots and Apple Casserole, page 183
Veal Loin Chops with Rosemary Sauce, page 117

After School with Friends

Peanut Butter Pizza, page 247
Celery Boats, page 242
Cracker Brittle, page 250
Orange Juice Shake, page 251

Holiday Open House

Egg Nog

Champagne Punch, page 35

Stuffed Baked Brie, page 12

Artichoke Crab Dip, page 28

Ham with Cloves and Beer, page 106

Assorted Rolls

Pork Tenderloin with Mustard Sauce, page 105

Fancy Chicken Log, page 26

Coffee Liqueur-Cinnamon Fruit Dip, page 31

Assorted Antipasto Tray

Scottish Shortbread Triangles, page 231

Sweetheart Fudge, page 232

Chocolate Pecan Ball with
Sugar Cookies, page 28

Index

Have You Heard...*A Tasteful Medley of Memphis*

Subsidium Publications
4711 Spottswood
Memphis, TN 38117
901-683-6557

Please send me _____ copies   @ $19.95 each: _____

TN Residents add 8.25% tax   @ $1.65 each: _____

Shipping and Handling   @ $4.00 each: _____

Total amount for order: _____

Your Name _____

Address _____

City _____ State _____ Zip _____

Phone (_____) _____

Enclosed is my check or money order in the amount of $ _____ payable to:
Subsidium Publications

Charge to my: MasterCard (   )   or my VISA (   )

Card # _____ Expiration date _____

Signature _____

Proceeds from the sale of
Have You Heard...*A Tasteful Medley of Memphis*
support the volunteer efforts of SUBSIDIUM, INC., on behalf of the Memphis Oral School for the Deaf. Thank you for your support.

Have You Heard...*A Tasteful Medley of Memphis*

Subsidium Publications
4711 Spottswood
Memphis, TN 38117
901-683-6557

Please send me _____ copies   @ $19.95 each: _____

TN Residents add 8.25% tax   @ $1.65 each: _____

Shipping and Handling   @ $4.00 each: _____

Total amount for order: _____

Your Name _____

Address _____

City _____ State _____ Zip _____

Phone (_____) _____

Enclosed is my check or money order in the amount of $ _____ payable to:
Subsidium Publications

Charge to my: MasterCard (   )   or my VISA (   )

Card # _____ Expiration date _____

Signature _____

Proceeds from the sale of
Have You Heard...*A Tasteful Medley of Memphis*
support the volunteer efforts of SUBSIDIUM, INC., on behalf of the Memphis Oral School for the Deaf. Thank you for your support.